Critical Acclaim for other books from PC Learning Labs

PC Learning Labs Teaches DOS 6.0

"With graphics and illustrations and lots of background snippets, you get the 'ah-so' exhilaration when puzzling jargons suddenly become clear."

—Francis Chin, *The Straits Times*

"For the beginner who really wants to make the best use of DOS, this is an excellent...highly recommended...learning tool."

—Hugh Bayless, *Monterey Bay Users Group Personal Computer Newsletter*

PC Learning Labs Teaches WordPerfect 5.1

"...a tightly focused book that doesn't stray from its purpose...it concentrates on the beginner, and it stays with the beginner."

—William J. Lynott, *Online Today*

"Excellent keystroke-by-keystroke instruction is provided by this handsome book."

—*Computer Book Review*

PC LEARNING LABS TEACHES POWERPOINT FOR WINDOWS

PC LEARNING LABS TEACHES POWERPOINT FOR WINDOWS

LOGICAL OPERATIONS

Ziff-Davis Press
Emeryville, California

Curriculum Development	Logical Operations
Writers	Richard P. Scott and Sue Reber
Editor	Janna Hecker Clark
Technical Reviewer	Dick Hol
Project Coordinator	B. Dahl
Proofreader	Cort Day
Production Coordinator,	
Logical Operations	Marie Boyers
Cover Illustration	Luis Dominguez
Cover Design	Kenneth Roberts
Book Design	Laura Lamar/MAX, San Francisco
Screen Graphics Editor	Cat Haglund
Technical Illustration	Steph Bradshaw
Word Processing	Howard Blechman, Cat Haglund, Allison Levin
Page Layout	Anna L. Marks, Cat Haglund, Tony Jonick
Indexer	Carol Burbo

Ziff-Davis Press books are produced on a Macintosh computer system with the following applications: FrameMaker®, Microsoft® Word, QuarkXPress®, Adobe Illustrator®, Adobe Photoshop®, Adobe Streamline™, MacLink® Plus, Aldus® FreeHand™, Collage Plus™.

Ziff-Davis Press
5903 Christie Avenue
Emeryville, CA 94608

ISBN 1-56276-154-4

Manufactured in the United States of America
10 9 8 7 6 5 4 3 2 1

CONTENTS AT A GLANCE

Table of Contents

INTRODUCTION

Welcome to *PC Learning Labs Teaches PowerPoint for Windows,* a hands-on instruction book designed to help you attain a high level of PowerPoint fluency in as short a time as possible. And congratulations on choosing PowerPoint 3.0, an easy-to-use, feature-packed desktop presentation program that will enable you to create professional-quality presentations with a minimum amount of training.

We at PC Learning Labs believe this book to be a unique and welcome addition to the ranks of "How To" computer publications. Our instructional approach stems directly from a decade's worth of successful teaching in a hands-on, classroom environment. Throughout the book, theory is mixed consistently with practice; a topic is explained and then immediately drilled in a hands-on activity. Included is the Data Disk, which contains sample presentation files that you will use in these activities.

When you've worked your way through this book, you will have a solid foundation of skills in

- Creating, editing, and enhancing presentations

- Working with text, images (drawings and clip art), color schemes, and charts (graphs)

- Importing and exporting data from and to other programs

- Printing presentation slides, notes, handouts, and outlines

This foundation will enable you to create sophisticated, professional-quality desktop presentations quickly and easily.

IMPORTANT NOTE

We recommend that you read through the rest of this Introduction before beginning Chapter 1. If, however, you are anxious to dive in, make sure that you first work through the upcoming section entitled "Creating Your Work Directory," as it is crucial to the successful completion of the hands-on activities in this book.

WHO THIS BOOK IS FOR

This book was written with the beginner in mind. While experience with personal computers is certainly helpful, little or none is required. You should know how to turn on your computer and how to use your keyboard. Everything beyond that will be explained in the text.

HOW TO USE THIS BOOK

This book is designed to be used as a learning guide, a review tool, and a quick reference.

 AS A LEARNING GUIDE

Each chapter in this book covers one broad topic or set of related topics. Chapters are arranged in order of increasing PowerPoint proficiency; skills acquired in a given chapter are used and elaborated upon in later chapters. For this reason, you should work through the chapters in the order they are presented.

Chapters are organized into explanatory topics and hands-on activities. Topics provide the theoretical understanding you need to master PowerPoint; activities allow you to apply this understanding to specific examples.

AS A REVIEW TOOL

Any method of instruction is only as effective as the time and energy you are willing to invest in it. For this reason, we encourage you to review the more challenging topics and activities presented in this book.

 ## AS A QUICK REFERENCE

General procedures—such as opening a new presentation or changing a presentation's color scheme—are presented as a series of bulleted steps; you can find these bullets (•) easily by skimming through the book. At the end of every chapter, you'll find a quick reference listing the mouse and keyboard actions needed to perform the techniques introduced in that chapter. In Appendix C, you'll find a list of PowerPoint's keyboard shortcuts.

WHAT THIS BOOK CONTAINS

This book is divided into the following chapters and appendices:

Chapter 12   Presentation Options
Chapter 13   Printing
Appendix A   Installation
Appendix B   Tool Palette and Toolbar Reference
Appendix C   Keystroke Reference

To attain full PowerPoint fluency, you should work through all the chapters. The appendices are optional.

The following features of this book are designed to facilitate your learning:

- Carefully sequenced topics that build on the knowledge you've acquired from previous topics.

- Frequent hands-on activities, designed to sharpen your PowerPoint skills.

- Numerous illustrations that show how your screen should look at key points within these activities.

- The Data Disk, which contains all the files you will need to complete the activities.

- A quick reference at the end of each chapter that lists in an easy-to-read table the keyboard and mouse actions needed to perform the techniques introduced in the chapter.

WHAT YOU NEED

To run PowerPoint and complete this book, you need a computer with a hard disk and at least one floppy-disk drive, a monitor, a keyboard, and a mouse (or compatible tracking device). Although you don't absolutely need a printer, we strongly recommend that you have one.

COMPUTER AND MONITOR

You need an IBM or IBM-compatible personal computer and monitor that are capable of running Microsoft Windows (version 3.1 or higher). A 286-based system is technically sufficient, but both Windows and PowerPoint will run somewhat slowly on it; we recommend that you use a 386 or higher (486, 586, and so on) computer.

You need a hard disk with at least 12 megabytes of free storage space (if PowerPoint 3.0 is not yet installed) or 1 megabyte of free space (if Power-Point 3.0 is installed).

Finally, you need an EGA or higher (VGA, SVGA, and so on) graphics card and monitor to display Windows and PowerPoint at their intended screen resolution. (**Note:** The PowerPoint screens shown in this book are taken from a VGA monitor. Depending on your monitor type, your screens may look slightly different.)

Windows 3.1 (or higher) must be installed on your computer; if it is not, see your Windows reference manuals for instructions. PowerPoint 3.0 must also be installed on your computer; for help installing it, see Appendix A.

 KEYBOARD

IBM-compatible computers come with various styles of keyboards; these keyboards work in the same way, but have different layouts. Figures I.1, I.2, and I.3 show the three main keyboard styles and how their keys are arranged.

PowerPoint uses three main areas of the keyboard:

- The *function keys*, which enable you to access PowerPoint's special features. On the PC-, XT-, and AT-style keyboards, there are 10 function keys at the left end of the keyboard; on the PS/2-style Enhanced Keyboard there are 12, at the top of the keyboard.

Figure I.1 **IBM PC–style keyboard**

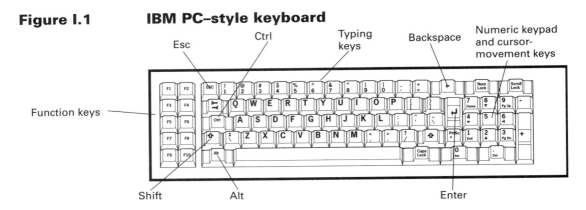

Figure I.2 **XT/AT–style keyboard**

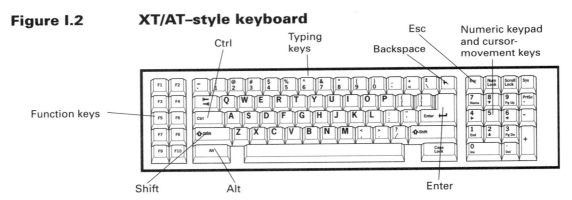

Figure I.3 **PS/2–style Enhanced Keyboard**

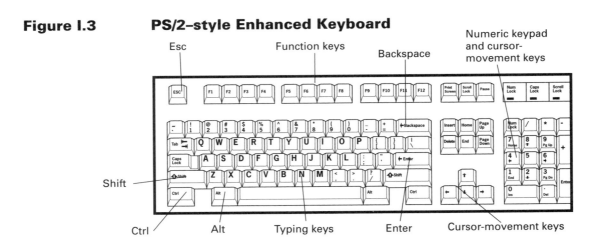

- The *typing keys*, which are located in the main body of all the keyboards. These include letters, numbers, punctuation marks, and, in addition, the Shift, Ctrl, and Alt keys, which you will need to access several of PowerPoint's special features.

- The *numeric keypad*, which groups the numbers (the same ones found across the top row of the typing keys) for convenient numeric data entry. The numeric keypad also contains these cursor movement keys: Up, Down, Left, and Right Arrows; Home, End, PgUp (Page Up), and PgDn (Page Down). To enter numeric data using the numeric keypad, *Num Lock* must be on (pressing the Num Lock key will toggle Num Lock on and off). To use the cursor movement keys on the keypad, Num Lock must be off. To enter numeric data when Num Lock is off, use the number keys on the top row of the typing area.

The Enhanced Keyboard has an additional cursor movement keypad to the left of the numeric keypad. This allows you to use the numeric keypad for numeric data entry (that is, to keep Num Lock on) and still have access to cursor movement keys.

 MOUSE OR COMPATIBLE TRACKING DEVICE

You need a mouse or tracking device to work through the activities in this book. Any standard PC mouse or compatible tracking device will do.

Note: Throughout this book, we direct you to use a mouse. If you have a different tracking device (a trackball, for example), simply use your tracking device instead of a mouse.

 PRINTER

Although you don't absolutely need a printer to work through the activities in this book, we strongly recommend that you have one. A laser printer is ideal, but an ink-jet or dot-matrix will do just fine. You must *select* your printer for use with PowerPoint; for help, see Appendix A.

CREATING YOUR WORK DIRECTORY

Throughout this book, you will be opening, editing, and saving several files. In order to keep these files together, you need to create a work directory for them on your hard disk. (A *directory* is like a folder in which a group of related files is stored.) Your work directory will also hold the sample files contained on the Data Disk included with this book.

Follow these steps to create your work directory. (**Note:** If PowerPoint 3.0 is not currently installed on your computer, please install it now, before you create your work directory. See Appendix A for instructions.)

1. Turn on your computer. After a brief internal self-check, your *operating environment* will load. If you are in Windows, skip directly to step 2. If you are in DOS, skip to step 4. If you are in a non-Windows, non-DOS environment (GeoWorks, for example), exit to DOS and then skip to step 4; for help exiting to DOS, follow the on-screen instructions or refer to your user's guide. If you don't know what operating system you are in, ask a colleague or technician for help.

2. Perform these actions to exit from Windows to DOS. Locate the *Program Manager* on your screen. The Program Manager is a Windows program that may appear in either of two guises: as a *window* (rectangular box) with "Program Manager" in its overhead title bar; or as an *icon* (small picture) with "Program Manager" beneath it. If your Program Manager appears as a window, skip directly to step 3. If your Program Manager appears as an icon, use the mouse to move the on-screen pointer to this icon, and then double-click (press the **left mouse button** twice in rapid succession) on the icon to open it into a window.

3. Use the mouse to move the on-screen pointer to the Program Manager's *Control Menu button*, the small, square box in the upper-left

corner of the Program Manager window. Double-click (press the **left mouse button** twice in rapid succession) on the dash within the Control Menu button. A box entitled "Exit Windows" will appear. Click the mouse pointer once on **OK** within this box. You have now exited from Windows to DOS. Skip directly to step 10.

4. You may see this prompt:

```
Current date is Tue 02-18-1994
Enter new date (mm-dd-yy):
```

(Your current date will be different.) If you do not see a date prompt, skip to step 7.

5. If the current date on your screen is wrong, type the correct date. Use a dash (-) to separate the month, day, and year (for example, 6-19-94).

6. Press **Enter**. After you type a command, you must press the Enter key to submit your command to the computer.

7. You may see this prompt:

```
Current time is 0:25:32:56p
Enter new time:
```

(Your current time will be different.) If you do not see a time prompt, skip to step 10.

8. If the current time on your screen is wrong, type the correct time. Use the 24-hour format *hh:mm* (for example, 10:58 for 10:58 a.m., and 22:58 for 10:58 p.m.).

9. Press **Enter** to send the time you specified to the computer's internal clock.

10. The DOS prompt will appear:

```
C:\>
```

(Your DOS prompt may differ somewhat from this.)

11. Type **dir** and press **Enter**. The contents of the current disk directory are displayed, followed by a final line reporting the number of free bytes on your hard disk. If you have 1,000,000 or more free bytes, skip directly to step 12. If you have fewer than 1,000,000 free bytes, you will not be able to create your work directory and perform the hands-on activities in this book. Before you go any further, you must delete enough files from your hard disk to bring the free-byte total up to approximately 1,000,000. For help doing this, refer to your DOS user's guide. (**Note:** Make sure to back up all your important files before deleting them!)

12. Insert the enclosed Data Disk (label up) into the appropriately sized disk drive and close the drive door, if necessary. Determine whether this is drive A or drive B. (On a single floppy-disk system, the drive is generally designated as A. On a double floppy-disk system, the upper drive is generally designated as A and the lower as B.)

13. Type **a:** if the Data Disk is in drive A, or type **b:** if the Data Disk is in drive B. Press **Enter** to change the current drive to that of the Data Disk.

14. Type **install c: powerwrk** (don't press Enter yet; remember to leave a space between *c:* and *powerwrk*). To create your work directory on a hard-disk drive other than drive C, substitute your hard-disk drive letter for the *c* in this command. For example, to create your work directory on a drive-D hard disk, you would type *install d: powerwrk*. POWERWRK is the name of your work directory.

15. Press **Enter** to create your work directory. If all goes well, the message

```
Work directory under construction.
Please wait .....................
```

will appear. And when the procedure is complete, the message

```
Work directory successfully completed!
```

will appear, followed by a line reporting the name of your work directory (c:\powerwrk, for example). If these two messages appear, skip directly to the Important Note following this step.

If all does not go so well, one of two messages will appear. The first message is

```
Installation aborted! c: drive does not exist.
Reenter the Install command using another drive.
```

This message indicates that the hard drive you specified in your step 14 command does not exist on your computer (your drive letter may be different). If you get this message, simply repeat steps 14 and 15, making sure to specify the correct letter of your hard drive.

The second message is

```
Installation aborted! c:\powerwrk directory already
exists.
Reenter the Install command using another directory
name.
```

This message indicates that a directory with the same name as your proposed work directory (POWERWRK) already exists on your specified hard disk. If this happens, repeat steps 14 and 15, specifying a new work directory name of your choice instead of *powerwrk*. For example, you might type *install c: mypower* or *install c: pwrfiles*, and so on. Your work directory name can be up to eight letters long. Do not use spaces, periods, or punctuation marks. Do not use the name *powerpnt*, as it is already used by the PowerPoint program.

Important Note: The hands-on activities in this book assume that your work directory is on drive C and is named POWERWRK. If you specified a different hard-disk drive or a different directory name, please remember to mentally substitute this drive and/or name whenever we mention drive C or POWERWRK.

CONVENTIONS USED IN THIS BOOK

The conventions used in this book are designed to help you learn Power-Point easily and efficiently. Each chapter begins with a short introduction and ends with a summary that includes a quick-reference guide to the techniques introduced in the chapter. Main chapter topics (large, capitalized headings) and subtopics (headings preceded by a cube) explain PowerPoint features. Hands-on activities allow you to practice using these features.

In these activities, keystrokes, menu choices, and anything you are asked to type are printed in boldface. Here's an example from Chapter 2:

4. Choose **File, Slide Show** to open the Slide Show dialog box.

Activities follow a *cause-and-effect* approach. Each step tells you what to do (cause) and then what will happen (effect). From the example above,

Cause: Choose the menu command **File, Slide Show**.

Effect: The Slide Show dialog box opens.

A plus sign (+) used with the Shift, Ctrl, and Alt keys indicates a multikey keystroke. For example, **Ctrl+r** means, "Press and hold down the Ctrl key, press the *r* key, and then release them both."

To help you distinguish between steps presented for your general knowledge and steps you should carry out at your computer as you read, we use the following system:

- A bulleted step, like this, is provided for your information and reference only.

1. A numbered step, like this, indicates one in a series of steps that you should carry out in sequence at your computer.

BEFORE YOU START

The activities in each of the following chapters are designed to proceed sequentially. In many cases, you cannot perform an activity until you have performed one or more of the activities directly preceding it. For this reason, we recommend that you allot enough time to work through an entire chapter at one sitting.

You are now ready to begin. Good learning and ... *Bon Voyage!*

CHAPTER 1:
GETTING STARTED

A Quick Review of
Mousing Skills

Starting
PowerPoint

Exploring the
Application and
Presentation
Windows

Opening a
Presentation File

Moving between
Slides in Slide View

Changing the View

Closing a
Presentation File

Exiting from
PowerPoint

Welcome to the world of computerized desktop presentation! PowerPoint 3.0 is a feature-rich, easy-to-use program that enables you to create presentation slides that combine text, charts (graphs), drawings, and clip-art graphics. You can display your PowerPoint slides on a computer screen, print them on paper or overhead transparencies, or process them as 35-millimeter slides.

This first chapter gets you up and running in PowerPoint and introduces you to the PowerPoint working environment. When you're done working through this chapter, you will know

- How to start PowerPoint
- How to open a presentation file
- How to move between slides in Slide view
- How to change the view
- How to close a presentation file
- How to exit from PowerPoint

A QUICK REVIEW OF MOUSING SKILLS

The mouse is a hand-held device that enables you to communicate with PowerPoint by manipulating (selecting, deselecting, moving, deleting, and so on) graphical and text objects that are displayed on your computer screen. When you move the mouse across the surface of your mousepad, a symbol called the *mouse pointer* moves across the screen. You use this mouse pointer to point to the on-screen object that you want to manipulate. On top of the mouse are one or more buttons. You use these buttons to communicate with Power-Point in several ways, as detailed in Table 1.1. **Note:** Read through the following table to familiarize yourself with standard PowerPoint mousing techniques. It's not necessary, however, to try to memorize these techniques. Instead, think of this table as a quick-reference guide, and refer back to it whenever you need to refresh your memory.

Table 1.1   **Mousing Techniques**

Technique	How to Do It
Point	Move the mouse until the tip of the mouse pointer is over the desired object. "Point to the word *File*" means "move the mouse until the tip of the mouse pointer is over the word *File*."
Click	Press and release the left mouse button. "Click on the word *File*" means "point to the word *File* and then press and release the left mouse button."

Table 1.1   **Mousing Techniques (Continued)**

Technique	How to Do It
Double-click	Press and release the left mouse button twice in rapid succession. "Double-click on the file name *PREVIEW1.PPT*" means "point to the file name *PREVIEW1.PPT* and then press and release the left mouse button twice."
Choose	Click on a menu command or a dialog-box button. "Choose File, Open" means "click on the word *File* (in the menu bar), and then click on the word *Open* (in the File menu)."
Drag	Press and hold the left mouse button while moving the mouse. "Drag the scroll box upward" means "point to the scroll box, press and hold the left mouse button, move the mouse upward, and then release the mouse button."
Scroll	Click on a scroll arrow or within a scroll bar, or drag a scroll box.
Select	Click on an object (to select the entire object), or drag over part of a text object (to select part of the text). "Select the file PREVIEW.PPT" means "click on the file name PREVIEW.PPT." "Select the first four letters of the title *Global Travel*" means "drag over the letters *Glob*."
Check	Click on a check box to check (turn on) that option. "Check the Match Case option" means "click on the Match Case check box to check it."
Uncheck	Click on a check box to uncheck (turn off) that option. "Uncheck the Match Case option" means "click on the Match Case check box to uncheck it."

STARTING POWERPOINT

Before you start PowerPoint, both Microsoft Windows and Power-Point 3.0 must be installed on your hard disk. If either of these programs is not installed, please install it now. For help installing

Microsoft Windows, see your Windows documentation. For help installing PowerPoint, see Appendix A of this book.

You also need to have created a work directory on your hard disk and to have copied the files from the enclosed Data Disk to this directory. If you have not done this, please do so now; for instructions, see "Creating Your Work Directory" in the Introduction.

Note: In this book, we present two types of procedures: bulleted and numbered. A *bulleted procedure*—one whose steps are preceded by bullets (•)—serves as a general reference; you should read its steps without actually performing them. A *numbered procedure*—one whose steps are preceded by numbers (1., 2., and so on)—is a specific hands-on activity; you should perform its steps as instructed.

Here's the general procedure for starting PowerPoint:

• Turn on your computer.

• If you are already in Windows, skip this step. If you are in a non-DOS operating environment, exit to DOS. At the DOS prompt, type *win* and press Enter to start Windows.

• Locate the Microsoft PowerPoint program icon. Double-click on this icon to start PowerPoint.

Let's follow this procedure to start PowerPoint:

1. Turn on your computer. After a brief self-check, your *operating environment* will automatically load. If your operating environment is Windows, skip directly to the next section, "Setting Your PowerPoint Defaults." If it is DOS, continue with step 2 of this activity. If you are in a non-DOS operating environment (for example, GeoWorks), exit from this environment to DOS and continue with step 2. (For help exiting to DOS, see the reference manuals for your operating environment.)

2. You may see this prompt:

```
Current date is Tue 10-18-1993
Enter new date (mm-dd-yy):
```

(**Note:** Your current date will be different.) If you do not see a date prompt, skip to step 5.

3. If the current date on your screen is wrong, type the correct date. Use a hyphen (-) to separate the month, day, and year (for example, 11-18-93).

4. Press **Enter**. Remember that after you type a command, you must press the Enter key to send this command to the computer.

5. You may see this prompt:

```
Current time is 0:25:32:56
Enter new time:
```

(Your current time will be different.) If you do not see a time prompt, skip to step 8.

6. If the current time on your screen is wrong, type the correct time. Use the 24-hour format *hh:mm* (for example, 10:30 for 10:30 a.m., and 22:30 for 10:30 p.m.).

7. Press **Enter** to set your computer's internal clock.

8. Observe that the DOS prompt

```
C:\>
```

appears. (Your DOS prompt may differ somewhat from this.)

9. Type **win** and press **Enter** to start Windows. After a few moments of furious hard-disk activity (which you can observe by watching your hard-disk drive pilot light), Windows appears on your screen.

 SETTING YOUR POWERPOINT DEFAULTS

At this point, we need to interrupt our start-up procedure to nip a potential problem in the bud. PowerPoint is a customizable program. Depending on how its *defaults* (standard settings) have been set—by you or, perhaps, a colleague—your PowerPoint program may look and behave quite differently from ours. To avoid the confusion these differences might create, you will need to set your PowerPoint defaults to match ours. This way, our programs will look and behave identically.

Note: You need to perform the following default-matching procedure only once. Thereafter, you can skip over this section when starting PowerPoint.

1. Observe your screen. You need to locate a Windows program named *Program Manager*. If Program Manager is running as an *icon* (a small picture with the words *Program Manager* beneath it, as shown in Figure 1.1), double-click on

this icon (move the mouse until the tip of the mouse pointer is over the icon, and then press the **left mouse button** twice in rapid succession) to open it into a window. If Program Manager is already running as a window (as shown in Figure 1.2), click (press the **left mouse button** once) on the window's *title bar* (the horizontal bar in which the words *Program Manager* appear) to activate it.

Figure 1.1   **Program Manager running as an icon**

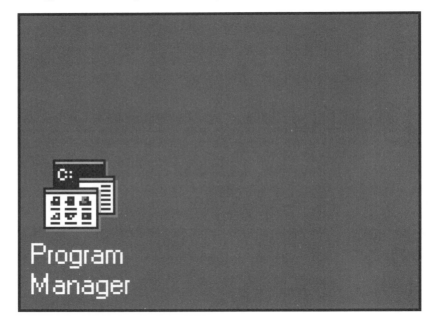

2. Click on the word **File** (point to *File* and press the **left mouse button** once) in the Program Manager *menu bar* (the horizontal bar directly under the title bar) to open the *drop-down File menu* (a list of file-related commands).

3. In the drop-down File menu, click on the **Run** command to open the Run dialog box. A *dialog box* is an on-screen box in which you enter information that PowerPoint needs in order to carry out your command. You'll work extensively with dialog boxes during the course of this book.

Figure 1.2 **Program Manager running as a window**

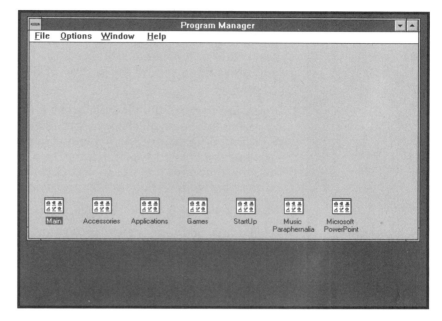

4. Type **dosprmpt** and press **Enter** to switch temporarily from Windows to DOS.

5. Type **cd \powerpnt** and press **Enter** to change the current directory to your PowerPoint directory.

6. If the message *Invalid directory* does *not* appear, skip the rest of this activity (steps 7 through 19) and continue with the next activity. If the *Invalid directory* message *does* appear, repeat the previous step, making sure to type a back-slash (\) and not a forward slash (/). If *Invalid directory* still appears, continue with step 7.

7. Type **exit** and press **Enter** to switch from DOS back to Windows.

8. Activate the **Program Manager** window by clicking on its title bar.

9. Choose **File, Run** (click on **File** in the Program Manager menu bar, and then click on **Run**) to open the Run dialog box. Type **win.ini** and press **Enter**. A window entitled Note-pad - WIN.INI appears. Inside this window are the contents

of WIN.INI, a special file that contains defaults for your Windows program.

10. Choose **Search, Find** (click on **Search**, and then click on **Find**) to open the Find dialog box. Type **[Microsoft PowerPoint 3]**— make sure to type square brackets [] and not parentheses ()— and press **Enter** to find the section of WIN.INI that deals with PowerPoint.

11. Press **Esc** to close the Find dialog box. Press the **down arrow** key as many times as necessary to display a line beginning with *DefaultDirectory*. (As explained in the Introduction, if you use the arrow keys—or Home, End, Ins, Del, and so on— on your numeric keypad, Num Lock must be turned off. You can toggle Num Lock on/off by pressing the Num Lock key.)

12. Your line will look something like this:

```
DefaultDirectory=C:\powerpnt
```

The first letter after the equal sign (=) identifies the hard-disk drive on which your PowerPoint directory is stored; in this example, the drive is C. The text from the first backslash (\) to the end of the line identifies the PowerPoint directory itself; in our example, the directory is \powerpnt.

13. Write down everything that appears to the right of the equal sign in your line. You'll need this information in a moment.

14. Choose **File, Exit** to close the Notepad - WIN.INI window. If a dialog box appears with the message *Do you want to save the changes?*, click on **No**.

15. Choose **File, Run** from the Program Manager menu bar.

16. Type **dosprmpt** and press **Enter** to switch temporarily from Windows to DOS.

17. Type **cd** and press **Enter**. A line similar to

```
C:\WINDOWS
```

appears. The first letter identifies your current hard-disk drive; in this example, the drive is C.

18. If your current drive is the same as the drive you wrote down in step 13, skip the rest of this step. If not, type the letter of the drive you wrote down, and then type a colon (:). For example, if the drive you wrote down is D, you would type the characters *d:*. Press **Enter** to change the current drive to the drive on which your PowerPoint directory is stored.

19. Type **cd** and then type a space. (Do not press Enter.) Type the name of the directory—not the drive or the subsequent colon—that you wrote down. Remember to begin the directory name with a backslash (\). For example, if you wrote down C:\powerpnt, you would type \powerpnt; if you wrote down D:\winapps\powerpnt, you would type \winapps\powerpnt. Press **Enter** to change the current directory to your PowerPoint directory. (**Note:** Please save the piece of paper on which you wrote your PowerPoint directory; you'll need it again in Chapter 6.)

PowerPoint's defaults are saved in a file called DEFAULT.PPT. In order to preserve your current defaults—so that you can restore them, if you wish, when you've completed this book—we'll create a copy of DEFAULT.PPT and name it DEFORIG.PPT:

1. Type **dir default.ppt** and press **Enter** to verify that DEFAULT.-PPT is stored in your PowerPoint directory.

2. If the message *File not found* appears, repeat the previous step. If *File not found* appears again, your PowerPoint directory does not contain DEFAULT.PPT, so you won't need to create a DEFORIG.PPT copy; skip to step 5.

3. Type **copy default.ppt deforig.ppt** and press **Enter** to create DEFORIG.PPT, an exact copy of DEFAULT.PPT.

4. Type **del default.ppt** to delete DEFAULT.PPT.

5. Type **exit** and press **Enter** to switch from DOS back to Windows. Your PowerPoint defaults now match the ones we used in writing this book.

 LOCATING THE MICROSOFT POWERPOINT PROGRAM ICON

Now that our PowerPoint defaults match, you can safely start the PowerPoint program. In order to do this, you must locate the *program icon* (a small on-screen picture that represents a program) entitled Microsoft PowerPoint.

Like PowerPoint, Windows is a customizable program. For this reason, we cannot know the details of your Windows setup. So please bear with us as we search for your Microsoft PowerPoint program icon:

1. Look for the Microsoft PowerPoint program icon depicted in Figure 1.3. If you see this icon on your screen right now, skip to step 4.

Figure 1.3

Program Manager running in window

Control Menu button

Microsoft PowerPoint program icon

Program-group window

Program-group icons

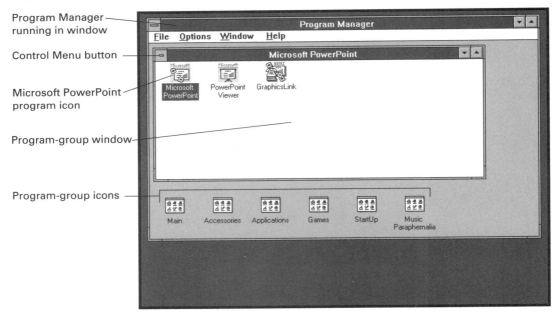

2. Activate the **Program Manager** window by clicking on its title bar. Program icons are stored in *program groups*; program groups are, in turn, stored in the Program Manager. Program groups can appear as windows (Microsoft PowerPoint in Figure 1.3) or as icons (Main, Accessories, Applications, Games, and so on in Figure 1.3). Normally, the Microsoft PowerPoint program icon is stored in a program group entitled Microsoft PowerPoint. If you see a program-group window entitled Microsoft PowerPoint, click on its title bar to activate it, and skip to step 4. If you see a program-group icon entitled Microsoft PowerPoint, double-click on the icon to open it into a window, and skip to step 4.

3. If you do not have a program-group window or icon entitled Microsoft PowerPoint in your Program Manager window, you'll have to search further for your Microsoft PowerPoint program icon. Look for a program-group window or icon with a title that seems appropriate for an application program like PowerPoint (Applications or Windows Applications would be good candidates). If this is a window, click on its title bar to activate it; if this is an icon, double-click on it to open it into a window. If you see the Microsoft PowerPoint program icon somewhere inside this window, skip to step 4. If not, double-click on the program-group window's **Control Menu button** (the boxed dash in the upper-left corner of the program-group window, as shown in Figure 1.3) to close the window. Repeat this step as many times as you need to find your elusive Microsoft PowerPoint program icon. Don't despair: If PowerPoint is installed on your computer, its program icon must be stored somewhere! It just may take a while to find it.

4. Double-click on the **Microsoft PowerPoint program icon** to start PowerPoint. Depending on how your PowerPoint program was last run, your screen will match that shown in Figure 1.4 or Figure 1.5. You'll learn about the difference between these two start-up screens in the next section.

   (**Note:** If your screen does not exactly match either Figure 1.4 or Figure 1.5, don't worry; we'll help you fix things in a moment.)

EXPLORING THE APPLICATION AND PRESENTATION WINDOWS

A *window* is a rectangular area on the screen, in which you view a program (PowerPoint, for example) or a document (a Power-Point slide, for example). When you start PowerPoint, two windows appear, one within the other. The outer window is called the *application window* because it contains the PowerPoint program's main options and commands. (**Note:** The terms *application* and *program* are synonymous.) The inner window is called the *presentation window*, because it contains the current presentation file and the tools, options, commands, and messages associated with this file. The next two sections discuss the PowerPoint application and presentation windows in detail.

Figure 1.4   **PowerPoint, after start-up**

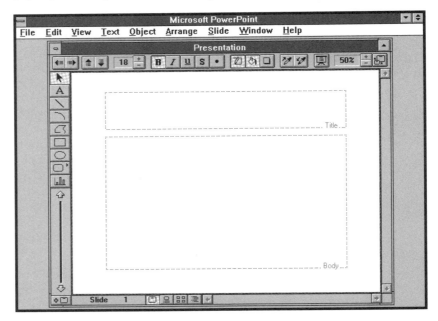

Figure 1.5   **PowerPoint, after start-up (alternate screen)**

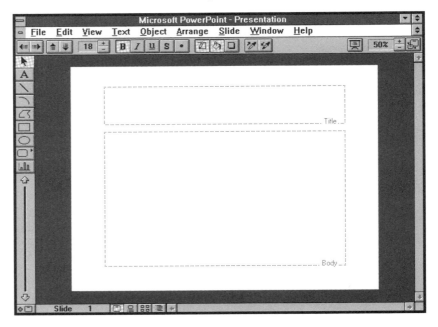

THE APPLICATION WINDOW

Let's remove the presentation window from the screen, so that we can observe the PowerPoint application window alone:

1. Choose **File, Close** (click on **File**, and then click on **Close**) from the PowerPoint menu bar to close the presentation window. The application window is left alone on screen, as shown in Figure 1.6.

Figure 1.6   **The PowerPoint application window**

Control Menu button

Title bar

Menu bar

Minimize button

Maximize/Restore button

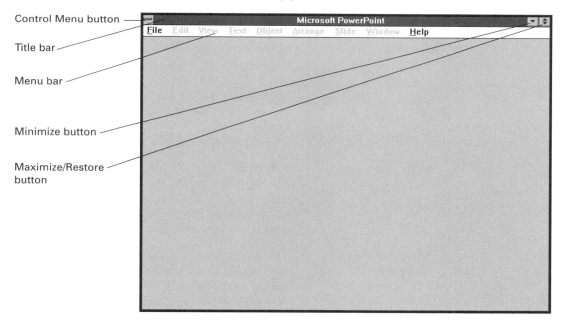

2. This application window can be thought of as a project supervisor that provides you with a set of options and commands to create and edit your presentations. Observe the elements shown in Table 1.2 and Figure 1.6.

Table 1.2   **PowerPoint Application-Window Elements**

Element	Description
Control Menu button	The boxed dash to the left of the title bar. You use it to change the size and position of the application window or to close it.
Title bar	The horizontal bar across the top of the application window. It contains the application title, Microsoft PowerPoint.
Menu bar	The horizontal bar beneath the title bar. It displays PowerPoint's menu options. Available options (options you can use in the current working context) are displayed in dark letters; in Figure 1.6, these include File and Help. Unavailable options (options you cannot use in the current working context) are *dimmed*, or displayed in light letters; in Figure 1.6, these include Edit, View, Text, Object, Arrange, Slide, and Window.
Minimize button	The downward-pointing, boxed arrow to the right of the title bar. It shrinks the application window to a program icon (the same type of program icon that you observed earlier in this chapter).
Maximize/Restore button	The button to the right of the Minimize button. When the application window is *maximized* (enlarged to fill the entire screen), this button contains an upward/downward-pointing arrow, and you use it to *restore* (shrink) the application window to its non-maximized size and location. When the application window is not maximized, this button contains an upward-pointing arrow, and you use it to maximize the application window. (**Note:** Since the application window in Figure 1.6 is maximized, the Maximize/Restore button contains an upward/downward-pointing arrow.)

Let's take a moment to explore some application-window elements:

1. Observe your Maximize/Restore button (the button in the upper-right corner of the window). If your application window is maximized (enlarged to full screen size), this button contains an upward/downward-pointing arrow; clicking on it restores (shrinks) the window to its nonmaximized size and location. If your application window is not maximized, this button contains an upward-pointing arrow; clicking on it maximizes the window.

2. Click on the **Maximize/Restore button** a few times to toggle your application window between its maximized and non-maximized states.

3. Place the application window in its nonmaximized state. The Maximize/Restore button should now contain an upward-pointing arrow. Click once on the **Control Menu button** (the boxed dash to the left of the PowerPoint title bar) to open the drop-down Control menu. (Do not double-click on the Control Menu button, as this will cause you to exit from PowerPoint.) Observe the various commands for moving and resizing the window. Click once again on the **Control Menu button** to close the drop-down Control menu.

4. Click on the **Maximize/Restore button** to maximize the application window. Click on the **Control Menu button** to reopen the drop-down Control menu. Note that several commands are now dimmed (Move, Size, and Maximize). As mentioned, PowerPoint dims a menu command to show that it is currently unavailable for your use. In this case, you cannot move, size, or maximize your application window, because it is already maximized. Click once again on the **Control Menu button** to close the drop-down Control menu.

PRACTICE YOUR SKILLS

Let's take a quick tour of the menu bar:

1. Click on **File** to open the File drop-down menu. Observe its contents. Note which commands are currently available (displayed in dark letters) and which are unavailable (dimmed). Click on **File** again to close the File menu.

2. Repeat the above step for the Help drop-down menu. Note that all Help commands are available.

THE PRESENTATION WINDOW

Now let's reopen the PowerPoint presentation window, so that we can examine it:

1. Choose **File, New** to open a new presentation window. (You'll learn more about using the File, New command in Chapter 2.)

2. Observe your presentation window's Maximize/Restore button. If your presentation window is maximized, this button is to the right of the menu bar and contains an upward/downward-pointing arrow. If your presentation window is not maximized, this button is to the right of the presentation-window title bar and contains an upward-pointing arrow.

3. If your presentation window is maximized, click on the **Maximize/Restore button** to restore the window to its nonmaximized size and location. Your screen should now match (or closely resemble) that shown in Figure 1.7.

Think of the PowerPoint presentation window as a workspace in which you create and edit your presentation slides. Observe the following elements, as shown in Table 1.3 and Figure 1.7:

Table 1.3   **PowerPoint Presentation-Window Elements**

Element	Description
Control Menu button	In a maximized presentation window, this button is a boxed dash to the left of the menu bar. In a nonmaximized presentation window (as shown in Figure 1.7), this button is a boxed dash to the left of the title bar. These buttons are equivalent; only their locations differ. You use the Control Menu button to change the size and position of the presentation window or to close it.

Figure 1.7   **Nonmaximized PowerPoint presentation window**

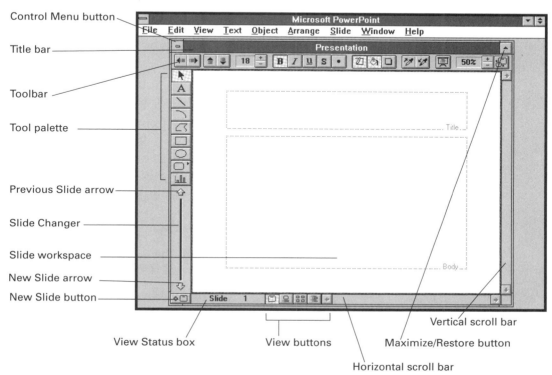

Table 1.3   **PowerPoint Presentation-Window Elements (Continued)**

Element	Description
Title bar	The horizontal bar across the top of the presentation window. It contains the presentation's title. Since you have not yet given a title to the new presentation you created in step 1, PowerPoint gives it the default title, Presentation.
Toolbar	The row of buttons at the top of the window. You click on these buttons to issue various PowerPoint commands.

Table 1.3   **PowerPoint Presentation-Window Elements (Continued)**

Element	Description
Tool Palette	The column of buttons on the left side of the presentation window. You use these buttons to draw, graph, and add text to a slide.
Slide Changer	The long vertical slot below the Tool Palette; it is flanked by a *Previous Slide arrow* and a *Next Slide arrow.* You use these items to move between slides in the current presentation.
Slide workspace	The large rectangular area in the middle of the window. This is the area in which you view, create, and edit your presentation slides.
New Slide button	The button beneath the Slide Changer. You use it to add a new slide to the current presentation.
View Status box	The box to the right of the New Slide button. PowerPoint uses this box to report information about the current slide and view.
View buttons	The group of four buttons to the right of the View Status box. You use these buttons to change the *view* in which the current presentation is displayed. (You'll learn more about views in the upcoming section, "Changing the View.")
Horizontal scroll bar	The long horizontal bar to the right of the View buttons, flanked by a *left scroll arrow* and a *right scroll arrow.* You use these items to *scroll* (move) the contents of the current slide to the right or left.

Table 1.3   **PowerPoint Presentation-Window Elements (Continued)**

Element	Description
Maximize/Restore button	In a maximized presentation window, this button is an upward/downward-pointing arrow to the right of the menu bar; you use it to restore the presentation window to its nonmaximized size and location. In a nonmaximized presentation window (as shown in Figure 1.7), this button is an upward-pointing arrow to the right of the title bar; you use it to maximize the presentation window.
Vertical scroll bar	The long vertical bar along the right border of the presentation window, flanked by an *up scroll arrow* and a *down scroll arrow*. You use these items to scroll (move) the contents of the current slide up or down.

Let's take a closer look at some of these presentation-window elements:

1. Observe the presentation-window title bar. As mentioned, since you have not yet named your new presentation, Power-Point has given it the default title, Presentation.

2. Click once on the presentation-window **Control Menu button**, the button to the left of the presentation-window title bar. (Make sure you click on the presentation-window Control Menu button, not the application-window Control Menu button.) Note that the presentation-window Control Menu commands are virtually identical to the application-window Control Menu commands you viewed in an earlier activity. Click again on the **Control Menu button** to close the Control menu.

3. Click on the **Maximize button** (the upward-pointing, boxed arrow in the upper-right corner of the presentation window) to maximize your presentation window.

4. Observe the changes to your screen display, as shown in Figure 1.8. The presentation window enlarged to fill all the

available space within the application window. The presentation-window title bar disappeared, and the current file name moved up to the application-window title bar (Microsoft PowerPoint - Presentation). The presentation-window Control Menu button moved to the left end of the menu bar (directly below the application-window Control Menu button), and the presentation-window Maximize/Restore button moved to the right end of the menu bar (directly below the application-window Maximize/Restore button).

Figure 1.8   **Maximized PowerPoint presentation window**

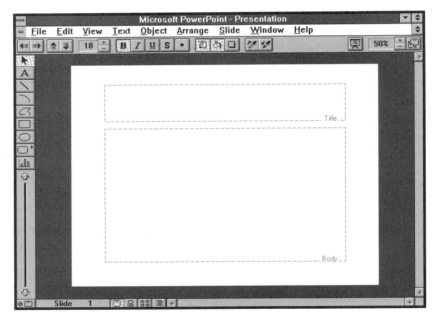

5. Choose **File, Close** to close the presentation window. The application window is left alone on screen.

OPENING A PRESENTATION FILE

A *file* is a collection of data (information) stored on a hard or floppy disk. A PowerPoint *presentation file* consists of one or more slides. Each slide can contain text, charts (graphs), drawings, and clip-art graphics. In order to view, edit, add, or delete slides in an existing presentation, you must first open the presentation file in which these slides are stored.

Here's the general procedure for opening a presentation file:

- Choose *File, Open* to open the Open dialog box.

- If necessary, change the current drive to the drive that contains the presentation file you want to open.

- If necessary, change the current directory to the directory that contains the presentation file you want to open.

- In the File Name list box, select the name of the presentation file that you want to open.

- Click on OK.

Let's use this procedure to open a presentation file stored in the POWERWRK work directory that you created in the Introduction. First, we'll take a closer look at PowerPoint's menu commands:

1. Click on **File** to open the drop-down File menu. Observe the commands in this menu. Note that some are followed by an *ellipsis* (...), and others are not. When you choose a command that is followed by an ellipsis (for example, Open...), PowerPoint displays a dialog box prompting you for further information that it needs to carry out your command. When you choose a command not followed by an ellipsis (for example, Exit), PowerPoint performs the command without displaying a dialog box. (**Note:** For the sake of clarity, we've chosen not to print command ellipses in this book. For example, when we ask you in step 3 to choose the File, Open... command, we'll simply say, "Choose File, Open.")

2. Click on **File** again to close the drop-down File menu.

3. Choose **File, Open** to open the Open dialog box, as shown in Figure 1.9.

4. Observe the current drive and directory, as reported in the *directory line*, the line beneath the heading *Directories* at the top of the dialog box. In Figure 1.9, the directory line reads *c:\powerpnt*, which means that the current drive is C and the current directory is POWERPNT. You must now change the current drive and directory to that of your POWERWRK work directory.

Figure 1.9   **The Open dialog box**

Directory line

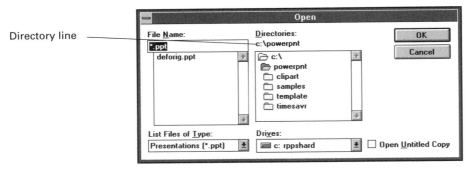

5. If the current drive is the drive on which you created your POWERWRK work directory, skip the rest of this step. Change the current drive to the drive on which you created your POWERWRK work directory. To do this, click on the **down arrow** to the right of the Drives drop-down list box to open the drop-down list of available drives, and then click on the desired drive. The directory line reports the new drive.

6. To change the current directory to your POWERWRK directory, double-click on the **c:** (or d:\, e:\, and so on) at the top of the Directories list box. Then, locate the powerwrk entry in this list box. You may need to scroll down through the list to find powerwrk; if so, click on the **down scroll arrow** (the downward-pointing arrow in the lower-right corner of the list box) as many times as needed.

7. Double-click on **powerwrk** (not on *powerpnt*!) to change your current directory to POWERWRK. The directory line should now read *c:\powerwrk* (or *d:\powerwrk, e:\powerwrk*, and so on); if it doesn't, repeat steps 3 through 6. This is the work directory that you created in the Introduction.

Now that you've changed to your POWERWRK directory, you can select and open a presentation file that is stored in it:

8. In the File Name list box, select (click once on) **preview1.ppt**. The file name is *highlighted* (displayed in reverse video), and it appears in the File Name text box, the box beneath the heading *File Name*. In addition, a miniature representation of the first slide of PREVIEW1.PPT appears on the right side of the dialog box.

9. Click on **OK** to open PREVIEW1.PPT. The mouse pointer changes to an hourglass to indicate that PowerPoint is busy and you cannot interrupt it. After a moment, the normal mouse pointer returns and the first slide of the presentation file PREVIEW1.PPT appears, as shown in Figure 1.10. This is the same slide you saw in miniature when you selected PRE-VIEW.PPT in the Open dialog box.

Figure 1.10   **PREVIEW1.PPT, newly opened**

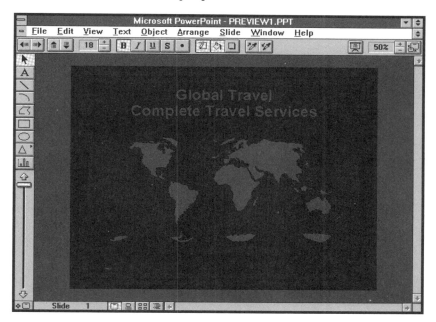

MOVING BETWEEN SLIDES IN SLIDE VIEW

PowerPoint provides four different *views* (working environments) in which you can work on your presentation slides. You are currently in Slide view; you use this view to work in detail on one slide at a time. (You'll learn about the remaining views in the upcoming section, "Changing the View.") When you are in Slide view, you can use the Slide Changer or the keyboard to move between slides in the current presentation.

Here's the general procedure for using the Slide Changer to move between slides:

- To move to the next slide, click on the Slide Changer's *Next Slide arrow*.

- To move to the previous slide, click on the Slide Changer's *Previous Slide arrow*.

- To move ahead or back more than one slide, drag the Slide Changer *lever* until your desired slide is displayed in the View Status box.

Here's the general procedure for using the keyboard to move between slides:

- To move to the next slide, press *Page Down* (or *PgDn* on the numeric keypad).

- To move to the previous slide, press *Page Up* (or *PgUp* on the numeric keypad).

Let's practice using the keyboard to move between the slides of PREVIEW1.PPT:

1. Observe the View Status box. It reports the current slide number, 1.

2. Press **Page Down** (or **PgDn**) to move to the next slide. (If you use the PgDn key on the numeric keypad, make sure that Num Lock is off.) Note that the View Status box reports your new slide number.

3. Repeat step 2 until you reach the last slide of the presentation, slide 9.

4. Press **Page Up** (or **PgUp**) to move to the previous slide, slide 8.

5. Repeat step 4 until you reach the first slide of the presentation.

Now let's use the Slide Changer to display this same sequence of slides:

1. Click once on the Slide Changer's **Next Slide arrow** (the downward-pointing arrow directly beneath the Slide Changer's vertical slot) to move to the next slide.

2. Repeat step 1 until you reach the last slide of the presentation, slide 9.

3. Click once on the Slide Changer's **Previous Slide arrow** (the upward-pointing arrow directly above the Slide Changer's vertical slot) to move to the previous slide, slide 8.

4. Repeat step 3 until you reach the first slide of the presentation.

Let's end this activity by using the Slide Changer to move between nonconsecutive slides. Suppose you wanted to move directly to slide 5, without displaying any of the slides in between:

1. Point to the lever (the short horizontal bar) at the top of the Slide Changer slot.

2. Press and hold down the **left mouse button** to "grab" the Slide Changer lever. Do not release the mouse button until we tell you to do so in step 4.

3. Move the mouse downward until the View Status box reads *Slide 5*.

4. Release the mouse button to display slide 5.

Note: The four-step procedure you just performed—pointing to an object, pressing and holding the left mouse button to "grab" the object, moving the mouse in the desired direction, and then releasing the mouse button—is called *dragging* an object (as explained in Table 1.1).

PRACTICE YOUR SKILLS

1. Use the keyboard to move to the following succession of consecutive slides:

   6, 7, 8, 9, 8, 7, 6, 5, 4, 3, 2, 1, 2

2. Use the Slide Changer to move to the following succession of consecutive and non consecutive slides:

   6, 1, 4, 2, 7, 8, 9, 6, 5, 4, 2, 5, 3, 2, 1

CHANGING THE VIEW

As mentioned, PowerPoint provides four different views in which you can display, create, and edit your presentation slides. These are Slide view, Notes view, Slide Sorter view, and Outline view. Each view lends itself to certain types of tasks:

- *Slide view* allows you to work in detail on one slide at a time. You can view a slide, create a new slide, and create/edit/delete slide text, graphs, clip art, and drawings.

- *Notes view* allows you to create notes for your individual slides. You can then use these notes as "cue cards" when narrating the presentation.

- *Slide Sorter view* allows you to work with an overview of the entire set of slides in the presentation. Slides are displayed in miniature, making it easy for you to rearrange, copy, and delete them.

- *Outline view* allows you to work with an overview of the presentation's text. You can create new slides and enter/edit slide text.

Here's the general procedure for changing the view:

- Click on *View* to open the drop-down View menu, and then click on the desired view: *Slides, Notes, Slide Sorter,* or *Outline*.

- Or, click on the *Slide View button*, the *Notes View button*, the *Slide Sorter View button*, or the *Outline View button*.

Let's practice changing views by using the View menu:

1. Click on **View** to display the drop-down View menu. Note that Slides is selected (preceded by a bullet).

2. Click on **Outline** to change to Outline view, as shown in Figure 1.11.

3. Observe the textual information on your screen. Scroll down to the end of the outline. (To do this, click repeatedly on the **down scroll arrow** in the bottom-right corner of the presentation window.) Now scroll back up to the beginning. (Click repeatedly on the **up scroll arrow**.) This is all the text in the PREVIEW1.PPT presentation. Note the numbers (1 through 9) on the left side of the screen; these represent the nine slides of PREVIEW1.PPT.

4. Observe the View buttons along the bottom of the presentation window. Note that the Outline View button (the one showing a miniature outline) is selected.

Figure 1.11 **PREVIEW1.PPT in Outline view**

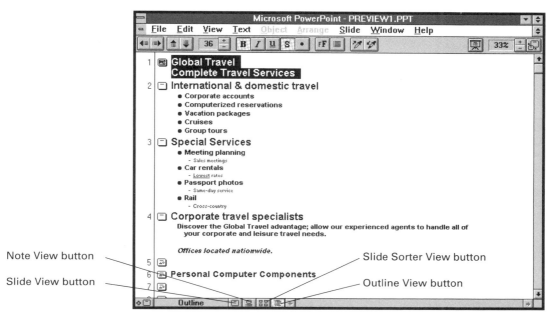

Note View button

Slide View button

Slide Sorter View button

Outline View button

5. Choose **View, Slide Sorter** to change to Slide Sorter view. Note that all nine slides of PREVIEW1.PPT are displayed in miniature, as shown in Figure 1.12. Later on, you'll learn how to copy and rearrange slides in the Slide Sorter.

6. Observe the View buttons. Note that the Slide Sorter View button (the one showing four miniature slides) is now selected.

Now let's use the View buttons to change views:

1. Click on the **Slide View** button (the one showing a single miniature slide) to change to Slide view.

2. Click on the **Slide Sorter View button** to change to Slide Sorter view.

PRACTICE YOUR SKILLS

1. Use the View buttons to change to Notes view.

2. Use the View buttons to return to Slide view.

Figure 1.12   **PREVIEW1.PPT in Slide Sorter view**

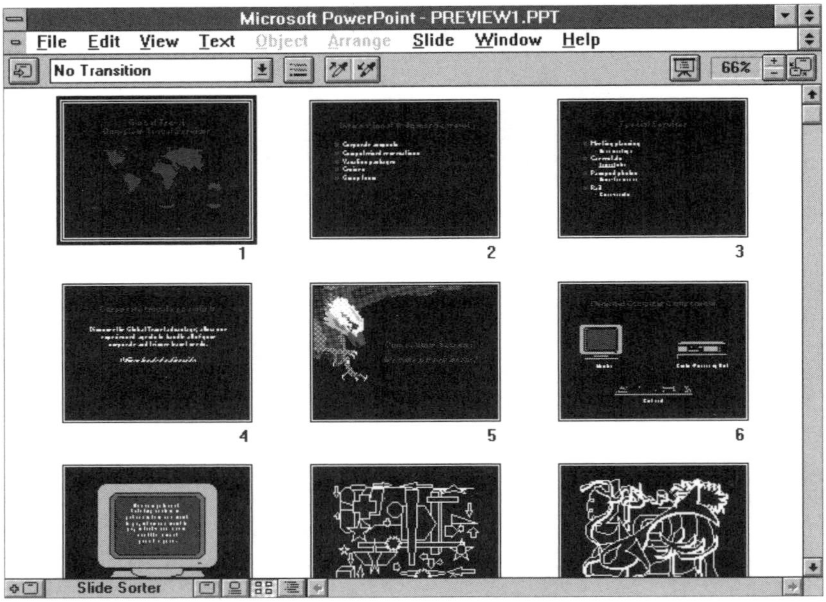

CLOSING A PRESENTATION FILE

When you are finished working on a presentation file, you should close it. Opening a file places a copy of it in your computer's active memory (RAM); closing the file removes it from memory, freeing this memory for use by another presentation.

Here's the general procedure for closing a presentation file:

* Choose File, Close.

Let's close the current presentation file, PREVIEW1.PPT:

1. Choose **File, Close**. The PREVIEW1.PPT presentation window disappears, and the application window remains alone on the screen.

EXITING FROM POWERPOINT

When you finish a PowerPoint work session and want to turn off your computer or to run another program, you must first exit from PowerPoint. Here's the general procedure to do this:

- Choose *File, Exit*.

Let's end this chapter by exiting from PowerPoint:

1. Choose **File, Exit**. You are returned to the Windows environment. You may now start another program from Windows, exit to DOS, or turn off your computer. For more information, see your Windows reference manuals.

SUMMARY

Congratulations on successfully working through this first chapter; you're well on your way to PowerPoint proficiency! You now know how to start PowerPoint, how to open a presentation file, how to move between slides in Slide view, how to change the view, how to close a presentation file, and how to exit from PowerPoint.

Here's a quick reference for the techniques you learned in this chapter:

Desired Result	How to Do It
Start PowerPoint	Turn on your computer; if you are already in Windows, skip to the final step; if you are in a non-DOS operating environment, exit to DOS; at the DOS prompt, type **win** and press **Enter** to start Windows; double-click on the Microsoft PowerPoint program icon
Open a presentation file	Choose **File, Open** to open the Open dialog box; if necessary, change the current drive and directory to the drive and directory that contains the presentation file you want to open; select the name of the presentation file you want to open; click on OK

Move between slides using the Slide Changer	To move to the next slide, click on the Slide Changer's **Next Slide arrow**; to move to the previous slide, click on the Slide Changer's **Previous Slide arrow**; to move ahead or back more than one slide, drag the Slide Changer lever until your desired slide is displayed in the View Status box
Move between slides using the keyboard	To move to the next slide, press **Page Down** (or **PgDn**); to move to the previous slide, press **Page Up** (or **PgUp**)
Change the view	Click on **View** to open the drop-down View menu, then click on the desired view (**Slides, Notes, Slide Sorter,** or **Outline**); or, click on the desired View button (**Slide, Notes, Slide Sorter,** or **Outline**)
Close a presentation file	Choose **File, Close**
Exit from PowerPoint	Choose **File, Exit**

A NOTE ON HOW TO PROCEED

If you wish to stop here, please feel free to do so now. If you feel energetic and wish to press onward, please proceed directly to the next chapter. Remember to allot enough time to work through an entire chapter in one sitting.

CHAPTER 2: BEGINNING A PRESENTATION

In Chapter 1, you learned basic PowerPoint survival skills. In this chapter, you'll put these skills into action by beginning work on the nine-slide presentation that you'll create over the course of this and the four following chapters. After learning the general procedure for creating a presentation, you'll open a new presentation, create blank slides, enter text in these slides, and save the presentation to a file on your hard disk.

When you're done working through this chapter, you will know

- How to run a slide show
- How to open a new presentation
- How to create slides and enter text in Slide view
- How to save a new presentation
- How to create slides and enter text in Outline view
- How to create nonbulleted body text
- How to save an existing presentation

RUNNING A SLIDE SHOW

You can display a presentation on your computer screen by running a slide show. One slide is displayed at a time; the application and presentation windows disappear to allow each slide to fill the entire screen. You can advance the slides manually, or have Power-Point advance them automatically.

Here's the general procedure for running a slide show manually:

- If it is not already open, open the presentation file containing the slides you want to show.
- Choose *File, Slide Show* to open the Slide Show dialog box.
- Click on *Show* to begin the slide show.
- To move forward one slide, click the left mouse button, press Enter, or press Page Down.
- To move backward one slide, click the right mouse button or press Page Up.
- When the last slide in the presentation is displayed, click the left mouse button or press Enter to end the show.

Note: You'll learn how to get PowerPoint to run a slide show automatically in Chapter 12.

SNEAK PREVIEW

Over the course of Chapters 2 through 6, you will create a nine-slide presentation that makes use of many of PowerPoint's basic slide creation and editing features. We'll begin this chapter by showing you a sneak preview of this presentation. As you observe these nine slides, remember that you'll soon possess the technical mastery to create them yourself!

If you are not running PowerPoint, please start it now. (For help, see "Starting PowerPoint" in Chapter 1 or the quick reference section at the end of Chapter 1.) Close all open presentations except for the default *start-up presentation* (named "Presentation") that automatically appears when you first start PowerPoint.

Let's run a slide show of PREVIEW1.PPT, a presentation that contains copies of the nine slides you'll create in this and the next four chapters:

1. If your application window is not maximized, maximize it.

2. Open **PREVIEW1.PPT** from your POWERWRK directory. As you'll recall from Chapter 1, you choose **File, Open** to open the Open dialog box, and (if necessary) change the current drive to the drive containing POWERWRK. Then change the current directory to POWERWRK. (Double-click on c:\ at the top of the Directories list box; scroll down, if necessary, to display the powerwrk entry in this list box; and double-click on powerwrk.) Select (click on) the file **preview1.ppt** in the File Name list box, and click on **OK**.

3. If your presentation window is not maximized, maximize it.

4. Choose **File, Slide Show** to open the Slide Show dialog box. Observe the various setup options. *Slides* determines which slides are shown, *Advance* determines how they are advanced, and *Loop Continuously Until 'Esc'* determines whether the entire show is looped (repeated). You'll learn how to use these options in Chapter 12. For now, we'll run the slide show using the default setup options: Slides is set to All, Advance is set to Manual, and Loop is turned off.

5. Click on **Show** to begin the slide show. The first slide of the presentation is displayed in full-screen view, as shown in Figure 2.1. This slide contains red title text (*Global Travel Complete Travel Services*), clip art (the global projection map), a shaded background (dark blue to light blue), and a three-dimensional border.

Figure 2.1    **Slide 1 of the PREVIEW.1 slide show**

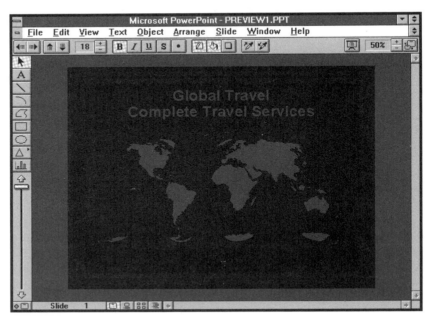

6. Click the **left mouse button** to display the next slide. It contains red title text (International & domestic travel), a bulleted list with red bullets and white text (Corporate accounts, Computerized reservations, and so on), and the same background and border as the previous slide.

7. Press **Enter** to display the next slide. You can advance to the next slide by pressing Enter, by clicking the left mouse button, or—as you'll see in the next step—by pressing Page Down. This slide contains red title text, a two-level bulleted list with red bullets and white text, and the same background and border as the previous two slides.

Notice a pattern here? Although the text and layout differ from slide to slide, several elements remain the same: the title-text size and color, the bulleted-text size and color, the background, and the border. These recurring elements give the presentation unity.

You'll learn more about unifying your presentation slides in Chapter 6. Now let's get back to our slide show:

1. Press **Page Down** to display the next slide. Note the red title text, the white body text (in this case, not formatted as a bulleted list), and the familiar background and border.

2. Display the next slide. (Use whichever technique you feel most comfortable with—the mouse, **Enter**, or **Page Down**.) Now here's something totally different! A black background, no border, a fierce eagle, and text that is in neither the standard title-text nor body-text location. PowerPoint allows you to "override" the unified style of a presentation in order to make a dramatic point—which this slide admirably succeeds in doing.

3. Display the next slide. It contains the standard title text, background, and border, along with three images, all with their own text labels.

4. Display the next slide. It contains the standard background and border, and a picture of a monitor with accompanying text.

The monitor in this slide is an enlarged version of the monitor you viewed on the previous slide. Let's redisplay the previous slide to verify this:

1. Click the **right mouse button** to display the previous slide. (You could also have pressed Page Up to do this.) Take a good look at the monitor in this slide.

2. Now redisplay the next slide (the enlarged monitor slide). Observe that this is the same image, proportionally enlarged to fill the entire slide.

3. Display the next slide. It contains an assortment of predefined shapes. You'll create a similar slide in Chapter 4.

4. Display the next slide. This—the ninth and last slide in the presentation—contains an assortment of *free-form shapes*. You'll create a similar slide in Chapter 4.

5. Click the **left mouse button** (or press **Enter** or **Page Down**) to end the slide show.

6. Choose **File**, **Close** to close PREVIEW1.PPT.

OVERVIEW OF THE PROCEDURE FOR CREATING A PRESENTATION

All the skills you'll learn in this book are geared toward helping you produce sophisticated, professional-quality slide presentations. The following five bulleted steps represent the general procedure you'll use in Chapter 3 through 6 to create the nine-slide presentation that you just previewed.

- Open a new, blank presentation in which to create your slides.

- In the newly opened presentation, create blank slides and enter their text.

- Save the presentation to a file on your disk; continue to save this file every 10 or 15 minutes while you're working on it.

- Add design elements by drawing on slides, adding charts (graphs) to slides, adding clip art to slides, and laying out slides.

- Generate output by printing slides, notes, or handouts; processing presentation as 35-millimeter slides; and running a slide show of the presentation.

Note: The above bulleted list represents the *general procedure* you follow to create a presentation. Please regard it as a guideline, not an inflexible law. At times, you may need to change the sequence of steps (for example, to work on slide design before entering text); or to skip back and forth between steps (for example, to create a slide, enter its text, add clip art to it, enter more text for it, customize its layout, and so on); or to skip a step entirely (for example, to create a text-only presentation, you might not need to add any design elements).

In this chapter, you'll learn how to begin a presentation by performing the first three steps of this procedure: opening a new presentation, creating slides and entering text, and saving the presentation. The remaining steps will be covered in Chapters 3 through 6.

OPENING A NEW PRESENTATION

Your first step in creating a presentation is to open a new presentation. Here's the general procedure for doing this:

- Choose *File, New*.

- If no presentations are open, PowerPoint opens a new, blank presentation. If a presentation is open, the New dialog box appears, offering you two options: *Use Format Of Active Presentation*, or *Use Default Format*. (These options are explained below.) Select your desired option and click on OK to open a new, blank presentation.

The first option in the New dialog box, Use Format Of Active Presentation, causes your new presentation to use the slide format (layout) and defaults of the currently active presentation. The second option, Use Default Format, causes your new presentation to use the slide format and defaults of PowerPoint's default presentation.

Let's open a new presentation:

1. Your screen should be empty, except for a maximized Power-Point application window. If any presentations are open, please close them.

2. Choose **File, New** to open a new, blank presentation, as shown in Figure 2.2. Note that the presentation window is maximized. When you open a presentation window, Power-Point automatically maximizes it if the last active presentation window was maximized. PREVIEW1.PPT—your last active presentation window—was maximized, so PowerPoint automatically maximized your new presentation window.

3. Observe the name of your new presentation, Presentation (as shown in the title bar). This is the default name for every new presentation, including the start-up presentation that appears when you first start PowerPoint. Soon, you'll learn how to rename a presentation and save it to a file on your hard disk.

CREATING SLIDES AND ENTERING TEXT IN SLIDE VIEW

After opening a new presentation, your next step in creating a presentation is to create blank slides and enter text in them. You can do this either in Slide view or in Outline view.

The advantage of entering your slide text in Slide view is that you can see what the actual slides look like (the text size, style, layout, and so on); the disadvantages are that you can see only one slide at a time, and that it is somewhat harder to enter and edit your text than in Outline view.

Figure 2.2   **Opening a new presentation**

Title object

Body object

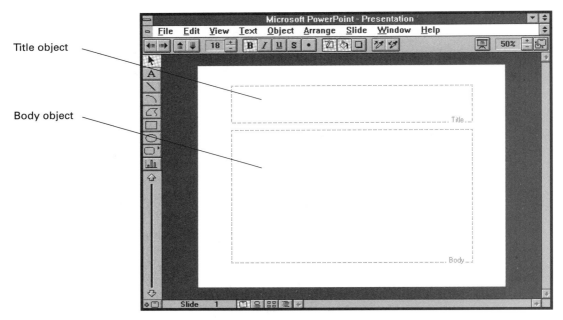

The advantages of entering your slide text in Outline view are that you can see an overview of all the text in your presentation, and that it is somewhat easier to enter and edit your text than in Slide view; the disadvantage is that you cannot see what the actual slides look like.

Novice PowerPoint users often prefer to enter their slide text in Slide view, while more advanced users often prefer to enter their slide text in Outline view.

Over the next few sections, we'll show you how to create slides and enter text in Slide view. In the second half of the chapter, we'll show you how to perform these same tasks in Outline view. By the end of the chapter, you should have a good idea in which view you feel more comfortable entering your slide text.

CREATING NEW SLIDES IN SLIDE VIEW

Here's the general procedure for creating a new slide in Slide view:

- Display the slide after which you want to add your new slide.
- Click on the *New Slide button* or press *Ctrl+N*.

Let's use this simple procedure to add a new slide to our presentation:

1. Observe the View Status box. The current slide is slide 1.

2. Click on the **New Slide button** (located beneath the Slide Changer, it shows a plus sign (+) next to a miniature slide) to create a new slide.

3. Observe the View Status box; the new slide is slide 2. As mentioned, clicking on the New Slide button adds a new slide *after* the current slide.

 ## ENTERING SLIDE TEXT IN SLIDE VIEW

When you are in Slide view, PowerPoint provides a *Title object* and a *Body object* in which you can enter your desired slide text. You enter a slide's title (and subtitle and so on) in the Title object, which is located at the top of the slide (as shown in Figure 2.2). You enter a slide's body text (bulleted items, descriptive paragraphs, and so on) in the Body object, which is located in the middle of the slide.

Here's the general procedure for entering text in Slide view:

- Select (click on) the Title object or the Body object.
- Type your desired title or body text.

 ## TEXT FORMATTING AND THE SLIDE MASTER

The format of the text you enter in the Title and the Body objects is determined by the format settings in a special slide called the *Slide Master*. For example, the text you enter in the Body object is automatically formatted as a bulleted list, because this is the format of the Body object text in the Slide Master. The bullet shape, size, and color, as well as the alignment of the bullet text items (left, right, center, or justified) are all determined by the Slide Master settings.

The Slide Master guarantees that all the title and body text in your presentation will be identically formatted, thus lending an overall consistency to the presentation. You'll learn more about the Slide Master in Chapter 6.

Let's enter a two-line title for the first slide of our new presentation:

1. Display slide 1. (Use the **Slide Changer** or the **Page Up** key.)

2. Click inside the **Title object** to select it. PowerPoint outlines the object to indicate that it is selected.

3. Type **Global Travel** to enter the first line of the title. Note that your text is automatically centered within the Title-object box. Why? Because the Title-object text in the Slide Master is set to be centered.

4. Press **Enter** to begin the second title line, and type **Complete Travel Services**.

5. Deselect the **Title object** by clicking outside the Title-object box. Your screen should match that shown in Figure 2.3.

Figure 2.3   **Entering a two-line title in Slide view**

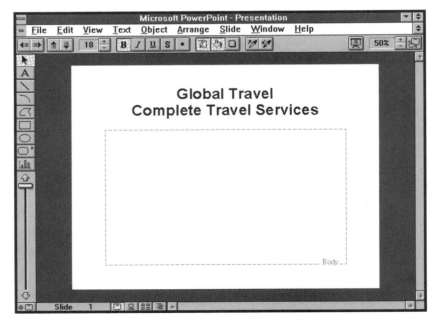

Now let's enter a title and some body text for slide 2:

1. Display slide 2 and select the **Title object**.

2. Type **International & domestic travel** to enter your slide title. Note that the text is automatically centered within the Title-object box, just like it was in slide 1. The Slide Master causes all the title and body text in your presentation to be identically formatted.

3. Select the **Body object**.

4. Type **Corporate accounts** to enter your first line of body text. Note that the text is automatically formatted as a bulleted item. As mentioned, this is the format of the Body-object text in the Slide Master. (Later on, you'll learn how to change the format of your title and body text.)

5. Press **Enter** to create a new bulleted item.

6. Type **Computerized reservations** to enter your second bulleted item.

PRACTICE YOUR SKILLS

1. Add the following two bulleted items to your body text. (Hint: Press **Enter** to create a new bulleted item.)

   Vacation packages

   Group tours

2. Deselect the Body object (by clicking outside the Body-object box). Your screen should match that shown in Figure 2.4.

SAVING A NEW PRESENTATION

Until you save a new presentation, it exists only in computer memory (RAM), a temporary storage place. For permanent storage, you must save the presentation in a file on a disk. To save a new presentation for the first time, you use the *File, Save As* command. Here's the general procedure for doing this:

• Choose *File, Save As* to open the Save As dialog box.

• If necessary, change the current drive and directory to the drive and directory in which you want to save your presentation.

Figure 2.4   **Entering a title and bulleted items for slide 2**

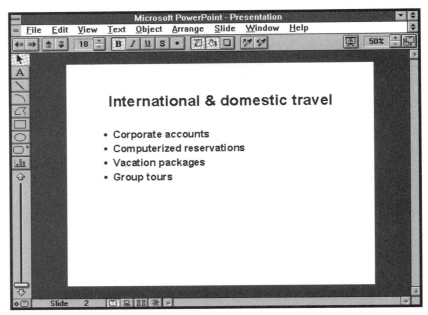

- In the File Name text box, type your desired file name. A file name can contain from one to eight characters (letters and numbers, but no spaces). Choose a descriptive file name to help you remember your presentation's contents. Do not include a *file-name extension*, a period followed by three letters (.PPT, for example). PowerPoint automatically adds the extension .PPT to your presentation's file name.

- Click on OK.

Let's use File, Save As to save our new presentation:

1. Choose **File, Save As** to open the Save As dialog box. Note the similarity between this and the Open dialog box (the dialog box that appears when you choose File, Open). Saving a file and opening a file are complementary actions: The former *writes* information to a specified disk location; the latter *reads* information from a specified disk location.

2. Observe the directory line beneath the heading *Directories*. Note that the current drive and directory are already set to those of POWERWRK (c:\powerwrk). Why? Earlier in this

chapter, you changed your current drive and directory to those of POWERWRK so that you could open the presentation file PREVIEW1.PPT. PowerPoint "remembers" the changes and uses them as the default settings for the rest of the current work session.

3. Type **mypres1** in the File Name text box.

4. Click on **OK** to save the current presentation as MYPRES1.PPT; as mentioned, PowerPoint automatically adds the extension .PPT to the end of a presentation's file name. Note that the title bar reports your file name, Microsoft PowerPoint - MYPRES1.PPT.

CREATING SLIDES AND ENTERING TEXT IN OUTLINE VIEW

In the first half of this chapter, you learned how to create slides and enter text in Slide view. Now you'll learn how to perform these same tasks in Outline view. As mentioned, experienced PowerPoint users often prefer to enter their slide text in Outline view for two reasons: They like to work with an overview of all their slides, and it is somewhat easier to enter and edit text in Outline view than in Slide view.

CREATING NEW SLIDES IN OUTLINE VIEW

Here's the general procedure for creating a new slide in Outline view:

• Place the insertion point anywhere within the text of the slide after which you want to add your new slide.

• Click on the *New Slide button* or press *Ctrl+N.*

Let's use Ctrl+N to create a new slide for our MYPRES1.PPT presentation:

1. Click on the **Outline View button** (the one showing a miniature outline) to change to Outline view.

2. Observe the differences between Outline view and Slide view. (You may want to switch back and forth between these two views while reading this step.) In Outline view, the menu-bar options Object and Arrange are dimmed, indicating that their drop-down menu commands are unavailable. The Tool-bar configuration has changed slightly, and the Tool Palette

has been completely removed, because you cannot draw on a slide in Outline view. The mouse pointer—when it is within the slide workspace—appears as an *I-beam*; this is the pointer that PowerPoint uses when you work with text. Finally, and most dramatically, the slides are no longer displayed in their actual "slide" form (as they are in Slide view or in a slide show); instead, only an outline of the slides' text is displayed.

3. Return to Outline view, if necessary.

4. Move the I-beam (the I-shaped mouse pointer) until it is positioned anywhere within the text of slide 2. Click the **left mouse button** to place the insertion point in the text. The *insertion point* marks the spot where what you type is inserted on the screen. In this case, you'll type a *Control-key combination* (a multiple keystroke involving the Ctrl key) rather than a character.

5. Press **Ctrl+n** (press and hold down the **Ctrl** key, press **n**, and then release both keys) to create a new slide, slide 3. Ctrl+N is a *keyboard shortcut* for the New Slide command. Power-Point provides many keyboard shortcuts, several of which you'll learn during the course of this book. Note that you do not need to use the Shift key to capitalize the letter in a keyboard shortcut; pressing Ctrl+n is equivalent to pressing Ctrl+N.

6. Type **My Slide** to assign a temporary title to this slide.

Now let's use the New Slide button to create a new slide:

7. Place the insertion point anywhere within the text of slide 2.

8. Click on the **New Slide button** to add a new slide after the current slide, slide 2. Your screen should match that shown in Figure 2.5. Note that My Slide was moved down to slide 4 to make room for your new (untitled) slide. When you add a new slide to a presentation, PowerPoint inserts it between the current and succeeding slides.

 ENTERING SLIDE TEXT IN OUTLINE VIEW

As you know, in Slide view, you enter title text in the Title-object box and you enter body text in the Body-object box. In Outline view, you still work with title and body text; however, this text is defined not by its location within a box, but by its degree of indentation within the outline.

Figure 2.5   **Creating slides in Outline view**

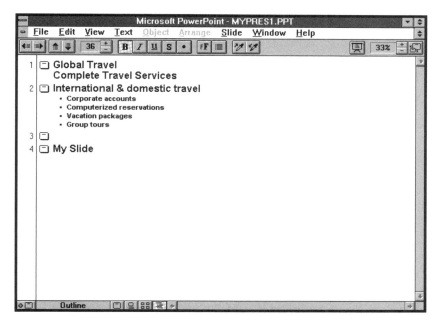

Title text is not indented; that is, it appears leftmost in the outline. You can see this in the Figure 2.5 titles, *Global Travel, Complete Travel Services, International & domestic travel*, and *My Slide*.

Body text is indented from one to five levels to the right of title text. The first level of indentation corresponds to a standard bulleted item on the slide. In Figure 2.5, the body-text items *Corporate accounts, Computerized reservations, Vacation packages*, and *Group tours*—all of which are indented one level—correspond to the four standard bulleted items shown in Figure 2.4. The second through fifth levels of body-text indentation correspond to level-2 through level-5 bulleted items. Figure 2.6 shows a sample slide in Outline view with all five levels of body-text indentation; Figure 2.7 shows this same slide in Slide view.

Here's the general procedure for entering text in Outline view:

- To enter title text, place the insertion point to the right of the slide icon and type your desired text.

Figure 2.6   **Level-1 through level-5 bulleted items in Outline view**

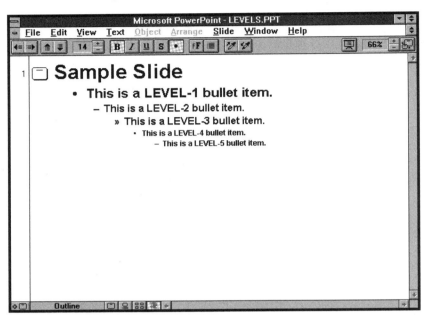

Figure 2.7   **Level-1 through level-5 bulleted items in Slide view**

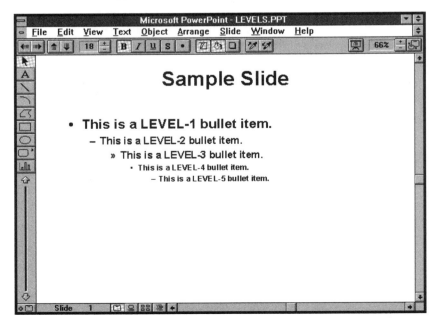

- To enter body text, place the insertion point at the end of the line after which you want to enter your text, press Enter to create a new line, press *Tab* or *Shift+Tab* (if necessary) to change your new line to the desired indentation level, and type your desired text.

- To *promote* a line (that is, to *decrease* its indentation by one level), place the insertion point in the line and click on the *Promote button* or press Shift+Tab.

- To *demote* a line (that is, to *increase* its indentation by one level), place the insertion point in the line, and click on the *Demote button* or press Tab.

Let's use this procedure to create a two-level bulleted list for slide 3. First, we'll enter the slide title:

1. If necessary, place the insertion point directly to the right of the slide 3 icon.

2. Type **Special Services** to enter the title for slide 3.

Now we'll enter the body text, a two-level bulleted list:

1. Press **Enter** to create a new line (and a new slide). We need to demote this line by one level to make it body text.

2. Click on the **Demote button** (the second button from the left on the Toolbar, it shows a thick right arrow) to increase the line's indentation by one level, from title text to level-1 body text. Note that the new slide icon disappears, and your new line becomes the first bulleted item of slide 3.

3. Type **Meeting planning** to enter the text for this first bulleted item.

4. Press **Enter** to create a new line. Observe that this is a level-1 bulleted item. We want to change it to a level-2 bulleted item, a *sub-bullet* under the level-1 bullet (*Meeting planning*) you just created. To do this, you need to demote the line by one level.

5. Press **Tab** to demote the line from a level-1 to a level-2 bulleted item. To demote a line, you can either click on the Demote button (as you did in step 2) or press Tab.

6. Type **Sales meetings** to enter the text for the level-2 bulleted item.

7. Press **Enter** to create a new, level-2 bulleted item. We need to promote this to a level-1 bulleted item.

8. Click on the **Promote button** (the leftmost button on the Toolbar, it shows a thick left arrow) to do this. You could also have pressed Shift+Tab to perform the promotion.

9. Type **Passport photos** to enter the text for the bulleted item.

10. Press **Enter** to create a new level-1 bulleted item, and then press **Tab** to demote it to a level-2 bulleted item.

11. Type **Same-day service** to enter the text for this bulleted item.

PRACTICE YOUR SKILLS

1. Add the following pair of level-1 and level-2 bulleted items to slide 3:

   Rail

   Cross-country

Your screen should now match that shown in Figure 2.8.

 ## CREATING NONBULLETED BODY TEXT

As you know, by default, PowerPoint formats the text you enter in the Body object as a bulleted list. There may be times, however, when you want to create nonbulleted body text. For example, you might find that a nonbulleted descriptive paragraph communicates a slide's message better than does a bulleted list.

Here's the general procedure for removing bullets from your body text:

- Select the body text whose bullets you want to remove. To select a single bulleted item, place the insertion point anywhere within the item. To select two or more adjacent bulleted items, drag from anywhere within the top item to anywhere within the bottom item.

- Click on the *Add Bullet button* on the Toolbar.

- To restore bullets to your body text, select the body text and click on the Add Bullet button. Clicking on the Add Bullet button once removes the bullets; clicking on it a second time restores the bullets.

Figure 2.8 **Creating a two-level bulleted list**

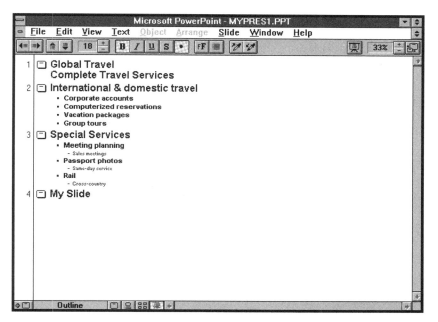

Let's enter a new title and two nonbulleted paragraphs for slide 4:

1. Select (drag over) **My Slide**, the current title of slide 4. The title is highlighted to indicate that it is selected.

2. Type **Corporate travel specialists** to enter a new title. Note that your new text replaced your old text (*My Slide*). Whenever you select text and then type, the new text replaces the selected text.

3. Press **Enter** and then press **Tab** to create a level-1 bulleted item under your new title.

4. Observe the Add Bullet button (located in the middle of the Toolbar, it shows a bullet). Note that it is selected. Now click on the **Add Bullet button** to remove the bullet from your new body-text line. Note that the button is deselected.

5. Type **Discover the Global Travel advantage; allow our experienced agents to handle all of your corporate and leisure
travel needs**. (including the period) to enter your nonbulleted body text. Observe that the text automatically wraps
around to a second line after the word *of*, and that this second line is indented.

6. Press **Enter** twice to create two new level-1 body-text lines.
Note that both of these lines inherit the nonbulleted attribute
of their parent line, *Discover the Global Travel advantage....*

7. Type **Offices located nationwide**. (including the period) to
enter a second nonbulleted body-text line. Your screen
should match that shown in Figure 2.9.

Figure 2.9   **Creating nonbulleted body text**

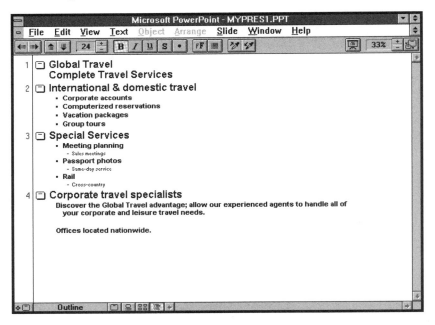

Now let's change to Slide view to see what the two slides we just created in Outline view actually look like:

1. Change to Slide view. Slide 4 should be displayed; if not, display it now. Your screen should match that shown in Figure 2.10.

Figure 2.10   **Slide 4 in Slide view**

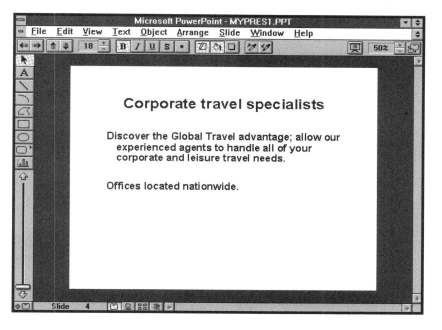

2. Observe the slide workspace. This is an accurate representation of how slide 4 will look when you display it in a slide show, print it out, or process it as a 35-millimeter slide.

3. Observe the first paragraph of body text. Note that it wraps around twice, once after *our* and once after *your*. In Outline view, as you'll recall, this paragraph wrapped around just once, after *of*. Change to Outline view to verify this. Outline view does not provide an accurate representation of how your text will look on the actual slide. To see this, you must change to Slide view.

4. Return to Slide view. Display slide 3. It should match that shown in Figure 2.11.

Figure 2.11   **Slide 3 in Slide view**

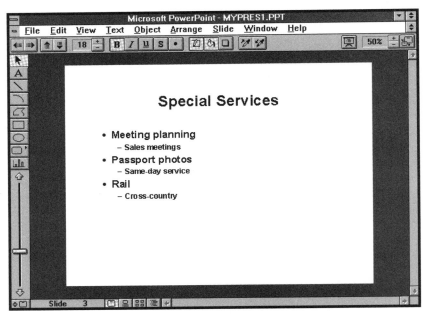

5. Switch back and forth between Outline view and Slide view to observe the differences in how slide 3's text is displayed in these two views.

SAVING AN EXISTING PRESENTATION

As you learned earlier in this chapter, to save a new presentation for the first time, you use the File, Save As command. To save changes to an existing presentation—a presentation that you've already saved at least once—you use the *File, Save* command. When you choose File, Save, PowerPoint saves the current version of your presentation under the same name and to the same disk location (directory and drive) that you specified when you used File, Save As to save the new presentation.

Here's the general procedure for saving an existing presentation:

- Choose *File, Save* or press *Ctrl+S*.

Let's use this simple procedure to save the current presentation, MYPRES1.PPT:

1. Choose **File, Save** to save the current version of your presentation under the same file name (MYPRES1.PPT) and to the same disk location (C:\POWERWRK) used for the previously saved version. Note that no dialog box appears. PowerPoint already knows all the salient information (file name, disk drive and directory), so it can perform your command without any further input from you.

2. Click on **File** to open the drop-down File menu. Observe the Save command; note that its keyboard shortcut, Ctrl+S, appears next to it. To learn keyboard shortcuts, keep an eye on the drop-down menus, or refer to Appendix C for a complete listing. Click on **File** again to close the File menu.

3. Press **Ctrl+s** to save your presentation again. As with all keyboard shortcuts, pressing Ctrl+S is equivalent to choosing the corresponding menu command (File, Save).

4. Close **MYPRES1.PPT**.

FILE-SAVING GUIDELINES

You should get into the habit of using File, Save (or Ctrl+S) to save your presentation files frequently. As a rule of thumb, save your current presentation every 10 to 15 minutes. That way, if your computer accidentally shuts off (due to a power outage, for example), you'll lose only 10 to 15 minutes of work. Never wait longer than a half hour before you save a file; to do so is to invite trouble!

KEEPING DIFFERENT VERSIONS OF THE SAME PRESENTATION

When you use File, Save to save an existing presentation, the current presentation file *overwrites* the previous version of the file, permanently erasing the previous file from your disk. If all you want to keep is your current version, this is fine. However, if you also want to keep the previous version, you must use File, Save As to save the current presentation file under a new name.

For example, let's say that you'd created and saved a presentation file named TRAVEL.PPT. Your manager asks you to revamp the presentation and to show her both, side by side, so that she can choose the better one for publication. You open TRAVEL.PPT, make the necessary changes, and then—realizing that if you choose File, Save to save your current version, you will lose the previous version—you choose File, Save As and name the current version TRAVEL1.PPT. Voilà! You've preserved both versions, TRAVEL.PPT and TRAVEL1.PPT.

SUMMARY

In this chapter, you began work on your MYPRES1.PPT presentation by creating four simple text slides. You learned how to run a slide show, how to open a new presentation, how to create slides and enter text in Slide view and in Outline view, how to create nonbulleted body text, and how to save both a new presentation and an existing presentation.

Here's a quick reference for the techniques you learned in this chapter:

Desired Result	How to Do It
Run a slide show manually	If necessary, open the presentation file; choose **File, Slide Show**; click on **Show**; to move forward one slide, click the **left mouse button**, press **Enter** or press **Page Down**; to move backward one slide, click the **right mouse button** or press **Page Up**; to end the show, display the last slide and click the **left mouse button** or press **Enter**

Desired Result	How to Do It
Create a slide presentation	Open a new blank presentation; create blank slides and enter their text; save the presentation (continue to save it every 10 or 15 minutes); add design elements by drawing on slides and adding charts (graphs) and clip art to slides, and then lay out slides; generate output by printing slides, notes, or handouts; process presentation as 35-millimeter slides; and run a slide show of the presentation
Open a new presentation	Choose **File, New**; if the New dialog box appears, select your desired option (Use Format Of Active Presentation or Use Default Format) and click on **OK**
Create a new slide in Slide view	Display the slide after which you want to add your new slide and click on the **New Slide button** or press **Ctrl+N**
Enter text in Slide view	Select the **Title object** or the **Body object** and type your desired title or body text
Save a new presentation	Choose **File, Save As**; if necessary, change the current drive and directory; enter your desired file name; click on **OK**
Create a new slide in Outline view	Place the insertion point anywhere within the text of the slide after which you want to add your new slide and click on the **New Slide button** or press **Ctrl+N**

Desired Result	How to Do It
Enter text in Outline view	For title text, place the insertion point to the right of the slide icon and type your desired text; for body text, place the insertion point at the end of the line after which you want to enter your text, press **Enter** to create a new line, use **Shift+Tab** (if necessary) to change your new line to the desired indentation level, and type your desired text; to promote a line, place the insertion point in the line and click on the **Promote button** or press **Shift+Tab**; to demote a line, place the insertion point in the line and click on the **Demote button** or press **Tab**
Remove/restore bullets from your body text	Select the desired body text and click on the **Add Bullet button**
Save an existing presentation	To keep only the current version of the presentation, choose **File, Save** or press **Ctrl+S**; to keep both the current version and the previous version of the presentation, choose **File, Save As**, enter your new file name and/or drive and/or directory, and click on **OK**

In the next chapter, we'll show you how to work with slide text. You'll learn how to get general and dialog-box help, how to edit slide text, how to rearrange bulleted items, how to apply text attributes, how to change indents, how to align text, how to change line spacing, and how to spell-check a presentation.

IF YOU'RE STOPPING HERE

If you need to break off here, please exit PowerPoint. If you want to proceed directly to the next chapter, please do so now.

CHAPTER 3: WORKING WITH SLIDE TEXT

Getting Help

Editing Slide Text

Spell-Checking a Presentation

In Chapter 2, you learned how to begin a presentation by creating slides and entering text in Slide view and in Outline view. In this chapter, you'll expand your slide-creation skills by learning how to further manipulate your slide text. We'll show you how to edit (modify) your text, rearrange it, change its appearance, and check its spelling. Mastery of these topics is crucial—a presentation is only as good as its words and images.

When you're done working through this chapter, you will know

- How to get help
- How to edit slide text
- How to add bulleted items to your slides
- How to rearrange bulleted items
- How to apply text attributes
- How to change indents
- How to align text
- How to change line spacing
- How to spell-check a presentation

GETTING HELP

Before diving into this chapter's main topic, working with slide text, we'd like to introduce you to *Help,* PowerPoint's on-line reference tool. You can use Help to get information about PowerPoint (commands, concepts, procedures, and so on) at any point during your work session. Think of Help as a very knowledgeable tech-support person sitting in the background and waiting patiently to answer your questions.

You can use Help to get both *general help* and *dialog-box help.* General help provides information on a vast array of PowerPoint topics. For example, let's say you forgot how to run a slide show of a presentation; you could refresh your memory by running Help and viewing the *Working with slide shows* topic. Dialog-box help provides information on the active dialog box. For example, let's say you opened the Slide Show dialog box (by choosing File, Slide Show) and didn't fully understand the Advance option; you could run Help to get information on Advance.

 GENERAL HELP

Here's the procedure for getting general help:

- Choose *Help, Contents* or press F1 to open the Help Contents window.
- To view the Help window for a topic, click on that topic.

- To search for a topic you want help with, click on the *Search button;* locate the desired search word by typing the initial part of the word or by scrolling through the search-word list; double-click on the desired search word to show its associated topics; double-click on the desired topic to view its Help window.

- To view previous Help windows, click on the *Back button.*

- To view the Contents window, click on the *Contents button.*

- To exit from Help, choose File, Exit from the Help menu bar.

If you are not running PowerPoint, please start it now. Close all open presentations, except for the start-up presentation. Let's get general help for some of the topics we've already covered in this book:

1. Choose **Help, Contents** to open the Help Contents window, as shown in Figure 3.1. The underlined items you see in this window are Help's main topics. The next four steps (2 through 5) are a miniprimer on scrolling. You can use these techniques to scroll through any PowerPoint window with scroll bars.

Figure 3.1   **The Help Contents window**

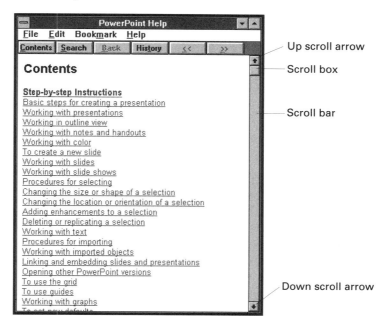

2. Click on the **down scroll arrow** (located in the lower-right corner of the Help window, as shown in Figure 3.1) to scroll the Help window down one line. Click five more times to scroll down five more lines.

3. Point to the down scroll arrow, and press and hold the **left mouse button** to scroll down smoothly to the bottom of the window. Do the same thing with the up scroll arrow to scroll back up to the top.

4. Click once within the **scroll bar**, just above the down scroll arrow, to scroll down one full screen of topics. Note that the scroll box moves downward to indicate your current position in the list. Click repeatedly to move to the end of the window. Click repeatedly just below the up scroll arrow to scroll back up to the top.

5. Drag the **scroll box** down to the middle of the scroll bar to move to the middle of the window. Use this technique to move to the bottom, and then back up to the top.

Now that you're comfortable with scrolling, let's select a topic and get help for it:

1. Click on the topic **Working with slides** (near the top of the window) to view its Help window. Note that two related topics are displayed: *To create a new slide* and *To delete a slide*.

2. Click on **To create a new slide** to view its Help window. Take a moment to read through the contents of this window. Note that it describes the slide-creation techniques you learned in Chapter 2.

3. Click on the **Back button** to return to the previous Help window, Working With Slides. Click on **Back** again to return to the original window, Contents. You can use the Back button to recall all the Help windows you viewed during the current Help session.

Let's say you wanted information on Save As, the command you use to save a new presentation. You could look through the Contents window for the appropriate topic. Or, you could use the Help Search feature to find the topic. Let's try out both of these techniques and see which is easier to use:

1. Scroll through the Contents window in pursuit of a topic that addresses the Save As command.

2. Find it? The topic you're looking for is *File*, under the sub-heading *Menu commands* (toward the bottom of the Contents window). Why this topic? Because—as you'll recall from Chapter 2—Save As is a menu command located in the drop-down File menu. Note how difficult it can be to locate a specific topic in the Contents window.

3. Click on the **File** topic to open its Help window. This window presents a list of all the commands contained in the File menu, including Save As. Clicking on a command displays a brief description of it; please *don't* do this now.

4. Click on the **Contents button** to return to the Contents window.

Now let's use Search to get help for the File, Save As command:

1. Click on the **Search button** to open the Search dialog box.

2. Type **s** to scroll the search-word list to words beginning with the letter *s*. Note that *save as command* appears in the list. In this case, you needed to type only the first letter of your desired search word to find it! In other cases, you may need to type the first few letters.

3. Double-click on **save as command** to display its single associated topic, *File menu,* in the lower list box.

4. Double-click on **File menu** to open its Help window. This is the same window that you opened in step 3 by clicking on File in the Contents window. Note how much easier it was in this case to use the Search feature than the Contents window to find information on a specific command. In other cases, it may be easier to use the Contents window; you'll have to play it by ear when you look for help.

Observe the line near the top of the Help window, *Click a command for a brief description.* Let's do this for the Save As command:

1. Click on the broken-underlined **Save As** entry in the File menu window. Help displays a brief description of the command along with a list of related topics. To choose a related topic, you simply click on it; please *don't* do this now.

2. Click on **Save As** again to remove the description.

3. Choose **File, Exit** from the Help menu bar to exit from Help. Do not choose File, Exit from the PowerPoint menu bar, as this will cause you to exit from the PowerPoint program.

DIALOG-BOX HELP

Now that you know how to get general help, let's find out how to get its counterpart, dialog-box help. Here's the general procedure for getting help for the active dialog box:

- Press F1 to open a Help window that provides information on the active dialog box.

- To exit from Help, choose File, Exit from the Help menu bar.

Let's use this technique to get information on the Save As dialog box:

1. Choose **File, Save As** to open the Save As dialog box. Note that the dialog box's title bar is highlighted, indicating that it is active.

2. Press **F1** to open the Help window for the Save As dialog box, as shown in Figure 3.2. This window provides information on the various components and options of the Save As dialog box (File Name, Directories, Save File of Type, Drives, and so on).

Figure 3.2   **The Save As dialog box Help window**

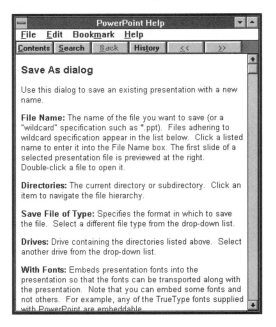

3. Scroll down to the end of the Help window, if necessary. Click on the related topic, **To save an existing presentation with a new name**, to open its Help window.

4. Click on **Back** to return to the previous window.

Note that dialog-box help looks and behaves just like general help; that's because they are two aspects of the same Help program. Think of Help as a comprehensive electronic reference manual. Getting general help (by choosing Help, Contents or pressing F1 when no dialog box is active) opens to the contents page of this manual; getting dialog-box help (by pressing F1 when a dialog box is active) opens to a page somewhere in the middle of the manual. Once you're in the manual, you can use the same basic techniques to navigate through it. Let's verify this:

1. Click on **Contents** to open the Contents window.

2. Click on the topic **Working with slides** to open its Help window. This is the same window you viewed in a previous activity, when you were getting general help.

3. Choose **File, Exit** from the Help menu bar to exit from Help.

4. Press **Esc** to close the Save As dialog box.

PRACTICE YOUR SKILLS

1. Get general help for the following PowerPoint features. (Hint: Use the **Contents** window or **Search** to locate the appropriate topic.) When you are finished getting help for the last feature, exit from Help.

Working with text

Freeform tool

Line spacing

Selecting objects

Deleting slides

2. Get dialog-box help for the following dialog boxes. (Hint: You must open a dialog box to get help for it.) When you are finished getting help for a dialog box, exit from Help, close the dialog box (by pressing **Esc**), and then open the next dialog box for which you want help.

File, Open dialog box

File, Slide Show dialog box

File, Print dialog box

File, Slide Setup dialog box

EDITING SLIDE TEXT

In Chapter 2, you learned how to enter text in Slide view and in Outline view. Here, you'll learn how to *edit* (modify) your slide text in both of these views. Over the next several sections, we'll show you how to

- Add bulleted items to your slides

- Rearrange bulleted items

- Apply text attributes

- Change indents

- Align text

- Change line spacing

 ## ADDING BULLETED ITEMS

Here's the general procedure for adding a bulleted item to a slide in Slide view or in Outline view:

- If you are in Slide view, select the Body object.

- Place the insertion point at the end of the bulleted item after which you want to add your new bulleted item.

- Press Enter to create the new bulleted item.

- If necessary, press Tab or Shift+Tab to change the indent level of your new bulleted item.

- Type your desired bullet text.

Let's open MYPRES1.PPT and add a bulleted item to slide 2 in Outline view:

1. Open **mypres1** from your POWERWRK directory. Maximize the presentation window, if necessary. This is the file that will hold the nine slides of the presentation you previewed in Chapter 2.

2. Change to Outline view.

3. Place the insertion point at the end of the level-1 bulleted item *Computerized reservations*.

4. Press **Enter** to create a new level-1 bulleted item.

5. Type **Cruises** to enter the text for this bulleted item. Your screen should match that shown in Figure 3.3.

Figure 3.3   **Adding a bulleted item in Outline view**

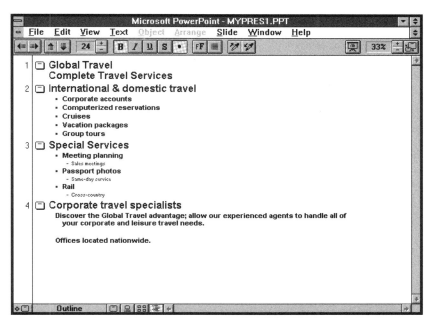

Now let's add a pair of bulleted items to slide 3 in Slide view:

1. Select slide 3 by clicking on the number **3** in the left margin of the outline.

2. Change to Slide view. Verify that slide 3 is displayed.

3. Select the **Body object** of slide 3.

4. Place the insertion point at the end of the level-2 bulleted item *Same-day service*.

5. Press **Enter** to create a new level-2 bulleted item, and then press **Shift+Tab** to promote this to a level-1 bulleted item.

6. Type **Car rentals** to enter the text for this bulleted item.

7. Press **Enter** and press **Tab** to create a new level-2 bulleted item.

8. Type **Lowest rates** to enter the text for this bulleted item. Deselect the Body object. Your screen should match that shown in Figure 3.4.

9. Choose **File, Save** to save the file.

Figure 3.4   **Adding bulleted items in Slide view**

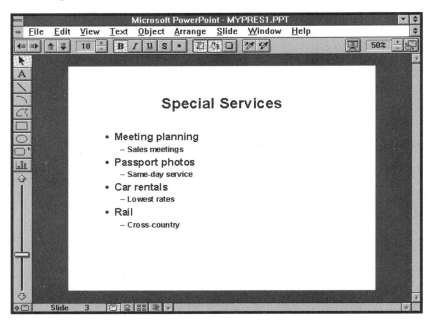

REARRANGING BULLETED ITEMS

PowerPoint allows you to quickly and easily rearrange the order of a slide's bulleted items in Slide view or in Outline view. You can do this either by dragging the bulleted items or by selecting the items and clicking on the *Move Up* and *Move Down buttons.*

Here's the general procedure for rearranging the order of bulleted items by dragging:

- If you are in Slide view, place the insertion point anywhere within the bulleted list.

- Point to the bullet of the bulleted item you want to move. The mouse pointer changes to a four-headed arrow.

- Press and hold down the left mouse button to grab this bulleted item (and all the sub-bulleted items beneath it).

- Drag the bulleted item(s) up or down to your desired new position, then release the mouse button.

Note: As you'll see in the next activity, when you move a bulleted item by dragging, you move the selected bulleted item along with all the sub-bulleted items beneath it.

Here's the general procedure for rearranging the order of bulleted items by using the Move Up and Move Down buttons:

- Select the bulleted item(s) you want to move. To select a single bulleted item, place the insertion point anywhere within the item. To select two or more adjacent bulleted items, drag from anywhere within the top item to anywhere within the bottom item.

- Click as many times as necessary on the Move Up or Move Down button to move the selected bulleted item(s) to your desired new position in the bulleted list.

Let's move a slide 3 bulleted item and its accompanying sub-bulleted item by dragging in Slide view:

1. Place the insertion point anywhere within the bulleted text of slide 3. To do this, click twice on the **Body object**. The first click selects the Body object; the second click places the insertion point within the object.

2. Point to the bullet of the *Car rentals* bulleted item. Note that the mouse pointer changes to a four-headed arrow.

3. Press and hold the **left mouse button** to grab this bullet. (Don't release the mouse button until we tell you to do so in step 5.) Note that both *Car rentals* and its sub-bulleted item *Lowest rates* are selected. As mentioned, when you move a bulleted item by dragging, you also move all the sub-bulleted items beneath it.

4. Drag upward until the *position marker* (the horizontal line extending across the Body object) is above the *Passport photos* bulleted item.

5. Release the mouse button to move the *Car rentals* and *Lowest rates* bulleted items to above *Passport photos*.

Now let's move a bulleted item in Outline view:

1. Change to Outline view.

2. Place the insertion point anywhere within the bulleted item *Vacation packages* in slide 2.

3. Click on the **Move Up button** (the third button from the left on the Toolbar, it shows an up arrow with miniature bulleted items beneath it) to move *Vacation packages* above *Cruises*.

4. Save the file.

APPLYING TEXT ATTRIBUTES

Text attributes determine the appearance of your slide text. These attributes include *font* (typeface, such as Times Roman or Courier), *size* (in points, where 72 points equals 1 inch in height), *style* (bold, italic, underlined, shadow, and so on), and *color* (black and white, grays, and a full spectrum of colors). To change the attributes of your text, you simply select the text and *apply* the desired new attributes. You can do this in Slide view or in Outline view; all text attributes are visible in both views (except for color, which is visible only in Slide view).

To apply the size, bold, italic, underline, and shadow attributes, you can use the text-editing buttons on the Toolbar. To apply any other attributes (such as font), you must use the Text menu. For example, to italicize text, you can simply click on the Italic button; to change the font, however, you need to choose the Font command from the Text menu.

Here's the general procedure for applying text attributes:

- Select the desired text. In Slide view, to select some of the text in a Title or Body object, select that object and then drag over the desired text; to select all the text, select the entire object. In Outline view, to select some of a slide's text, drag over the desired text; to select all the text, click on the slide number.

- Click on the desired text-editing button (as shown in Figure 3.5). Or, choose the desired command from the Text menu.

Figure 3.5   **Text-editing buttons**

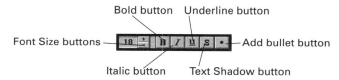

Bold button   Underline button

Font Size buttons —   — Add bullet button

Italic button   Text Shadow button

- To remove a text attribute, simply repeat the previous two steps. Clicking once on a text-editing button (or choosing a Text menu command) applies the attribute; clicking on the button (or choosing the command) a second time removes the attribute.

Let's practice applying text attributes in Outline view. We'll begin by using the Underline button to underline a word:

1. In Outline view, drag to select the word **Lowest** in slide 3. Make sure not to select the space after *Lowest*.

2. Click on the **Underline button** (as shown in Figure 3.5) to underline *Lowest*.

3. Deselect the text. Note that the underline attribute is visible in Outline view.

Now we'll use the Font Size buttons to change the size of slide 2's text:

1. Click on the number **2** in the left margin to select all of slide 2's text.

2. Click on the **Font Size Plus (+) button** (as shown in Figure 3.5) to increase the size of slide 2's text. Observe this change in the outline and in the Font Size list box (to the left of the Font Size buttons).

3. Click on the **Font Size Plus (+) button** again to increase the text size by another step.

4. Click on the **Font Size Minus (-) button** twice to return slide 2's text to its original size.

Now we'll change the font of slide 2's text. In order to do this, you'll have to use the Text menu (rather than a text-editing button):

1. If necessary, select all of slide 2's text (by clicking on **2** in the left margin).

2. Choose **Text, Font** to open the Font submenu, which contains a list of your available fonts (typefaces). *Drop-down menus* (Text, in this case) appear beneath the menu item you click on; *submenus* (Font) appear to the right of the drop-down menu item you click on. The font of slide 2's text is preceded by a bullet. Jot down the name of this font.

3. Click on any other font in the Font submenu to change the font of slide 2's text. Observe this change in the outline.

4. Use the procedure laid out in steps 2 and 3 to try out a few other fonts. When you've had enough, return slide 2's text to its original font (the one you jotted down).

Now let's practice applying text attributes in Slide view:

1. Change to Slide view and display slide 4.

2. Click twice on the **Body object** to place the insertion point in the object. Select the nonbulleted item **Offices located nationwide**.

3. Click on the **Italic button** (as shown in Figure 3.5).

4. Deselect the Body object. Your screen should match that shown in Figure 3.6.

5. Save the file.

Figure 3.6   **Italicizing text in Slide view**

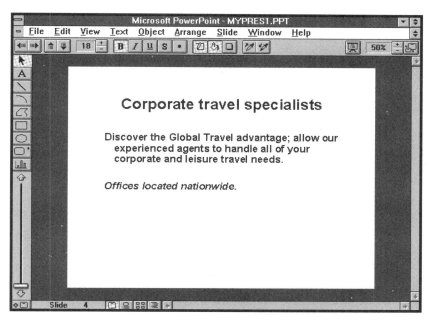

CHANGING INDENTS

Before you learn about indents, you need to understand what PowerPoint means by the term *paragraph*. A paragraph is a unit of text that begins with a character and ends with a *carriage return*. A carriage return is the invisible character that you insert by pressing Enter; it creates a new line of text (or a new bulleted item).

Paragraphs can consist of a single text line or of several lines. Let's verify this by taking a quick tour through the slides of MYPRES1.PPT:

1. In Slide view, display slide 1. The Title object contains two separate paragraphs (*Global Travel* and *Complete Travel Services*) rather than a single two-line paragraph. Why? Because, as you'll remember from Chapter 2, after typing *Global Travel*, you pressed Enter and then typed *Complete Travel Services*. If, instead, you had typed *Global Travel Complete Travel Services* (without pressing Enter) and let PowerPoint wrap the text automatically, the title would have been a single two-line paragraph.

2. Display slide 2. The Title object contains one paragraph; the Body object contains five paragraphs (five separate bulleted items).

3. Display slide 3. The Title object contains one paragraph; the Body object contains eight paragraphs (four bulleted items and four sub-bulleted items).

4. Display slide 4. The Title object contains one paragraph. The Body object contains three (not two!) paragraphs:

- The nonbulleted, three-line item beginning with *Discover* and ending with *needs.* You pressed Enter only after typing this entire item; PowerPoint wrapped the text automatically.

- The *Offices located nationwide.* item.

- The blank line between these two text items.

Now that you understand paragraphs, we can move on to indents. *Indents* determine how far the lines of a paragraph are shifted to the right. A slide's body text, as you'll remember, has up to five levels of text. Each of these levels has, in turn, two types of indents: The *first-line indent* (marked by the upper indent triangle, as shown on the ruler in Figure 3.7) is the place where the first line of a paragraph at that level will start; the *trailing-line indent* (marked by the lower indent triangle) is the place where any subsequent lines of a paragraph at that level will start.

Note: Every text object on a slide has a ruler associated with it. Normally, these rulers are kept hidden, because they clutter the screen. To change the indents of the text in a given text object, however, you need to display the ruler of this text object.

Here's the general procedure for changing indents:

- Select the text object whose indents you want to change.

- Choose *Text, Show Ruler* to display the ruler for this text object.

- To change the first-line indent for an indent level, drag that level's upper indent triangle to the desired position on the ruler.

- To change the trailing-line indent for an indent level, drag that level's lower indent triangle to the desired position on the ruler.

- To change both the first-line indent and the trailing-line indent for an indent level, drag the line that connects that level's upper and lower indent triangles to move both triangles to the desired position.

- Choose *Text, Hide Ruler* to remove the ruler.

Figure 3.7 **Indents, as shown on the ruler**

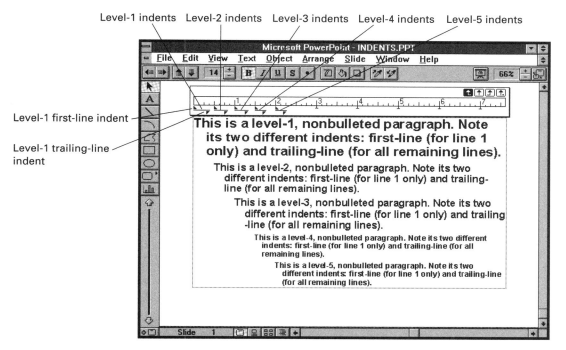

Let's use this procedure to change the indents of slide 4's body paragraphs:

1. Select the **Body object** of slide 4.

2. Choose **Text, Show Ruler** to display the ruler for the Body object. Note the two level-1 indent triangles. (The level-2 through level-5 indent triangles are not displayed, because this Body object contains only level-1 text.) The upper triangle marks where the first line of the selected paragraphs starts. The lower triangle marks where the remaining lines start.

3. Drag the **upper indent triangle** rightward to line up its left (vertical) edge with the ½-inch mark on the ruler. The first-line indent is now set to half an inch. Observe the change in your paragraphs' layouts, as shown in Figure 3.8. The first line is now indented more than the remaining lines.

Figure 3.8   **Changing the first-line indent**

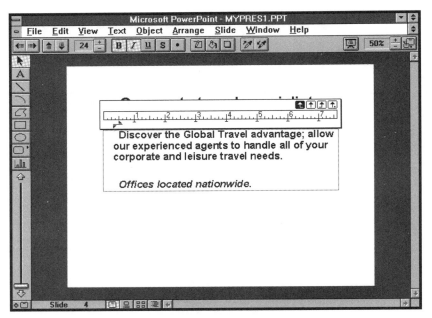

4. Drag the **lower indent triangle** rightward to line up its left (vertical) edge with the 1-inch mark on the ruler. The trailing-line indent is now set to 1 inch. Observe the change in your paragraphs' layouts.

5. Drag the line connecting the upper and lower indent triangles to the leftmost edge of the ruler. Note that dragging the connecting line moves both triangles as a unit, without changing the distance between them. The first-line indent is now set to 0 inches, and the trailing-line indent is set to half an inch.

6. Drag the **lower indent triangle** to the leftmost edge of the ruler. Both the first-line indent and the trailing-line indent are now set to 0 inches. Your screen should match that shown in Figure 3.9.

Figure 3.9   **Changing both indents to 0 inches**

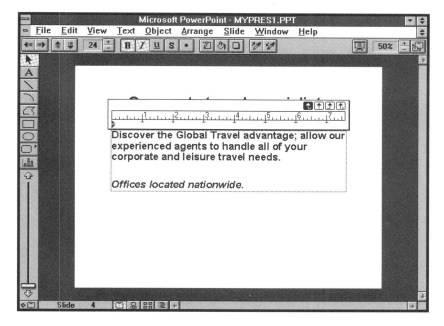

7. Choose **Text, Hide Ruler** to hide the ruler.

8. Deselect the Body object.

9. Save the file.

ALIGNING TEXT

Alignment determines the position of your slide text within its text-object box. Text can be left-aligned, right-aligned, centered, or justified, as follows (see Figure 3.10):

• *Left-aligned* text lines begin at the left edge of the text-object box.

Figure 3.10   **Alignment types**

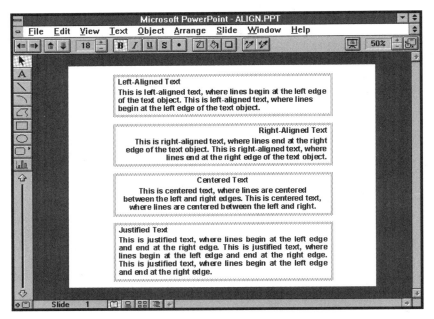

- *Right-aligned* text lines end at the right edge of the text-object box.

- *Centered* text lines are centered between the left and right edges of the text-object box.

- *Justified* text lines begin at the left edge and end at the right edge of the text-object box.

Here's the general procedure for aligning text:

- Select the text to be aligned.

- Choose *Text, Alignment* to open the Alignment submenu.

- Click on the desired alignment (*Left, Center, Right,* or *Justify*).

Let's use this simple procedure to change the alignment of slide 4's body text:

1. Select the **Body object** of slide 4.

2. Choose **Text, Alignment** to open the Alignment submenu.

3. Observe that the current alignment setting is Left. By default, PowerPoint left-aligns body text.

4. Click on **Right** to right-align slide 4's body text within its Body object box.

PRACTICE YOUR SKILLS

Slide 4's text layout looks imbalanced, like it's tipping over to the right. Let's try a different alignment:

1. Justify the body text. This layout looks better, but is still somewhat off.

2. Center the body text. Now we've got it!

3. Save the file.

CHANGING LINE SPACING

Line spacing determines two things: the amount of space between the individual lines of a multiline paragraph, and the amount of space between paragraphs. Here's the general procedure for changing the line spacing of your slide text:

• Select the paragraph(s) whose line spacing you want to change.

• Choose *Text, Line Spacing* to open the Line Spacing dialog box.

• To change the spacing between lines of a multiline paragraph, click on the Line Spacing *up arrow* (to increase the spacing) or the *down arrow* (to decrease the spacing).

• To change the spacing between separate paragraphs, click on the Before Paragraph or After Paragraph *up arrow* (to increase the spacing) or the *down arrow* (to decrease the spacing). Before Paragraph determines the amount of space before each paragraph; After Paragraph determines the space after each paragraph.

• Click on OK.

Let's change the spacing between the lines of a paragraph:

1. Select the first paragraph of slide 4's body text. (To do this, place the insertion point anywhere within the paragraph.)

2. Choose **Text, Line Spacing** to open the Line Spacing dialog box. Observe the current line-spacing value, 0.90 lines.

3. Click on the Line Spacing **up arrow** 12 times to increase the line spacing to 1.50 lines. Note that the layout of your selected paragraph (largely hidden behind the Line Spacing dialog box) has changed to reflect your new line spacing.

4. Drag the **Line Spacing dialog box** (by its title bar) below the selected paragraph to uncover the paragraph. Now you can clearly see how your line-spacing changes affected the paragraph's layout.

PRACTICE YOUR SKILLS

We've overdone it; the paragraph looks too loose. Let's tighten things up a bit:

1. Change the first paragraph's line spacing to **1.05** lines. There, that looks better.

2. Click on **OK** to remove the Line Spacing dialog box.

3. Save the file.

4. Close the file.

SPELL-CHECKING A PRESENTATION

Correct spelling is a vital part of a successful presentation. No matter how impressive a slide looks, if its title is misspelled, you'll lose credibility with your audience. PowerPoint provides a spell checker that searches your entire presentation—all the text objects in all of your slides, outlines, notes, and handouts—for spelling errors.

Here's the general procedure for spell-checking a presentation:

- Change to Outline view. (You can spell-check in Slide view, but doing so in Outline view is easier.)

- Press Ctrl+Home to move the insertion point to the top of the outline.

- Choose *Text, Spelling* to open the Spelling dialog box.

- Click on the *Check Spelling button* to begin the spell-check. When PowerPoint finds a misspelled or unrecognized word (a word that is not in its internal dictionary), it highlights the word in the outline and displays the word in the Spelling text box. At this point, you have several choices. (Please refer to Figure 3.11 when reading through the next few items. It shows a Spelling dialog box from an in-progress spell-check.)

Figure 3.11   **Spelling dialog box**

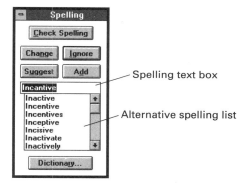

- If the word is misspelled and you know the correct spelling, type the correctly spelled word in the Spelling text box and then click on the *Change button* to correct the word in the outline. To continue the spell-check, click on the Check Spelling button.

- If the word is misspelled and you do not know the correct spelling, click on the *Suggest button* to display a list of alternative spellings, click on the correct spelling (you may need to scroll through the list), and then click on the Change button. To continue the spell-check, click on the Check Spelling button.

- If the word is not misspelled (for example, if it is a correctly spelled proper name that is not in PowerPoint's dictionary), click on the *Ignore button* to leave the word as is. PowerPoint automatically searches for the next misspelled word.

- If you want to add the word in the Spelling text box to your custom dictionary, click on the *Add button;* the next time the spell checker encounters the word (in this or any other presentation), it will consider the word correctly spelled. After you click on Add, PowerPoint automatically searches for the next misspelled word.

- To modify (add words to, delete words from) the custom dictionary, click on the *Dictionary button* to open the Custom Dictionary dialog box. To add a word, type the desired word in the Custom Dictionary text box and click on the *Plus (+) button;* repeat this for all the words you want to add. To delete a word, click on the word in the Custom Dictionary list box (you may have to scroll) and then click on the *Minus (-) button;* repeat this for all the words you want to delete. When you are finished modifying the custom dictionary, click on the *Close button.*

- To exit from the spell checker, double-click on the Control Menu button of the Spelling dialog box. You can do this at any time during the spell-checking procedure.

Let's open a presentation file from the POWERWRK directory and spell-check it:

1. Open **spell.ppt** from your POWERWRK directory.

2. Change to Outline view and press **Ctrl+Home** to move the insertion point to the top of the outline.

3. Choose **Text, Spelling** to open the Spelling dialog box.

4. Click on the **Check Spelling button** to begin the spell-check. PowerPoint highlights the word *servces* in the outline and displays it in the Spelling text box. This is obviously a misspelling of *services.* Since you know the correct spelling, you can enter it manually.

5. Type **services** to enter the correct spelling in the Spelling text box.

6. Click on **Change** to change the misspelled word in the outline (*servces*) to the correctly spelled word you typed in the Spelling text box (*services*).

7. Click on **Check Spelling** to continue the spell-check. PowerPoint highlights the word *MacArthur* and displays it in the Spelling text box. The proper name *MacArthur* is not in PowerPoint's dictionary.

8. Click on **Ignore** to leave *MacArthur* as is. (You could have clicked on Add if you'd wanted to leave *MacArthur* as is *and* add it to your custom dictionary. Instead, we'll use a different

method to add it to the custom dictionary at the end of this activity.) PowerPoint automatically continues the spell-check and stops at the word *Incantive*.

9. Let's say you weren't sure how to spell this word correctly. Click on **Suggest** to display a list of alternative spellings for *Incantive*.

10. Click on **Incentive** to select it. Note that *Incentive* is now displayed in the Spelling text box.

11. Click on **Change** to change *Incantive* in the outline to *Incentive*.

12. Click on **Check Spelling** to continue the spell-check. Power-Point displays the message *No misspelled words were found*. This means that you've completed the spell-check of your entire presentation.

13. Click on **OK** to return to the Spelling dialog box.

Now, as promised, we'll add *MacArthur* to the custom dictionary:

1. Click on **Dictionary** to open the Custom Dictionary dialog box.

2. Type **MacArthur**.

3. Click on the **Plus (+) button** to add *MacArthur* to the custom dictionary. Note that it appears in the list box.

4. Click on **Close** to close the Custom Dictionary dialog box.

PRACTICE YOUR SKILLS

1. Delete *MacArthur* from your custom dictionary.

2. Double-click on the **Control Menu button** of the Spelling dialog box to close the dialog box.

3. Save the file as **myspell.ppt**. (Hint: Use **File, Save As**.)

4. Close the file.

SUMMARY

In this chapter, you learned how to work with your slide text. You now know how to get general and dialog-box help, how to edit slide text, how to rearrange bulleted items, how to apply text attributes, how to change indents, how to align text, how to change line spacing, and how to spell-check a presentation.

Here's a quick reference for the techniques you learned in this chapter:

Desired Result	How to Do It
Get general help	Choose **Help, Contents** or press **F1** (with no active dialog box); to view a topic, click on it; to search for a topic, click on the **Search button**, double-click on the desired search word, double-click on the desired topic; to view previous Help windows, click on the **Back button**; to view the Contents window, click on the **Contents button**; to exit from Help, choose **File, Exit**
Get help for the active dialog box	Press **F1**
Add a bulleted item to a slide	If you are in Slide view, select the **Body object**; place the insertion point at the end of the bulleted item after which you want to add your new bulleted item; press **Enter** to create the new bulleted item; if necessary, press **Tab** or **Shift+Tab** to change the indent level of your new bulleted item; type your desired bullet text
Rearrange the order of bulleted items by dragging	If you are in Slide view, place the insertion point anywhere within the bulleted list; point to the bullet of the bulleted item you want to move; drag the bullet (and all its sub-bulleted items) to your desired new position
Rearrange the order of bulleted items by using the Move Up and Move Down buttons	Select the bulleted item(s) you want to move and click as many times as necessary on the **Move Up** or **Move Down button** to move the selected bulleted item(s) to your desired new position

Desired Result	How to Do It
Apply text attributes	Select the desired text; click on the desired text-editing button or choose the desired command from the Text menu; to remove a text attribute, repeat the previous two steps
Change indents	Select the desired text object; choose **Text, Show Ruler** to display its ruler; drag the desired first-line indent triangles and/or trailing-line indent triangles to the desired position on the ruler; choose **Text, Hide Ruler** to remove the ruler
Align text	Select the desired text; choose **Text, Alignment**; select the desired alignment (**Left, Center, Right**, or **Justify**)
Change line spacing	Select the desired paragraph(s); choose **Text, Line Spacing**; to change the spacing between lines of a multiline paragraph, click on the Line Spacing **up arrow** or **down arrow**; to change the spacing between separate paragraphs, click on the Before Paragraph or After Paragraph **up arrow** or **down arrow**; click on **OK**
Spell-check a presentation	Change to Outline view; press **Ctrl+Home** to move to the top of the outline; choose **Text, Spelling**; click on the **Check Spelling** button and follow the prompts; to modify the custom dictionary, click on the **Dictionary button** and add/delete your desired words; to exit from the spell checker, double-click on its **Control Menu button**

In the next chapter, you'll find out how to draw and create text objects on your slides. You will learn how to draw basic shapes (lines, rectangles, squares, ellipses, circles, and arcs), how to draw other predefined shapes (arrows, triangles, stars, diamonds, and so on), how to draw free-form objects, and how to create text objects. You will also learn how to edit objects (select and deselect, resize, move, align, and delete them), how to undo your last action, and how to enhance objects (change their shapes, fill colors, shadows, and line styles).

IF YOU'RE STOPPING HERE

If you need to break off here, please exit PowerPoint. If you want to proceed directly to the next chapter, please do so now.

CHAPTER 4: DRAWING ON YOUR SLIDES

Drawing Primer

Creating Text Objects

Editing Objects

Enhancing Objects

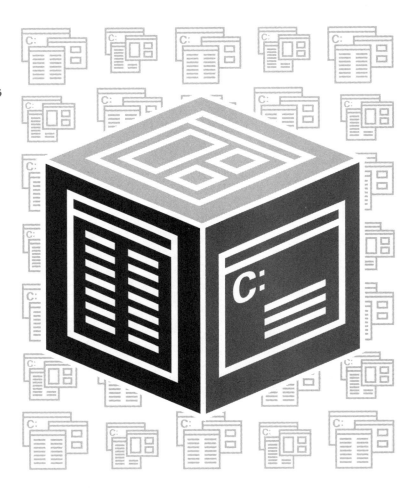

A strong presentation consists of both effective words and effective images. In Chapters 2 and 3, you learned the fundamentals of working with words. In Chapters 4 and 5, you'll learn how to work with images. Here, we'll show you how to draw on your slides and how to edit and enhance your drawn objects.

Note: Normally, we ask you to work through an entire chapter in one sitting. However, since this chapter is so long, we've given you an opportunity to work through it in two separate sittings. You'll find a section entitled "If You Want to Pause Here" about halfway through the chapter. You can decide then whether to pause or continue.

When you're done working through this chapter, you will know

- How to draw basic shapes—lines, rectangles, squares, ellipses, circles, and arcs

- How to draw other predefined shapes—arrows, triangles, stars, diamonds, and so on

- How to draw free-form objects

- How to create text objects

- How to edit objects—select and deselect, resize, move, align, and delete them

- How to undo your last action

- How to enhance objects—change their shapes, fill colors, shadows, and line styles

DRAWING PRIMER

PowerPoint's Tool Palette contains nine drawing tools, as shown in Figure 4.1 and Table 4.1.

Figure 4.1   **Drawing Tools**

—Selection tool
—Text tool
—Line tool
—Arc tool
—Freeform tool
—Rectangle tool
—Ellipse tool
—Shape tool
—Graph tool

Table 4.1   **Drawing Tools**

Tool	Used To
Selection tool	Select, deselect, move, and resize objects
Text tool	Create text objects
Line tool	Draw straight lines
Arc tool	Draw arcs (curved lines)
Freeform tool	Draw free-form shapes
Rectangle tool	Draw rectangles and squares
Ellipse tool	Draw ellipses (ovals) and circles
Shape tool	Draw predefined shapes
Graph tool	Draw graphs

Over the next several sections of this chapter, you'll learn how to use the first eight of these tools. You'll explore the Graph tool in Chapter 8.

DRAWING STRAIGHT LINES

Here's the general procedure for drawing a straight line on a slide:

- Select the Line tool.
- To draw a horizontal, vertical, or diagonal line, press and hold the Shift key.
- Press and hold the left mouse button.
- Drag in the slide to draw the line.
- Release the mouse button.
- If necessary, release the Shift key.

If you are not running PowerPoint, please start it now. Close all open presentations, except for the start-up presentation. Let's begin by opening MYPRES1.PPT, creating a new slide, and then drawing two lines on it:

1. Open **mypres1** from your POWERWRK directory. Maximize the presentation window, if necessary.

2. Display slide 4, the last slide of the presentation.

3. Click on the **New Slide button** to add a new slide (slide 5). You won't be using either the Title object or the Body object of this slide, so let's get rid of them now.

4. Select the **Title object** of slide 5 and press **Del** to delete it. Select the **Body object** and press **Del** to delete it.

First, let's draw a straight line that slants up slightly to the right:

1. Select the **Line tool** (as shown in Figure 4.1) by clicking on it.

2. Move the mouse pointer onto the slide workspace. Note that the pointer changes to a cross hair. Position the center of the cross hair about half an inch below and to the right of the upper-left corner of the slide. (**Note:** In the slide workspace of a maximized presentation window, the actual slide is represented by the white area, not by the gray area surrounding it.)

3. Press and hold the **left mouse button**. Drag rightward and slightly upward to draw a slanting straight line resembling the one shown in Figure 4.2. Release the mouse button to complete the line.

Now let's draw a horizontal line:

1. Position the mouse cross hair about half an inch below the left end of the line you just drew.

2. Press and hold the **Shift key**. Press and hold the **left mouse button**.

3. Drag to the right to draw a horizontal line resembling the one shown in Figure 4.2. (As long as you are holding down Shift, you do not need to drag absolutely horizontally to do this.)

4. Release the mouse button, and then release the Shift key to complete the line. (Make sure to release the mouse button *before* you release the Shift key, or your line may not turn out to be exactly horizontal.)

Figure 4.2   **Drawing a slanting line and a horizontal line**

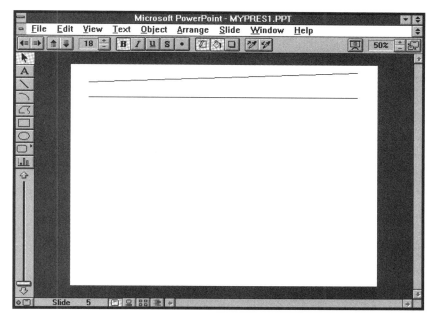

5. Click on any blank area of the slide to deselect your newly
   drawn line. Your screen should match (or closely resemble)
   that shown in Figure 4.2.

DRAWING RECTANGLES AND SQUARES

Here's the general procedure for drawing a rectangle or a square
on a slide:

- Select the Rectangle tool.

- To draw a square, press and hold the Shift key.

- Press and hold the left mouse button.

- Drag in the slide to draw the rectangle or square.

- Release the mouse button.

- If necessary, release the Shift key.

Let's draw a rectangle on our new slide:

1. Select the **Rectangle tool** (as shown in Figure 4.1).

2. Position the mouse cross hair about half an inch below the left end of the horizontal line you drew in the last activity.

3. Press and hold the **left mouse button**.

4. Drag down and to the right to draw a long, thin rectangle resembling the one shown in Figure 4.3.

Figure 4.3   **Drawing a rectangle and a square**

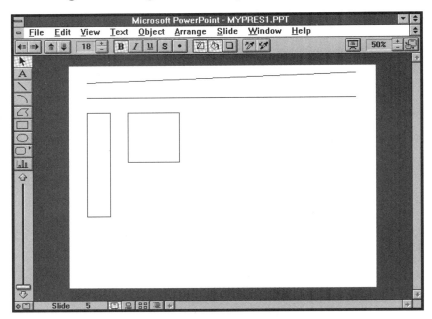

5. Release the mouse button to complete the rectangle.

Now let's draw a square:

1. Position the mouse cross hair about half an inch to the right of the upper-right corner of the rectangle you just drew.

2. Press and hold the **Shift key**. Press and hold the **left mouse button**.

3. Drag down and to the right to draw a square resembling the one shown in Figure 4.3.

4. Release the mouse button, and then release the Shift key. (Make sure to release the mouse button *before* you release the Shift key, or your square may not turn out to be perfectly square.)

5. Deselect your square (by clicking on a blank area of the slide). Your screen should match (or closely resemble) that shown in Figure 4.3.

 DRAWING ELLIPSES AND CIRCLES

Here's the general procedure for drawing an ellipse (oval) or a circle on a slide:

- Select the Ellipse tool.
- To draw a circle, press and hold the Shift key.
- Press and hold the left mouse button.
- Drag in the slide to draw the ellipse or circle.
- Release the mouse button.
- If necessary, release the Shift key.

Let's add an ellipse to our slide:

1. Select the **Ellipse tool**.

2. Position the mouse cross hair about half an inch to the right of the upper-right corner of the square you drew in the last activity.

3. Press and hold the **left mouse button**.

4. Drag to the right and down to draw a long, thin ellipse resembling the one shown in Figure 4.4. Release the mouse button.

Now let's draw a circle:

1. Position the mouse cross hair about half an inch below the left end of the ellipse you just drew.

2. Press and hold the **Shift key**. Press and hold the **left mouse button**. Drag down and to the right to draw a circle resembling the one shown in Figure 4.4. Release the mouse button and then release the Shift key.

Figure 4.4   **Drawing an ellipse and a circle**

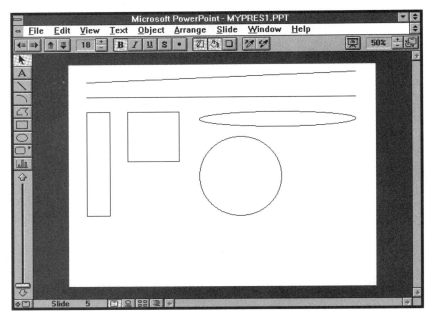

3. Deselect the circle. Your screen should match (or closely resemble) that shown in Figure 4.4.

DRAWING ARCS (CURVED LINES)

Technically, an *arc* is a 90-degree (quarter) segment of an ellipse or a circle. In effect, though, an arc is simply a curved line. Here's the general procedure for drawing an arc on a slide:

- Select the Arc tool.

- To draw a circular arc (rather than an elliptical arc), press and hold the Shift key.

- Press and hold the left mouse button.

- Drag in the slide to draw the arc.

- Release the mouse button.

- If necessary, release the Shift key.

Let's add an elliptical arc to our slide; that is, an arc with the curve of an ellipse rather than a circle:

1. Select the **Arc tool**.

2. Position the mouse cross hair about half an inch above and to the right of the lower-left corner of the slide. (Remember, the actual slide is represented by the white— not the gray—area.)

3. Press and hold the **left mouse button**.

4. Drag up and to the right to draw an elliptical arc resembling the one shown in Figure 4.5. Release the mouse button. Observe that the arc's curve is that of an ellipse (oval), rather than that of a circle.

Figure 4.5   **Drawing an elliptical arc and a circular arc**

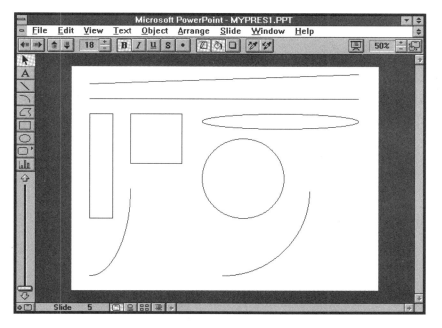

Now let's draw a circular arc:

1. Position the mouse cross hair about half an inch above the midpoint of the bottom edge of the slide.

2. Press and hold the **Shift key**. Press and hold the **left mouse button**. Drag up and to the right to draw a circular arc resembling the one shown in Figure 4.5. Release the mouse button, and then release the Shift key. Observe that the arc's curve is that of a circle, rather than that of an ellipse.

3. Deselect the circular arc. Your screen should match (or closely resemble) that shown in Figure 4.5.

4. Choose **File**, **Save** to save the presentation file.

DRAWING PREDEFINED SHAPES

Thus far, you've learned how to draw four types of objects on your slides: lines, rectangles/squares, ellipses/circles, and arcs. Although the size and proportions of these objects vary, their basic shapes are predefined. For example, you can use the Rectangle tool to draw a long narrow rectangle, a short wide rectangle, or a perfect square, but you can't use it to draw a butterfly. In this section, you'll learn how to use the Shape tool to draw other predefined shapes, including arrows, triangles, stars, diamonds, and three-dimensional boxes.

Here's the general procedure for drawing a predefined shape on a slide:

- If the Shape tool already displays the shape you want to draw, select it and skip the rest of this step. Otherwise, point to the Shape tool, press and hold the left mouse button to open the Shape palette, release the mouse button, and then click on the shape you want to draw.

- To maintain the proportions of the selected shape, press and hold the Shift key.

- Press and hold the left mouse button.

- Drag in the slide to draw the selected shape.

- Release the mouse button.

- If necessary, release the Shift key.

Let's create a new slide and fill it with predefined shapes:

1. Click on the **New Slide button** to create a new slide (slide 6).

2. Delete slide 6's Title object and Body object. We won't be entering any text on this slide.

3. Point to the Shape tool. Press and hold the **left mouse button** to open the *Shape palette*, which contains PowerPoint's 24 predefined shapes. Release the mouse button.

4. Click on the triangle shape (the fourth shape from the top in the first vertical column) to select it. Note that the Shape tool now displays this triangle shape.

5. Position the mouse cross hair about half an inch below and to the right of the upper-left corner of the slide.

6. Press and hold the **left mouse button**. Do not release this button until we tell you to do so in the next step. Drag all around the slide to get a feeling for how you can change the size and proportions of the triangle.

7. Continue dragging until your triangle resembles the left triangle in Figure 4.6, and then release the mouse button.

Figure 4.6   **Drawing predefined triangle shapes**

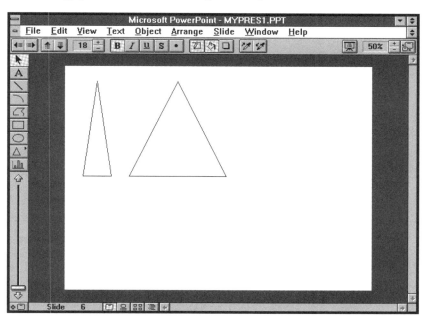

Observe that the proportions of your triangle do not match the proportions of the triangle shape displayed in the Shape tool; your triangle is much thinner. As mentioned, you need to hold down the Shift key while dragging in order to maintain the proportions of your selected shape. Let's do this now:

1. Position the mouse cross hair about an inch to the right of the top of the triangle you just drew.

2. Press and hold the **Shift key**. Press and hold the **left mouse button**. Drag down and to the right to draw a triangle resembling the one to the right in Figure 4.6. Note that this triangle has the same proportions as the one displayed in the Shape tool. Release the mouse button, and then release the Shift key.

3. Deselect the triangle. Your screen should match (or closely resemble) that shown in Figure 4.6.

PRACTICE YOUR SKILLS

1. Time to have fun! Using the procedure just described, fill slide 6 with as many types of predefined shapes as you have the stamina to draw. Don't worry about the overlapping objects; it's perfectly okay to do this. When you're done, compare your slide with the one we created, shown in Figure 4.7. Who wins?

2. Save the file.

DRAWING FREE-FORM OBJECTS

All the objects you've drawn thus far have been predefined Power-Point shapes (lines, rectangles/squares, ellipses/circles, arcs, and the Shape-tool shapes). In this section, you'll learn how to use the Freeform tool to draw *free-form* (nonpredefined) shapes. Here's the general procedure for doing this:

• Select the Freeform tool.

• Position the mouse cross hair where you want to start drawing your free-form object.

• Press and hold the left mouse button.

• Drag the pointer to draw your free-form object.

Figure 4.7   **A cornucopia of predefined objects**

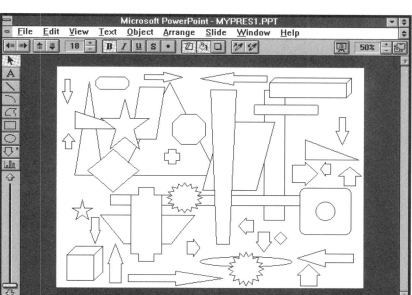

- Complete your free-form object in either of the following ways:

  - To create an *open object*—one whose end point does not connect to its starting point, such as a spiral—release the mouse button (if necessary) and double-click on your desired end point for the object.

  - To create a *closed object*—one whose end point connects to its starting point, such as a circle—release the mouse button (if necessary) and click on the starting point of the object.

Let's draw an open free-form object:

1. Click on the **New Slide button** to create a new slide (slide 7).

2. Delete slide 7's Title object and Body object.

3. Select the **Freeform tool**.

4. Position the mouse cross hair in the center of the slide.

5. Press and hold the **left mouse button**. Without releasing the button, drag in ever-widening circles to draw a spiral object resembling the one shown in Figure 4.8.

Figure 4.8   **Drawing open and closed free-form objects**

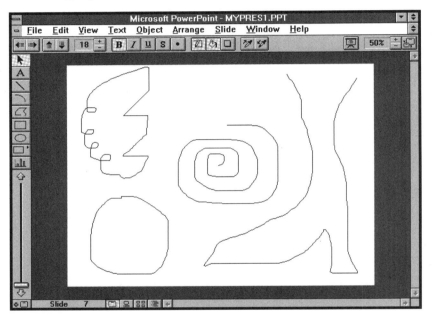

6. When you've reached the end point of your spiral, release the mouse button and—without moving the pointer—double-click to complete the object. This is an open object; its end point does not connect to its starting point.

Let's draw another open object:

1. Select the **Freeform tool**.

2. Follow the technique outlined in steps 5 and 6 above to draw an open object resembling the boot-like object shown on the right side of the slide in Figure 4.8.

Now let's draw a closed free-form object:

1. Select the **Freeform tool**.

2. Do your best to draw a perfect circle in the lower-left quadrant of the slide. When you've reached the end point of your circle (which should be right on top of the starting point), release the mouse button and click on the starting point to connect these two points, thus closing the object.

3. Observe your results. Note how difficult (impossible!) it is to use the Freeform tool to draw a perfect circle (as evidenced by our woeful attempt in Figure 4.8). The moral is this: To draw a precise geometric shape (rectangle/square, ellipse/circle, and so on), use the appropriate drawing tool (Rectangle tool, Ellipse tool, and so on), not the Freeform tool.

 ## DRAWING STRAIGHT FREE-FORM LINES

The free-form objects you just drew are composed almost exclusively of curved lines. You may at times, however, want to draw one or more straight lines in a free-form object. You can do this in either of the following ways:

- While drawing your free-form object, drag in a straight line. You'll need a very steady hand to achieve good results using this technique, particularly if you are attempting to draw lines that are neither horizontal nor vertical.

- Or, while drawing your free-form object, release the mouse button, move the pointer to draw the straight line, and then press and hold the left mouse button to continue drawing in free-form (or click to begin drawing another straight line). (**Note**: To draw a horizontal, vertical, or diagonal line, hold down the Shift key while you move the mouse pointer.)

Let's use each of these techniques to draw a closed free-form object composed of both free-form and straight lines. In order to do this, you must press, hold, and release the left mouse button and the Shift key at precisely the right times, so please be sure to follow our directions exactly:

1. Select the **Freeform tool**.

2. Position the cross hair about half an inch above the uppermost point in your imperfect circle.

3. Press and hold down the **left mouse button**. Do not release the button until we tell you to do so in step 8.

4. Begin drawing the object depicted in the upper-left quadrant of Figure 4.8 by dragging a curved line up and to the right about 1 inch. (Don't release the mouse button!)

5. Now attempt to draw a straight horizontal line by dragging left about half an inch (refer to Figure 4.8).

6. Attempt to draw a straight diagonal line by dragging diagonally up and to the right about half an inch. Note how difficult it is to draw a nonhorizontal, nonvertical straight line by dragging.

7. Attempt to draw a straight vertical line by dragging up about half an inch.

8. Release the mouse button (finally!) but do not move the mouse.

Now we'll use the second technique to draw a copy of these three straight lines:

1. Press and hold the **Shift key**. Do not release this key until we tell you to do so in step 2 of the next activity.

2. Draw a straight horizontal line by moving the mouse pointer about half an inch to the left (refer to Figure 4.8).

3. Without moving the mouse pointer, click to begin another straight line.

4. Draw a straight diagonal line by moving the mouse pointer diagonally about half an inch up and to the right. Note how much easier it is to draw a diagonal line by using this technique than by dragging.

5. Click to begin another straight line.

6. Draw a straight vertical line by moving the mouse pointer up about half an inch. Observe how much better these straight lines look than the ones you drew by dragging.

Now we'll return to free-form drawing and complete the object depicted in Figure 4.8:

1. Press and hold the **left mouse button**.

2. Release the Shift key (finally!).

3. Drag to draw the rest of the object in Figure 4.8.

4. Close the object by clicking on its starting point.

PRACTICE YOUR SKILLS

1. Time for more fun! Fill slide 7 with free-form drawings. Follow your imagination; be creative! Observe your results in relation to ours, shown in Figure 4.9. How do our masterpieces compare?

2. Save the file.

Figure 4.9   **Free-form jamboree**

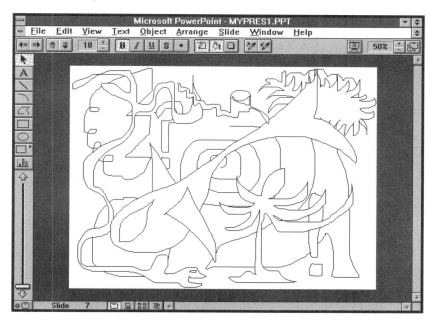

CREATING TEXT OBJECTS

In Chapters 2 and 3, you learned how to add text to your slides' Title and Body objects. PowerPoint does not limit your slide text to these two predefined text objects. Just as you can create any number of drawn objects on a slide, you can create any number of text objects.

You create text objects to add text that does not belong to either the title-text or body-text categories; for example, a caption for a piece of clip art, or a footnote for a bulleted item in your body text.

Here's the general procedure for creating a text object on a slide:

- Select the Text tool.

- Position the mouse pointer where you want your text to begin on the slide.

- Drag to create a box as wide as your desired text object.

- Type your desired text. PowerPoint automatically wraps the text, if necessary, to fit within the width of the text box you created in the previous step.

- When you are finished entering your text, click on any blank area of the slide to complete your text object.

Let's use this procedure to create a simple text object:

1. Click on the **New Slide button** to create a new slide (slide 8), and then delete its Title object and Body object.

2. Select the **Text tool**.

3. Position the mouse pointer about half an inch below and to the right of the upper-left corner of the slide.

4. Press and hold the **left mouse button**. Drag to create a box about half as wide as the slide and an inch high. As you'll see in the next step, it doesn't matter how high you make your box, because PowerPoint always reduces it to a one-line-high text box.

5. Release the mouse button. A dotted text box appears. Its width is the width you dragged in the previous step; its height, as mentioned, is one line. Observe the blinking insertion point at the left end of the text box. (You'll have to look carefully; it's nearly invisible.) This marks where your text will appear.

6. Type the following paragraph (without pressing Enter). As you type, observe how PowerPoint automatically wraps the text to fit your text-box width. Observe also how PowerPoint automatically expands the text box vertically to accommodate all your text lines.

   Discover the Global Travel advantage; allow our experienced agents to handle all of your corporate and leisure travel needs.

7. Click on any blank area of the slide to complete your text object. The dotted text box disappears and the object is deselected, as shown in Figure 4.10. (Your lines may wrap at different places than ours.)

Figure 4.10 **Creating text objects**

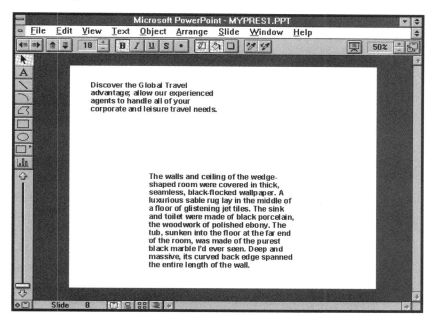

PRACTICE YOUR SKILLS

1. Create the other text object shown in Figure 4.10. Again, your lines may wrap differently.

2. Center the contents of both text boxes.

3. Save the file.

EDITING OBJECTS

Now that you know how to draw objects and create text objects on your slides, it's time to learn how to edit them. Over the next several sections, you'll learn how to:

• Select and deselect objects

- Undo your last action
- Resize objects
- Move objects
- Align objects
- Delete objects

 ## SELECTING AND DESELECTING OBJECTS

In order to edit an object, you must first select it. Here's the general procedure for doing this:

- Click on the Selection tool, if it is not already selected.
- Click on the desired object. A selection box appears around the object to indicate that it is selected.
- To deselect the currently selected object, click on any blank area of the slide.

Note: This is the same procedure you've used to select and deselect the Title and Body objects.

You may, at times, want to select multiple objects. For example, later in this chapter you'll add a shadow effect to several objects by selecting them all and then applying a shadow to the entire group at once (rather than selecting one object, applying a shadow, selecting the next object, applying a shadow, and so on). Here's the general procedure for selecting multiple objects:

- Press and hold the Shift key.
- Select (click on) all your desired objects, one by one.
- Release the Shift key.
- To add an object to a multiple selection, press and hold the Shift key, click on the desired object, and release the Shift key.
- To remove (deselect) an object from a multiple selection, press and hold the Shift key, click on the selected object you want to remove, and release the Shift key.
- To deselect all objects in a multiple selection, click on any blank area of the slide.

Let's begin by selecting and deselecting single objects:

1. Display slide 5, the slide that contains the simple objects you drew at the beginning of this chapter.

2. Select the slanted line at the top of the slide by clicking on it. Note the selection box that appears around the line to indicate that it is selected.

3. Deselect the line by clicking on any blank area of the slide.

4. Use this technique to select and deselect first the square, then the circle, and finally the elliptical arc.

Now let's create and modify a multiple selection:

1. All of slide 5's objects should be deselected. If they are not, click on any blank area of the screen to do this.

2. Press and hold the **Shift key**. Do not release this key until we tell you to do so in step 4.

3. Select (click on) the two lines, the rectangle, the square, the ellipse, and the circle.

4. Release the Shift key. Observe your multiple selection, which consists of all six objects you selected in the previous step.

Let's say you decided to add the two arcs to your multiple selection:

1. Press and hold the **Shift key**.

2. Select the two arcs to add them to the multiple selection.

3. Release the Shift key. All eight objects on your slide should now be selected, as shown in Figure 4.11.

Now let's say you wanted to remove the circle from your multiple selection:

1. Press and hold the **Shift key**.

2. Click on the circle to remove it from the multiple selection.

3. Release the Shift key.

Let's finish up by deselecting all the objects in your multiple selection:

1. Press **Del**. Oh no! You've made a terrible mistake. Instead of deselecting the objects, you've deleted them!

Figure 4.11   **Selecting all of slide 5's objects**

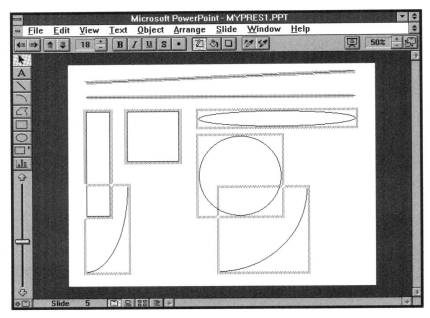

Relax... PowerPoint provides a very handy command that can rescue you from calamities like this. (Please don't touch your keyboard or mouse until we tell you to do so in the next activity.)

 UNDOING YOUR LAST ACTION

You can use the *Edit, Undo* command to undo (reverse) your last PowerPoint action. Here's the general procedure for doing this:

- Immediately after performing the action you want to reverse, choose Edit, Undo.

- To reverse your last Undo command, choose Edit, Undo immediately again.

Let's use Edit, Undo to recover our lost objects:

1. Choose **Edit**, **Undo** to reverse the last action you performed, deleting all the objects in your multiple selection. The deleted objects reappear!

2. Choose **Edit**, **Undo** again to reverse the Undo command you just issued. The objects are again deleted.

3. Choose **Edit**, **Undo** once again to reverse the second Undo command. The objects reappear. You can use the Edit, Undo command in this manner to toggle between the "before" and "after" conditions of an action.

4. Save the file.

IF YOU WANT TO PAUSE HERE

As mentioned, because this chapter is so long, we're giving you an opportunity to work through it in two sittings. If you want to pause here and finish the chapter later, perform the following steps. If you want to forge ahead and finish the chapter now, skip to the next section, "Resizing Objects."

To pause at this point in the chapter,

1. Close the file.

2. Exit PowerPoint.

When you're ready to finish the chapter,

1. Start **PowerPoint**.

2. Open **mypres1** from your POWERWRK directory.

3. Continue with the next section, "Resizing Objects."

RESIZING OBJECTS

Once you've drawn an object or created a text object on a slide, you may find that you need to reduce or enlarge the object to fit the overall slide layout. PowerPoint enables you to resize objects quickly and easily. Here's the general procedure for doing this:

• Select the object.

• To maintain the proportions of the selected object, press and hold the Shift key.

• Point to the desired selection handle. Press and hold the left mouse button to grab the handle.

- To reduce the object, drag the handle diagonally toward the center of the object. To enlarge the object, drag the handle diagonally away from the center of the object.

- Release the mouse button.

- If necessary, release the Shift key.

Let's practice resizing objects:

1. Display slide 5, if necessary.

2. Select the circle. Observe the four selection handles. You can drag any of these handles to resize the circle.

3. Enlarge the circle by dragging its lower-right selection handle about an inch diagonally away from the center of the circle. Feel free to overlap the arc, if it gets in your way.

4. Observe your enlarged circle carefully. Is it, in fact, still a perfect circle? Or have you subtly distorted its proportions, turning it into a nearly circular ellipse?

If you have a good eye and a steady hand, it's possible to maintain the proportions of a object you resize by dragging along the true diagonal. However, it's much easier—and more reliable—to hold down the Shift key while resizing.

Let's try this technique. First, we'll return the enlarged circle to its original size and proportions. Rather than dragging to do this, we'll use the Edit, Undo command:

1. Choose **Edit**, **Undo** to undo your circle-resizing action.

2. Select the circle, if necessary.

3. Point to the lower-right selection handle. Press and hold the **Shift key**. Press and hold the **left mouse button** to grab the selection handle.

4. Drag the handle about 1 inch diagonally away from the center of the square.

5. Release the mouse button. Release the Shift key. Voilà! An enlarged perfect circle, as shown in Figure 4.12.

It's easy to use the Shift-drag method to proportionally resize a object, if that object's selection box (the box that surrounds a selected object) is square or nearly square. For example, you had no trouble (right?) proportionally enlarging the circle, which has a

Figure 4.12   **Enlarging a circle proportionally**

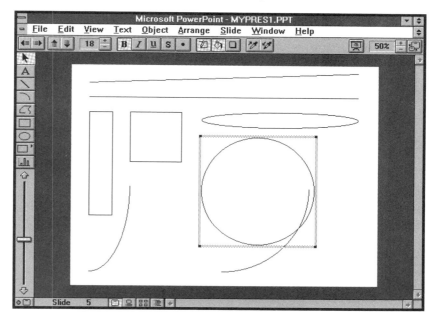

square selection box, as you can see on your screen. It's somewhat more challenging to proportionally resize a object whose
selection box is rectangular. Let's see why:

1. Select the rectangle on the far left of the slide. Note that its
   selection box is rectangular.

2. Point to the lower-right selection handle. Press and hold the
   Shift key. Press and hold the **left mouse button** to grab the
   selection handle.

3. Drag the handle about an inch diagonally away from the center of the rectangle. Note that the rectangle enlarges horizontally (to the right), not proportionally (to the right and down).

4. Release the mouse button and then release the Shift key.
   Choose **Edit**, **Undo** to return the disproportionally enlarged
   rectangle to its original size and position.

5. Let's try again: Point to the rectangle's lower-right selection
   handle. Press and hold the **Shift key**. Press and hold the **left
   mouse button** to grab the selection handle.

6. This time, drag the handle away from the rectangle's center in a direction about halfway between the diagonal and straight down, as shown in Figure 4.13. The rectangle should now grow proportionally, rather than just horizontally.

Figure 4.13   **Enlarging a rectangle proportionally**

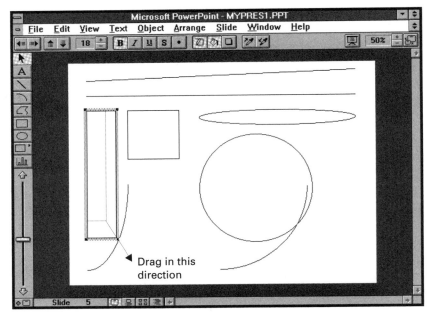

Drag in this direction

7. Release the mouse button and then release the Shift key to complete your proportionally enlarged rectangle.

Follow these simple rules when proportionally resizing:

- To proportionally resize a object in a square selection box, hold Shift and drag along the true diagonal.

- To proportionally resize a object in a rectangular selection box, hold Shift and drag along a diagonal angled toward the longer side of the selection box.

PRACTICE YOUR SKILLS

Using Figure 4.14 as a guide, perform the following four steps:

1. Proportionally enlarge the ellipse by dragging its lower-left handle.

2. Proportionally reduce both arcs by dragging their upper-right handles. (Hint: Drag toward—not away from—the center.)

3. Deselect the arcs. Your screen should resemble that shown in Figure 4.14.

4. Save the file.

Figure 4.14 **Proportionally resizing objects**

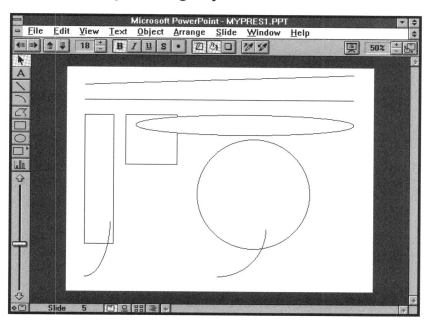

 MOVING OBJECTS

Along with resizing your objects, you may want to move them to improve the slide layout. Here's the general procedure for doing this:

• Select the object.

- Point to the middle of the object (not to a selection handle).
- Drag the object to your desired new location.

PRACTICE YOUR SKILLS

1. Use the above procedure to move the objects on slide 5 to match (or closely resemble) the arrangement shown in Figure 4.15.

2. Save the file.

Figure 4.15   **Moving objects**

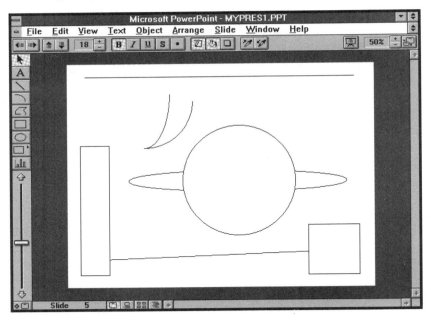

ALIGNING OBJECTS

Sloppily laid-out objects can seriously undermine the effectiveness of a slide. To help you optimize the clarity and harmony of a slide's layout, PowerPoint enables you to align its objects; that is, it allows you to position these objects so that they line up precisely across or down the slide. For example, in an organization chart depicting the hierarchical structure of a company, you'd want to horizontally align the text boxes of employees who are at the same level. PowerPoint provides two utilities that allow you to easily align objects in your slides: the *grid* and *guides*.

The grid is an invisible crosshatch of vertical and horizontal lines (12 to an inch) that covers the entire slide workspace. When the *Arrange, Snap To Grid* option is turned on, the edge of any object that you move will *snap* (move automatically) to the nearest grid line.

The guides are a single vertical and a single horizontal line, both extending across the entire slide workspace. When the *Arrange, Show Guides* option is turned on, the center or edge of any object that you move near either guide will snap to that guide.

Let's create a new slide, draw a number of rectangles on it, and then use the grid to align their top edges:

1. If necessary, display slide 5. Click on the **New Slide button** to create a new slide (slide 6). Note that you can create a new slide between two existing slides (in this case, between slides 5 and 7).

2. Select both the **Title object** and the **Body object**, and then press **Del** to delete both objects at the same time.

3. Using Figure 4.16 as a guide, draw five rectangles of different sizes from left to right across the slide. (Your rectangles needn't match ours exactly.) Make sure to leave a gap at the right, as shown in Figure 4.16.

4. Click on **Arrange** to open the drop-down Arrange menu. Observe the Snap To Grid option. If it is already turned on (preceded by a check), click on **Arrange** again to close the Arrange menu, and then skip the rest of this step. Otherwise, click on the **Snap To Grid** option to turn it on.

5. Move the first (leftmost) rectangle to the upper-left corner of the slide, as shown in Figure 4.17.

6. Now move the second rectangle (proceeding from left to right) so that its top edge aligns with the first rectangle's top edge. Note that it is quite easy to align the two objects, because the Snap To Grid option causes the rectangles to snap to the invisible grid lines (12 to an inch) as you drag.

7. Align the top edges of the remaining three rectangles with those of the first two. Use the grid to space the rectangles equidistantly across the slide, as shown in Figure 4.17.

Figure 4.16   **Drawing five rectangles**

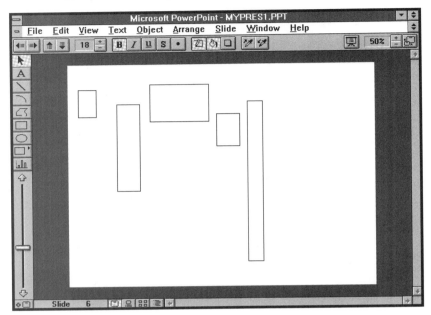

Figure 4.17   **Using the grid to align the rectangles' top edges**

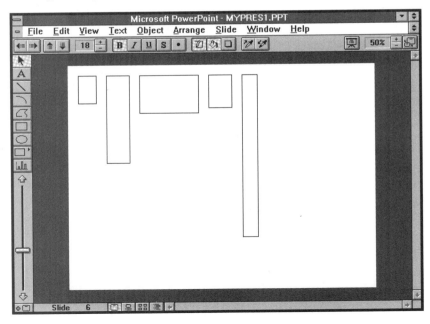

Now let's create some circles and attempt to align their centers by using the grid:

1. Draw five perfect circles (not ellipses), ranging in size from about the diameter of a dime to that of a half-dollar, down the gap at the right side of the slide.

2. Attempt to align the centers of the circles along an imaginary vertical line down the right side of the slide, as shown in Figure 4.18. Space the circles equidistantly down the slide. Note that—try as you might—you cannot align the circles' centers exactly. Why not? Because the grid aligns objects' edges, not their centers.

Figure 4.18   **Attempting to align circles' centers by using the grid**

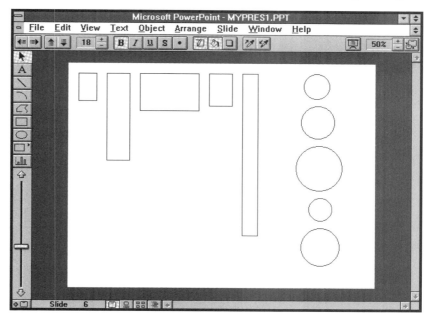

In order to align the circles by their centers, you must use the guides. Let's do this now:

1. Click on **Arrange** to open the drop-down Arrange menu. Observe the Show Guides option; it should be turned off. If, instead, it is turned on (preceded by a check), click on **Arrange**

to close the Arrange menu, and then skip the rest of this step. Otherwise, click on the **Show Guides** option to turn it on.

2. Dotted vertical and horizontal lines appear in your slide workspace. These are the PowerPoint guides. They are used as drawing aids, and will not show up when you print the slide or display it in a slide show.

3. Drag the **vertical guide** to the right until it lines up as closely as possible with the centers of your five circles.

4. Drag the **horizontal guide** upward as far as you can; the position indicator will read *3.75* (meaning that the guide is 3.75 inches above the center of the slide). We want to put this guide aside before we begin aligning the circles with the vertical guide. If, instead, you let the horizontal guide overlap (or come near) a circle, the circle might accidentally snap to the horizontal guide as well as the vertical guide. This, in turn, might cause uneven spacing between your circles.

5. Point to the uppermost circle. Press and hold the **left mouse button**; do not move the mouse. If your vertical guide is close enough to the circle's center, the center will automatically snap to the guide, without your having to drag. If this does not happen, drag the circle until its center snaps to the vertical guide.

6. Repeat this for the remaining four circles. Your circles should match those shown in Figure 4.19.

PRACTICE YOUR SKILLS

Now let's use the horizontal guide to realign the top edges of our five rectangles:

1. Drag the **horizontal guide** downward until the position indicator reads *2.75*. This is where we'll realign the top edges of our rectangles.

2. Drag the leftmost rectangle straight downward—making sure not to move it left or right—until its top edge snaps to the horizontal guide.

3. Repeat this for the four remaining rectangles. Your screen should match that shown in Figure 4.19. As you can see, aligning to a guide is easier (and more reliable) than aligning to a grid line.

Figure 4.19 **Using the guides to align objects**

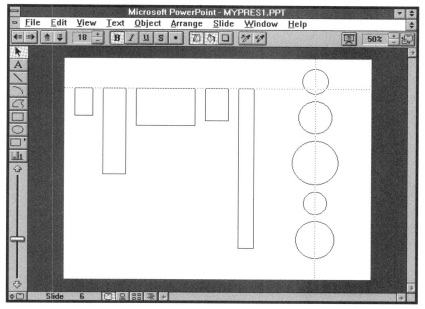

4. Choose **Arrange**, **Show Guides** to remove the guides from the screen.

5. Save the file.

 DELETING OBJECTS

Earlier in this chapter, you had a near-traumatic experience when you deleted your objects. We're sure that you'll never forget how to delete objects; however, for the record, here's the general procedure:

• Select the object(s) you want to delete.

• Press Del.

PRACTICE YOUR SKILLS

Hone your already formidable object-deletion skills by deleting all the objects from slides 5 and 6. (Yes, this time we really mean it!)

ENHANCING OBJECTS

We'll finish up this chapter by showing you how to enhance the appearance of your slide objects. Over the next several sections, you'll learn how to:

- Change the shape of an object
- Fill an object with a specified color or pattern
- Add a shadow to an object
- Change the style of the line with which an object is drawn

 CHANGING OBJECT SHAPES

You may, at times, want to change the shape of a drawn object. For example, you might want to change a simple rectangle to a more dramatic, three-dimensional rectangle, or to change a simple five-pointed star to a glorious, multipointed starburst.

You could do this by deleting the old object and drawing the new object in its place. This technique, however, is tedious and time-consuming. It's far more convenient to use the *Object, Change Shape* command. Choosing this command allows you to quickly and easily change the shape of any object that you've drawn with the Ellipse, Rectangle, or Shape tools. Here's the general procedure for doing this:

- Select the object.
- Choose Object, Change Shape to open the Shape palette.
- Select your desired new shape.

Let's use this technique to change the shape of an object you drew on slide 7:

1. Display slide 7, your cornucopia of predefined objects.

2. Select a prominent object that is not overlapped by another object.

3. Choose **Object, Change Shape** to open the Shape palette. These are the same 24 shapes that are contained in the Shape palette associated with the Shape tool.

4. Select a new shape of your choice in the Shape palette. Observe that the selected object changes to this new shape, while maintaining its original size and proportions.

PRACTICE YOUR SKILLS

1. Use this technique to change the shape of several of the objects in slide 7.

2. When you've had enough of shape-shifting, save the file.

FILLING A SHAPE WITH A COLOR OR PATTERN

You can use the *Object, Fill* command to fill the inside of a closed object with a specified color or pattern. Here's the general procedure for doing this:

- Select the desired object.

- Choose Object, Fill to open the Fill submenu.

- Select one of the following options from the submenu:

  - *None*, to remove the object's current fill

  - *Background*, to fill the object with the slide's background color

  - *Shaded*, to fill the object with a shaded color

  - *Patterned*, to fill the object with a two-color pattern

  - Any of the colors displayed in the submenu, to fill the object with that color

  - *Other Color*, to open the Other Color dialog box, from which you can choose a fill color not shown in the Fill submenu

You can use the *Fill button* on the Toolbar (as shown in Figure 4.20) to change an object's fill colors. Here's the general procedure for doing this:

- Select the desired object.

- To remove a filled object's current fill color (that is, to make the object transparent), click on the Fill button.

- To fill an unfilled (transparent) object with the default fill color, click on the Fill button.

Figure 4.20   **Line, Fill, and Object Shadow buttons**

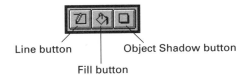

Line button   Object Shadow button

Fill button

Let's fill some of the objects in slide 8:

1. Display slide 8, your free-form jamboree.

2. Select a prominent closed object, preferably one that over-laps other objects but is not itself overlapped.

3. Choose **Object**, **Fill** to open the Fill submenu.

4. Select (click on) **RD8** to fill the selected object with a shade of red.

Now let's use the Fill button to remove this fill color:

1. If necessary, select the object you just filled with RD8.

2. Click on the **Fill button** (as shown in Figure 4.20) to remove the object's current fill color. Observe that the object becomes transparent (devoid of any fill color), revealing those objects that it overlaps.

3. Click on the **Fill button** again to fill the object with the default fill color (white). Observe that the object once again hides those objects that it overlaps.

PRACTICE YOUR SKILLS

1. Fill several of the closed objects in slide 8 with your desired fill colors. Make sure to use some colors from the Other Color dialog box (which you open by clicking on **Other Color** at the bottom of the Fill submenu).

2. Select the spiral in the middle of slide 8 and fill it with a color. (If your spiral is not visible, select and fill any other open object.) In order to fill an open object, like a spiral, PowerPoint first closes the object by connecting its end point and its start-ing point, thus distorting the object's original shape.

3. Choose **Edit**, **Undo** to remove the spiral's fill color and return it to its original (open) shape.

4. Save the file.

ADDING A SHADOW TO AN OBJECT

PowerPoint enables you to add a shadow effect to an object. Here's the general procedure for doing this:

- Select the desired object.

- Click on the **Object Shadow button** on the Toolbar.

- To change the shadow color, choose **Object, Shadow** and select your desired color from the Shadow submenu.

- To remove the shadow, click on the Object Shadow button again.

Let's add a shadow to several of the objects in slide 8:

1. In slide 8, select a prominent object.

2. Click on the **Object Shadow button** (as shown in Figure 4.20) to add a default gray shadow to the selected object.

3. Click again on the **Object Shadow button** to remove the object's shadow. The Object Shadow button acts as a toggle; clicking on it either adds or removes the selected object's shadow.

4. Using the technique outlined in steps 1 and 2, add a default gray shadow to several (at least four) objects.

Now let's change the shadow color for these objects:

1. Select all your shadowed objects.

2. Choose **Object, Shadow** to open the Shadow submenu.

3. Select **BK** to change the shadow for all your selected objects from gray to black. Note that the multiple selection you performed in step 1 allowed you to accomplish your desired task (recoloring the shadows) in one step, instead of several.

CHANGING AN OBJECT'S LINE STYLE

You can use the *Object, Line Style* command to change the style of the line with which an object is drawn. Here's the general procedure for doing this:

- Select the desired object.

- Choose Object, Line Style to open the Line Style submenu.

- Select your desired line style from the submenu.

- To hide or show the line with which the object is drawn, click on the *Line button* on the Toolbar.

Let's change the line style of a few of slide 8's objects:

1. In slide 8, select a nonshadowed object.

2. Choose **Object, Line Style** to open the Line Style submenu.

3. Select the third style from the top of the submenu to increase the thickness of the line with which the selected object is drawn.

4. Click on the **Line button** (as shown in Figure 4.20) to hide the selected object's line.

5. Click on the **Line button** again to redraw this line. Note that the line is back to its original thickness, rather than the thickness you applied in step 3. When you click on the Line button to show a hidden line, PowerPoint draws this line in the default thickness.

PRACTICE YOUR SKILLS

1. Change the line style of several other nonshadowed and shadowed objects in slide 8.

2. Save the file and close it.

PRACTICE YOUR SKILLS

Congratulations on making it through the first four chapters of this book! You've learned a whole slew of important PowerPoint techniques in these chapters. The following two activities are designed to increase your fluency with these techniques.

Note: In case you need to refresh your memory about a certain procedure, the relevant chapter number is included in parentheses at the end of each step.

Other "Practice Your Skills" activities appear at key points throughout the course of this book. Please don't think of these activities as tests, but rather as opportunities to hone your Power-Point skills. It is only through repetition that you'll internalize the techniques you've learned.

Follow these steps to create the slides shown in Figures 4.21 and 4.22:

Figure 4.21   **Corporate Services slide**

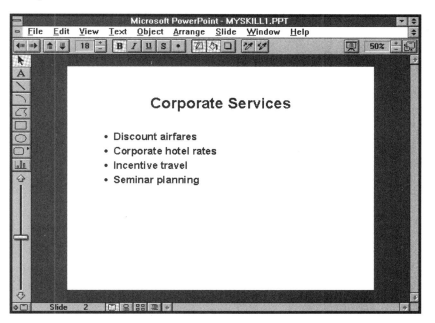

1. Open the file **skills1.ppt** (Chapter 1).

2. Add a new slide (slide 2) to the presentation and enter the title **Corporate Services** (Chapter 2).

Figure 4.22   **Leisure Services slide**

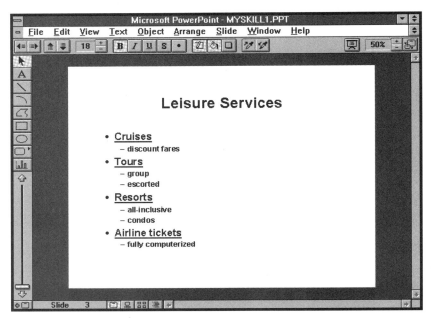

3. In Slide view, add the following level-1 bulleted items to the slide (Chapter 2):

   Discount airfares

   Corporate hotel rates

   Incentive travel

   Seminar planning

4. Save the presentation as **myskill1** (Chapter 2).

5. In Outline view, add another new slide (slide 3) to the presentation and enter the title **Leisure Services** (Chapter 2).

6. In Outline view, add the following two-level bulleted list to the slide (Chapter 2):

   Cruises

      discount fares

Tours

    group

    escorted

Airline tickets

    fully computerized

Resorts

    all-inclusive

    condos

7. Move the bulleted item *Resorts* and its two sub-bulleted items to above *Airline tickets* (Chapter 3).

8. Underline all the level-1 bulleted text items (Chapter 3).

9. Save the file (Chapter 2).

10. In Slide view, use the Slide Changer to view slides 2 and 3 (Chapter 1). They should match those shown in Figures 4.21 and 4.22.

11. Close the file (Chapter 1).

Follow these steps to create the slide shown in Figure 4.23:

1. Open a new presentation file (Chapter 2).

2. Delete the Title object and Body object from slide 1 (Chapter 4).

3. Draw the nine objects (but not the text) depicted in Figure 4.23 (Chapter 4). (Hint: Use the **Shift key** where necessary to maintain an object's original proportions.) Position the objects as shown in Figure 4.23. However, don't worry about their exact locations; you'll get to that later.

4. Save the presentation as **myskill2** (Chapter 2).

5. Create the text object in the bottom center of the slide (Chapter 4). (Hint: Don't press Enter when typing the text.)

6. Center and bold this text, and increase its size to 24 points (Chapter 3). If necessary, resize the text box to force the lines to wrap, as in Figure 4.23.

Figure 4.23   **A sample slide combining words and images**

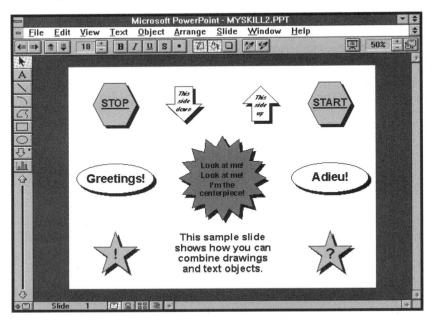

7. Use the guides to align the centers of all ten objects (nine drawn objects and one text object), as shown in Figure 4.23.

8. In a blank area of the slide, create a text object that consists of the word **STOP** (Chapter 4).

9. Change this object's text attributes (size, bold, underline, and so on) to match those shown in Figure 4.23 (Chapter 3).

10. Position your text object within its corresponding object, as shown in Figure 4.23. (Hint: To fine-tune an object's position, hold down the **Alt key** while moving it. This temporarily turns off the Snap To Grid option, thus allowing you to move the object in finer increments.)

11. Using the technique outlined in steps 8 through 10, create the remaining eight text objects and position them within their corresponding objects, as shown in Figure 4.23. Set the text attributes and line spacing to match that shown in Figure 4.23.

12. Add a shadow to all the drawn objects (Chapter 4). (Hint: Select all the drawn objects—not the text objects!—and then click on the **Object Shadow button**.)

13. Change the shadow color to **BK** (black) (Chapter 4).

14. Fill the five objects depicted in Figure 4.23 with appropriate colors (Chapter 4). Your screen should now match that shown in Figure 4.23.

15. Save the file and close it (Chapter 1).

SUMMARY

In this chapter, you began working with slide images. You learned how to draw basic shapes (lines, rectangles, squares, ellipses, circles, and arcs), how to draw other predefined shapes (arrows, triangles, stars, diamonds, and so on), how to draw free-form objects, and how to create text objects. You also learned how to edit objects (select and deselect, resize, move, align, and delete them), how to undo your last action, and how to enhance objects (change their shapes, fill colors, shadows, and line styles).

Here's a quick reference for the techniques you learned in this chapter:

Desired Result	How to Do It
Draw a straight line	Select the **Line tool**; to draw a horizontal, vertical, or diagonal line, press and hold the **Shift key**; press and hold the **left mouse button**; drag in the slide to draw the line; release the mouse button; if necessary, release the Shift key
Draw a rectangle or a square	Select the **Rectangle tool**; to draw a square, press and hold the **Shift key**; press and hold the **left mouse button**; drag in the slide to draw the rectangle or square; release the mouse button; if necessary, release the Shift key

Desired Result	How to Do It
Draw an ellipse or a circle	Select the **Ellipse tool**; to draw a circle, press and hold the **Shift key**; press and hold the **left mouse button**; drag in the slide to draw the ellipse or circle; release the mouse button; if necessary, release the Shift key
Draw an arc	Select the **Arc tool**; to draw a circular arc, press and hold the **Shift key**; press and hold the **left mouse button**; drag in the slide to draw the arc; release the mouse button; if necessary, release the Shift key
Draw a predefined shape	Select the desired shape from the Shape palette; to maintain the proportions of the selected shape, press and hold the **Shift key**; press and hold the **left mouse button**; drag in the slide to draw the select shape; release the mouse button; if necessary, release the Shift key
Draw a free-form object	Select the **Freeform tool**; drag to draw your free-form object; to create an open object, double-click on the desired end point; to create a closed object, click on the starting point
Draw a straight line in a free-form object	Drag in a straight line; or, release the mouse button, move the pointer to draw the straight line, and then press and hold the **left mouse button** to continue drawing in free-form or click to begin drawing another straight line

Desired Result	How to Do It
Create a text object	Select the **Text tool**, drag to create a box as wide as your desired text object, type your desired text, click on any blank area of the slide to complete the text object
Select an object	Click on the **Selection tool**, if it is not already selected, and click on the desired object
Select multiple objects	While holding down the **Shift key**, select all your desired objects
Remove object(s) from a multiple selection	While holding down the **Shift key**, click on the selected object(s) that you want to remove
Deselect all currently selected objects	Click on any blank area of the slide
Undo your last PowerPoint action	Choose **Edit, Undo**
Resize an object	Select the object; to maintain the proportions of the selected object, press and hold the **Shift key**; to reduce the object, drag the desired selection handle diagonally toward the center of the object; to enlarge the object, drag the handle diagonally away from the center of the object; release the mouse button; if necessary, release the Shift key
Move an object	Select the object and drag it (by its middle) to your desired new location
Align objects using the grid	Turn on the **Arrange, Snap To Grid** option and move the objects to align their edges to the grid lines

Desired Result	How to Do It
Align objects using the guides	Turn on the **Arrange, Show Guides** option; move the guides to your desired positions; move the objects to align their edges or centers to the guides
Delete an object	Select the object and press **Del**
Change an object's shape	Select the object; choose **Object, Change Shape**; select your desired new shape from the Shape palette
Specify a fill color for an object	Select the desired object; choose **Object, Fill**; select the desired option from the Fill submenu
Use the Fill button to change an object's fill colors	Select the desired object; to remove a filled object's current fill color, click on the **Fill button**; to fill an unfilled object with the default fill color, click on the **Fill button**
Add a shadow to an object	Select the desired object; click on the **Object Shadow button**; to change the shadow color, choose **Object, Shadow** and select your desired color from the Shadow submenu; to remove the shadow, click on the **Object Shadow button** again
Specify a line style for an object	Select the desired object; choose **Object, Line Style**; select your desired line style from the Line Style submenu; to hide or show the line with which the object is drawn, click on the **Line button**

In the next chapter, you'll complete our two-part series on working with images by exploring clip art and color. You'll learn how to add clip art to a slide, and how to resize, crop, ungroup, and scale your clip art. You'll also learn how to change an entire color scheme, how to change individual color-scheme colors, how to recolor clip art, and how to uncrop clip art.

IF YOU'RE STOPPING HERE

If you need to break off here, please exit PowerPoint. If you want to proceed directly to the next chapter, please do so now.

CHAPTER 5: CLIP ART AND COLOR SCHEMES

Clip Art

Working with Color

Exiting PowerPoint with an Open, Unsaved File

In Chapter 4, you learned how to draw objects on your slides and how to edit and enhance these objects. In this chapter, the second in our two-part series on working with images, you'll learn how to add *clip art* (predrawn, precolored graphic images) to your slides; how to resize, crop, and recolor clip art; and how to change your presentation's *color scheme* (the palette of colors used to draw the various elements of a slide—title text, body text, lines, fills, and so on).

When you're done working through this chapter, you will know

- How to add clip art to a slide
- How to resize clip art
- How to crop clip art
- How to ungroup clip art into its component parts
- How to scale clip art
- How to change an entire color scheme
- How to change individual colors of a color scheme
- How to recolor clip art
- How to uncrop clip art

CLIP ART

In Chapter 4, you added images to your slides by drawing them yourself. In some cases, this was easy (as when you were working with predefined shapes); in others, a bit more challenging (as when you created free-form shapes). Here you'll learn how to add sophisticated predrawn, precolored images to your slides without doing any drawing at all. These images are called *clip-art objects* or simply *clip art*. PowerPoint provides you with a generous library of clip art, including images of animals, household objects, humorous cartoons, internationally recognized landmarks, international maps, scenic landscapes, and much more.

 ### ADDING CLIP ART TO A SLIDE

Adding clip art to a slide is a two-step procedure. First, you copy the clip-art object from the file in which it is contained to the *Clipboard*, a temporary storage location used to transfer data (images, text, and so on) between slides or presentations. Then, you paste the clip-art object from the Clipboard to your slide. Here's the general procedure for adding clip art to a slide:

- In Slide view, display the slide to which you want to add the clip art.
- Choose *File, Open Clip Art* to open the Open Clip Art dialog box.

- If necessary, change the current drive and directory to the drive and directory in which the clip art is stored.

- Double-click on the desired clip-art file to open it in Outline view.

- Double-click on the desired clip-art slide number to display it in Slide view.

- Select the clip-art object.

- Choose Edit, Copy to copy the selected clip-art object to the Clipboard.

- Close the clip-art file.

- If necessary, display the slide (in Slide view) to which you want to add the clip art.

- Choose Edit, Paste to paste the clip-art object from the Clipboard to this slide.

If you are not running PowerPoint, please start it now. Close all open presentations except the start-up presentation. Let's begin this chapter's activities by adding a clip-art object to slide 1 of MYPRES1.PPT:

1. Open **MYPRES1.PPT** from your POWERWRK directory.

2. Delete slide 1's Body object. You'll fill this empty space with your clip-art object.

3. Choose **File, Open Clip Art** to open the Open Clip Art dialog box.

4. In the File Name list, double-click on the clip-art file name **intlmaps.ppt** (short for "International Maps") to open it in Outline view.

5. Scroll through the outline. INTLMAPS.PPT contains 23 different clip-art maps that you can use in your presentations. Observe the eighth entry, World Map. This is the map we want to add to slide 1.

6. Double-click on the number **8** in the left margin to display the World Map slide in Slide view, as shown in Figure 5.1.

7. Select the map object by clicking on it.

Figure 5.1 **World Map clip-art slide**

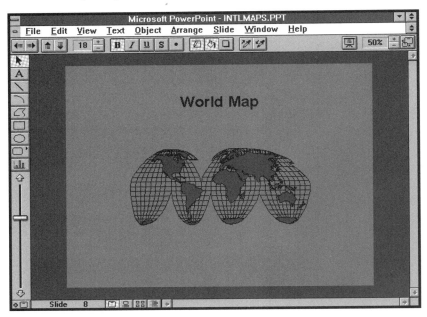

8. Choose **Edit, Copy** to copy the map to the Clipboard. Note that PowerPoint does not inform you that the slide has been copied. The Clipboard operates behind the scenes.

9. Choose **File, Close** to close the INTLMAPS.PPT clip-art file. Verify that slide 1 of MYPRES1.PPT is displayed on the screen. This is our target slide.

10. Choose **Edit, Paste** to paste the clip-art map from the Clipboard to slide 1. Your screen should match that shown in Figure 5.2.

11. Choose **File, Save** to save the file.

RESIZING CLIP ART

You resize a clip-art object just as you would resize any other PowerPoint object. Here's the general procedure for doing this:

- Select the clip-art object.

Figure 5.2   **Pasting the clip-art map to slide 1**

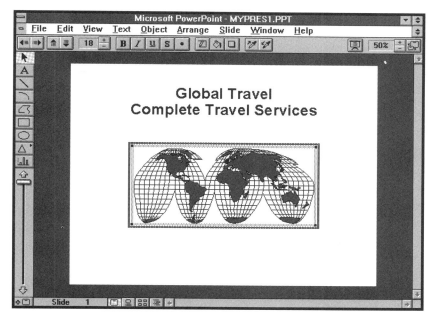

- To maintain the proportions of the object, press and hold the Shift key.

- To keep the object centered as you resize it, press and hold the Ctrl key. (See the paragraph directly following this procedure for more details about this step.)

- Point to the desired selection handle. Press and hold the left mouse button to grab the handle.

- To reduce the object, drag the handle diagonally toward the center of the object. To enlarge the object, drag the handle diagonally away from the center of the object.

- Release the mouse button.

- If necessary, release the Ctrl key.

- If necessary, release the Shift key.

This is the same procedure you used in Chapter 4 to resize your drawn and text objects, with the addition of one very useful technique. By holding down the Ctrl key while you drag the object's selection handle, you resize the object from the center outward (or inward); that is, the center of the object remains fixed as you enlarge (or reduce) the object. This technique is not limited to clip art; you can use it on any resizable PowerPoint object (drawn object, text object, and so on).

Important Note: PowerPoint's clip-art files (such as the INTLMAPS-.PPT file you opened earlier in this chapter) are designed to hold original, unmodified clip-art objects. For this reason, you should *never* resize or otherwise modify (crop, recolor, and so on) a clip-art object in its file of origin (such as INTLMAPS.PPT). Instead, copy the object to your target presentation file, and then modify this *copied* object, thus leaving the original object intact.

Let's enlarge our clip-art map nonproportionally:

1. Select the clip-art map on slide 1, if necessary.

2. Drag the upper-right selection handle about an inch directly to the right to enlarge the map horizontally. Observe that this significantly distorts the map's original proportions.

3. Choose **Edit, Undo** to return the map to its original proportions.

4. Drag the lower-right selection handle about an inch directly downward to enlarge the map vertically. This also distorts the map's proportions.

5. Choose **Edit, Undo** to return the map to its original proportions. As mentioned in Chapter 4, you can use the Edit, Undo command to toggle between the "before" and "after" conditions of an action, a feature we'll take full advantage of in this activity.

Now let's enlarge the map proportionally:

1. Press and hold the **Shift key.** Drag the lower-right selection handle to enlarge the map proportionally by about an inch. As explained in Chapter 4, since the map's selection box is rectangular instead of square, you'll have to drag about half-way between the diagonal and straight to the right—that is, along a diagonal angled toward the longer side of the box.

2. Release the Shift key and then release the mouse button. Observe the results, shown in Figure 5.3. You've enlarged your map proportionally, but in doing so, you've changed its position on the slide.

Figure 5.3   **Enlarging proportionally without using the Ctrl key**

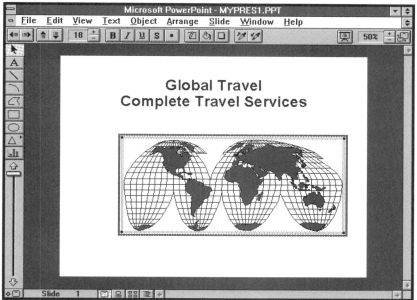

3. Choose **Edit, Undo** to return the map to its original size and position.

Now let's use the Ctrl key to enlarge the map from the center outward, without changing its position:

1. Press and hold the **Ctrl key**. Press and hold the **Shift key**. Drag the lower-right selection handle to enlarge the map proportionally by about an inch.

2. Release the mouse button, release the Shift key, and then release the Ctrl key. Observe the results, shown in Figure 5.4. You've enlarged your map proportionally without changing its centered position on the slide.

3. Choose **Edit, Undo** to return the map to its original size.

PRACTICE YOUR SKILLS

1. Without changing its position, reduce the map proportionally to about the size of a postage stamp.

Figure 5.4   **Enlarging proportionally using the Ctrl key**

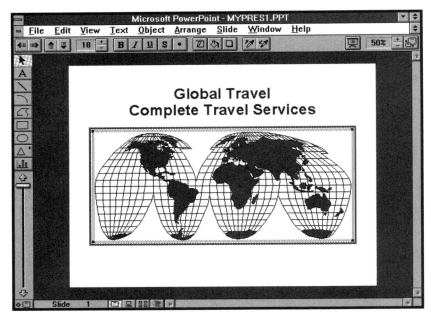

2. Choose **Edit, Undo** to return the map to its original size.

3. Without changing its position, return the map to the enlarged size shown in Figure 5.4. This is the size we'll use for the actual slide.

 CROPPING CLIP ART

PowerPoint allows you to quickly and easily *crop* (trim) a clip-art object. You use this feature just as photographers and layout artists do: to remove the undesirable part of an image in order to emphasize the part that remains. For example, in the next activity, you'll crop a clip-art image of an eagle so that only the head and feet remain. Then you'll enlarge the cropped image and use it as a dramatic illustration in a slide.

Here's the general procedure for cropping a clip-art object:

• Select the clip-art object.

- Choose *Object, Crop Picture*. The mouse pointer becomes a *Cropping tool.*

- Drag one of the clip-art object's selection handles to crop the image as desired.

- If necessary, repeat the previous step until the image is cropped to your satisfaction.

- Click on any blank area of the slide to deselect both the clip-art object and the Cropping tool.

(**Note:** At the end of this chapter, you'll learn how to uncrop a cropped clip-art object.)

Let's use this procedure to create the cropped eagle image, as described earlier in this section. We'll begin by pasting the eagle clip art onto a blank slide:

1. Display slide 5. This blank slide originally contained several simple objects (lines, rectangles, ellipses, and so on) that you drew at the beginning of Chapter 4.

2. Choose **File, Open Clip Art** to open the Open Clip Art dialog box.

3. Double-click on the clip-art file name **animals.ppt** to open it in Outline view.

4. Observe the outline. ANIMALS.PPT contains 12 different clip-art animals that you can use in your presentations. Observe the last entry, Eagle. This is the image that we want to paste onto slide 5.

5. Double-click on the number **12** in the left margin to display the Eagle slide in Slide view, as shown in Figure 5.5.

6. Select the eagle object, and then choose **Edit, Copy** to copy it to the Clipboard.

7. Choose **File, Close** to close the ANIMALS.PPT clip-art file. Verify that slide 5 of MYPRES1.PPT is displayed.

8. Choose **Edit, Paste** to paste the eagle clip-art object from the Clipboard onto slide 5.

Figure 5.5   **The original eagle clip-art object**

Now let's crop the eagle until only its head and feet remain:

1. Choose **Object, Crop Picture**. Move the mouse pointer onto the slide. Note that the pointer changes to the squarish Cropping tool.

2. Using this tool, grab the eagle's upper-left selection handle and drag downward until the top, dashed line of the object box is about one-eighth of an inch above the top of the eagle's head (the white part).

3. Release the mouse button and observe the results. Your cropped eagle should resemble the one shown in Figure 5.6. If it doesn't, choose **Edit, Undo** and repeat step 2.

4. Using the **Cropping tool**, drag the eagle's lower-left selection handle to the right until the dashed vertical line is about one-eighth of an inch to the left of the leftmost edge of the eagle's feet (the orange part).

Figure 5.6   **The eagle, after one round of cropping**

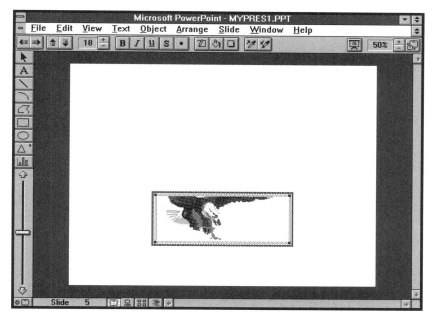

5. Drag the eagle's lower-right selection handle to the left until the dashed vertical line is about one-eighth of an inch to the right of the rightmost edge of the eagle's beak, as shown in Figure 5.7.

Now let's proportionally enlarge our cropped eagle:

1. Click on any blank area of the slide to deselect both the eagle clip-art object and the Cropping tool.

2. Reselect the eagle, and proportionally enlarge it (by dragging the upper-right selection handle while holding down the **Shift key**) until the object box is about three-quarters as high as the slide, as shown in Figure 5.8.

Now let's relocate our cropped, enlarged eagle and add some appropriate text to the slide:

1. Move the eagle object to the upper-left corner of the slide, as shown in Figure 5.9.

Figure 5.7   **The eagle, fully cropped**

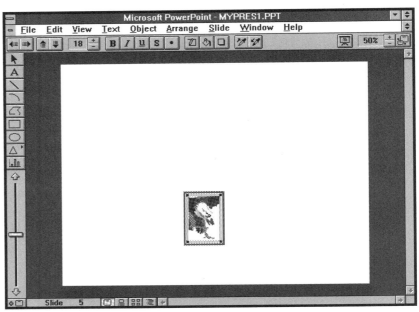

Figure 5.8   **Proportionally enlarging the cropped eagle**

Figure 5.9   **Moving the eagle and adding text**

2. Create a text object consisting of the following two paragraphs:

   Competitors beware:

   We take no prisoners!

3. Center both paragraphs. Verify that both paragraphs are in bold. Italicize the second paragraph.

4. Increase the text size to 36 points. To make the lines break as they do in Figure 5.9, resize the text box, if necessary. Move the text box to the location shown in Figure 5.9.

5. Use **Text, Color** to change the text color to **RD8** (red). Your screen should match that shown in Figure 5.9.

6. Save the file.

UNGROUPING CLIP ART

Every PowerPoint clip-art object consists of two or more sub-objects that are grouped together as a single unit. For example, the eagle object that you just cropped consists of two subobjects: the eagle's head and the rest of its body.

In effect, every clip-art object is itself a minilibrary of clip-art sub-objects. You can use this fact to your advantage. For example, in the next activity you'll *ungroup* a clip-art image of a personal computer into its component parts, rearrange these parts on the slide, and then label them.

Here's the general procedure for ungrouping a clip-art object:

- Select the object.

- Choose *Arrange, Ungroup*.

- If a dialog box informs you that the selected object is an imported object, not a group, and asks you whether you want to convert the imported object to PowerPoint objects, click on Yes.

Note: Once you ungroup a clip-art object, you cannot crop or recolor the resulting subobjects. (You'll learn how to recolor clip-art objects later in this chapter.)

Now, as promised, we'll ungroup a clip-art image of a personal computer into its component parts:

1. Display slide 6, another blank slide whose contents you deleted in Chapter 4.

2. Choose **File, Open Clip Art** to open the Open Clip Art dialog box.

3. Double-click on the clip-art file name **business.ppt** to open it in Outline view. Observe the first slide in the outline, Personal Computer.

4. Double-click on the number **1** in the left margin to display the Personal Computer slide in Slide view.

5. Select both the computer clip-art object and the **Title object** (Personal Computer). Choose **Edit, Copy** to copy both of these objects to the Clipboard.

6. Choose **File, Close** to close the BUSINESS.PPT clip-art file. As mentioned, you should *never* ungroup or otherwise modify a clip-art object in its file of origin (BUSINESS.PPT, in this case).

7. Verify that slide 6 of MYPRES1.PPT is displayed on the screen. Choose **Edit, Paste** to paste the computer object and the Title object from the Clipboard onto slide 6.

8. Deselect both objects, and then select only the computer object.

9. Choose **Arrange, Ungroup** to ungroup the computer object into its component subobjects. A dialog box appears.

10. Ignore the dialog-box message (which addresses a high-level Windows issue with which you needn't be concerned), and click on **OK** to perform the ungrouping.

11. Observe the results. You've ungrouped the single computer clip-art object into four separate subobjects: the monitor, the monitor stand, the central processing unit (the box beneath the monitor stand), and the keyboard.

12. Verify this by clicking on a blank area of the slide to deselect the subobjects, and then selecting each of the four subobjects, one by one.

We want the monitor to be "attached" to the monitor stand. To do this, we'll have to *group* these two subobjects:

1. Deselect all subobjects, and then—using the mouse and the **Shift key**—select both the monitor and the stand subobjects.

2. Choose **Arrange, Group** to group the monitor and the stand into a single object.

PRACTICE YOUR SKILLS

Perform the following steps to create the slide shown in Figure 5.10:

1. Decrease the title text size to **32** points, and change the title to **Personal Computer Components**.

2. Move the **Title object** upward four grid units (one-third of an inch). Be careful not to slide it left or right.

3. Position the three computer subobjects approximately as shown in Figure 5.10.

4. Display the guides. (Hint: Choose **Arrange, Show Guides**.)

5. Use the horizontal guide to align the bottom edges of the monitor and central processing unit objects to 0.50 inches below the center of the slide.

6. Use the horizontal guide to align the bottom edge of the keyboard object to 2.50 inches below the slide center.

Figure 5.10   **Personal Computer Components slide**

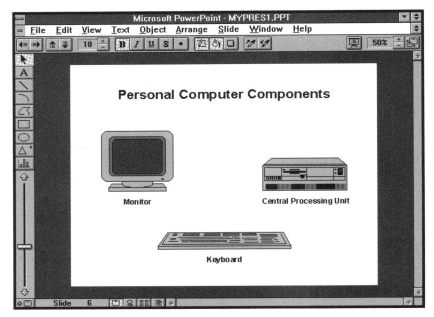

7. Use the vertical guide to align the left edge of the monitor object to 4.00 inches to the left of the slide center.

8. Use the vertical guide to align the right edge of the central processing unit to 4.00 inches to the right of the slide center.

9. Use the vertical guide to align the center of the keyboard with the center of the slide (0.00 inches).

10. Create the three additional text objects shown on Figure 5.10: **Monitor**, **Central Processing Unit**, and **Keyboard**.

11. Center the text within these objects. If necessary, change the text to 18-point bold.

12. Use the horizontal guide to align the bottom edges of the Monitor and Central Processing Unit text objects to 1.08 inches below the slide center.

13. Manually center these two text objects beneath their respective images. (Hint: If necessary, hold down **Alt** while dragging left or right to move the text objects in fine increments.)

14. Use the horizontal guide to align the bottom edge of the Keyboard text object to 3.08 inches below the slide center. Use the vertical guide to align the center of this text object with the center of the slide.

15. Remove the guides. Your slide should now match that shown in Figure 5.10.

16. Save the file.

SCALING CLIP ART

Earlier in this chapter, you learned how to proportionally resize a clip-art object around a fixed center point by holding down the Ctrl and Shift keys as you dragged one of the object's selection handles. Here you'll learn how to *scale* a clip-art object; that is, how to proportionally resize the object around a fixed center point by specifying a *scale percentage*. Specifying a scale of 200 percent doubles the size of the selected object; specifying 50 percent halves the size of the object; and so on.

Here's the general procedure for scaling a clip-art object:

● Select the clip-art object.

● Choose *Object, Scale* to open the Scale dialog box.

● If necessary, move the dialog box out of the way of the object you are scaling.

● In the Scale To box, type your desired scale percentage.

● Observe the results. Repeat the previous step, if necessary.

● Click on OK.

Note: You can use this procedure to scale any resizable Power-Point object.

Let's create a new slide, copy the monitor object to it, and then practice scaling this object:

1. Verify that slide 6 is displayed. Click on the **New Slide button** to create a new slide (slide 7). Delete slide 7's Title and Body objects.

2. Display slide 6.

3. Select the monitor object and choose **Edit, Copy** to copy it to the Clipboard.

4. Display slide 7.

5. Choose **Edit, Paste** to paste the monitor object from the Clipboard to slide 7. Note that copying an object from one slide to another within the same presentation file (as you just did) is essentially the same as copying an object from a slide in a clip-art file to a slide in a different presentation file (as you did in the section "Adding Clip Art to a Slide" at the beginning of this chapter). In both cases, you select the object, copy it to the Clipboard, and then paste it onto the target slide.

6. Press **Ctrl+y** (the keyboard shortcut for choosing Arrange, Show Guides) to display the guides. Use them to center the monitor within the slide. Press **Ctrl+y** again to remove the guides.

7. Select the monitor object, if necessary. Choose **Object, Scale** to open the Scale dialog box.

8. Type **50** (without pressing Enter) to scale the monitor down to 50 percent of its original size; that is, to proportionally reduce the monitor object by half without changing its slide position.

Chances are that the Scale dialog box is blocking your view of the scaled-down monitor. Let's fix that:

1. Move the dialog box (by dragging its title bar) to the upper-left corner of your screen to free up as much of the slide as possible, as shown in Figure 5.11. It's perfectly okay to move the dialog box on top of presentation-window and application-window elements (the Toolbar, menu bar, title bar, Tool Palette, and so on).

2. Observe the screen. Note that you can now see your scaled-down monitor.

3. Press **Backspace** twice to delete the *50* you typed in step 8. Type **25** (without pressing Enter) to scale the monitor down to 25 percent of its original size. Observe this change on your slide.

Figure 5.11   **Moving the Scale dialog box out of the way**

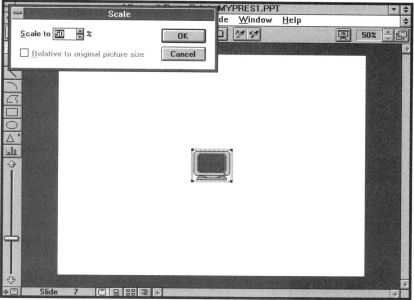

Now let's scale the monitor to fill the entire slide:

1. Use **Backspace** to delete the *25* you typed in step 3 in the last activity. Type **200** to double the monitor's original size. Hmmmm...not big enough.

2. Delete the *200* and type **300** to triple the monitor's original size. Still not quite big enough.

3. Delete the *300* and type **350**. Bingo! A perfect fit.

4. Click on **OK** to close the Scale dialog box.

PRACTICE YOUR SKILLS

1. Complete the slide by creating the text object shown in Figure 5.12. Change the text to 28-point bold. Center the text within the object. Center the object within the monitor.

2. Save the file.

Figure 5.12   **The completed monitor slide**

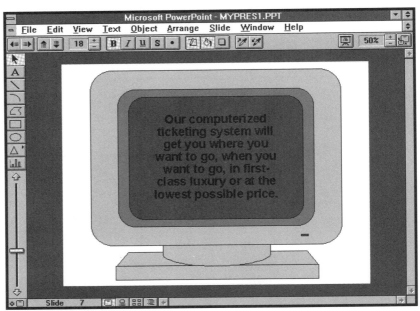

WORKING WITH COLOR

Color is a critical (and, sadly, often neglected) factor in the overall effectiveness of a presentation. For example, a vivid palette of colors—one consisting, perhaps, of neon blues, reds, and yellow—could be just what you need to wake up a sleepy audience. Conversely, an understated palette—one consisting of black, white, and gray shades—might be perfect for a sedate business crowd.

Over the next several sections, we'll introduce you to the exciting world of slide colors by showing you how to change your presentations' color schemes and how to recolor your clip art.

CHANGING AN ENTIRE COLOR SCHEME

Every PowerPoint presentation has a *color scheme*, a set of eight compatible colors that are used for specific slide elements. Table 5.1 lists these eight colors by element and provides a brief description of each.

Table 5.1   **Color-Scheme Colors**

Color Name	Description
Background	The color of a slide's background (the area behind the slide's objects)
Lines & Text	The color of drawn lines (ellipses, squares, straight lines, free-form objects, and so on), Body-object text, and text created with the Text tool
Shadows	The color of objects' shadows
Title Text	The color of the Title-object text
Fills	The color inside filled objects
Accents	The set of three colors used for graphs (bar-chart bars, pie-chart slices, and so on) and for secondary slide items

Here's the general procedure for changing an entire color scheme:

- Change to Slide view or Slide Sorter view. (You can also change the color scheme in Outline view, but doing so in Slide view or Slide Sorter view lets you see your new color scheme immediately.)

- If you are changing the color scheme of a single slide, select this slide.

- Choose *Slide, Color Scheme* to open the Color Scheme dialog box.

- Click on the *Choose A Scheme button* to open the Choose A Scheme dialog box.

- Select a background color in the Background list box.

- Select a color for line and text in the Text list box.

- Select a set of shadow, title-text, fill, and accent colors in the Remaining list box.

- Click on OK to return to the Color Scheme dialog box.

- To change the color scheme of the current slide only, select the *This Slide* option in the Apply To box. To change the color scheme of all the presentation's slides, select the *All Slides* option.

- Click on OK.

Let's begin this activity by opening a new presentation file and exploring a very useful PowerPoint feature:

1. Observe that MYPRES1.PPT is open. We're not done working on this presentation, so we won't close it yet.

2. Open the **COLOR.PPT** file from your POWERWRK directory. You now have two presentation files open at the same time, MYPRES1.PPT and COLOR.PPT. MYPRES1.PPT is currently hidden behind the active file, COLOR.PPT.

3. Verify this by clicking on **Window** to open the drop-down Window menu. Your two open files, MYPRES1.PPT and COLOR.PPT, are listed at the bottom of the drop-down menu. The numbers preceding the file names (*1* and *2*) indicate the order in which you opened the files. The check preceding *COLOR.PPT* indicates that it is the active file. The unchecked file, MYPRES1.PPT, is hidden.

4. Click on **1 MYPRES1.PPT** to make it the active file. *COLOR.PPT* disappears; the file is not closed, however, just hidden.

5. Choose **Window, 2 COLOR.PPT** to make COLOR.PPT the active file again.

You can use the procedure just outlined in steps 2 through 5 to work on two or more presentations at the same time. You'll find this feature particularly useful when you're working on interdependent presentations or when you're copying objects between different presentations.

Now let's examine COLOR.PPT's color scheme:

1. Display slide 4 of COLOR.PPT.

2. Choose **Slide, Color Scheme** to open the Color Scheme dialog box. Observe the set of eight colors (Background, Lines & Text, Shadows, and so on) that make up the current color scheme.

3. Move the Color Scheme dialog box to the right side of the screen, as shown in Figure 5.13, so that you can see the slide and the color-scheme colors at the same time.

Figure 5.13   **Moving the Color Scheme dialog box out of the way**

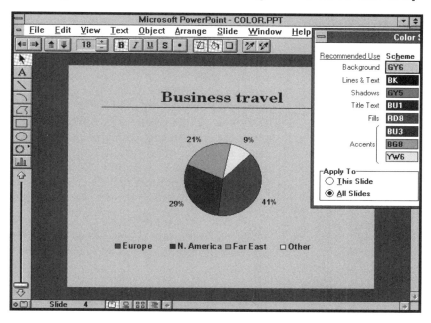

4. Observe the name of the current background color in the Color Scheme dialog box (*GY6*, or light gray). Now observe this color in the background of the slide.

5. Repeat step 4 for the remaining seven color-scheme colors. (**Note:** There are no shadowed objects on the slide, so the shadow color is not used.) Observe that the fill color and the three accent colors are used to color the four slices of the pie chart.

Now let's practice changing the color scheme. First we'll create a sedate, black/white/grays scheme:

1. Move the **Color Scheme dialog box** back to the middle of the slide, so that the entire dialog box is visible.

2. Click on the **Choose A Scheme button** to open the Choose A Scheme dialog box.

3. Observe that three list boxes are displayed: Background, Text, and Remaining Colors. The color you select in the Background list box determines the background color of your color scheme. The color you select in the Text list box determines the line and text color. The set of six colors you select in the Remaining Colors list box determines the shadow, title-text, fill, and accent colors.

4. Note that the Background list box displays a palette of colors, but that the Text list box and the Remaining Colors list box are both empty. Why? Because when you create a color scheme, PowerPoint guides you in selecting a set of eight compatible, balanced colors. As soon as you select the background color (in the Background list box), PowerPoint displays a palette of compatible line and text colors (in the Text list box). Likewise, as soon as you select the line and text color, PowerPoint displays a palette of compatible shadow, title-text, fill, and accent colors (in the Remaining Colors list box).

5. In the Background list box, click on the **WT** box to select a white background for your new color scheme. Observe that the Text list box displays a palette of compatible line and text colors.

6. In the Text list box, click on the **BK** box to select black as the line and text color. Observe that the Remaining Colors list box displays a palette of compatible shadow, title-text, fill, and accent colors.

7. In the Remaining Colors list box, click on the third set of colors from the left in the top row to select a palette of gray shades for your remaining colors.

8. Click on **OK** to return to the Color Scheme dialog box.

9. In the Apply To box, select the **All Slides** option, if necessary.

10. Click on **OK** to apply your new black/white/grays color scheme to all four of COLOR.PPT's slides. If a dialog box appears informing you that PowerPoint cannot find the file HPDSKJET.DRV, double-click on **Close** to remove this dialog box.

11. Observe slides 4, 3, 2, and 1. Note that the global-projection clip-art object on slide 1 contains the color green, even though you did not include this color in your new scheme. Clip-art color is not affected by the presentation's color scheme. At the end of this chapter, you'll learn how to recolor clip art.

PRACTICE YOUR SKILLS

As you'll remember, COLOR.PPT was originally done up tastefully in a gray background and muted foreground colors. The black/white/grays color scheme you created in the previous activity was even more sedate. In this activity, you'll create a pair of dramatic color schemes. This way, you'll have observed the full spectrum of color schemes, from the sedate to the tasteful to the dramatic.

1. Change to Slide Sorter view. Working in this view lets you see how your new color scheme affects all your presentation's slides. Verify that slide 1 is selected (outlined in black); you cannot change the color scheme in Slide Sorter view unless a slide is selected.

2. Create a new, dramatic color scheme and apply it to all the presentation's slides. Use striking, contrasting colors. Imagine that you needed to wake up a roomful of executives who are badly in need of a coffee infusion. (Hint: You can scroll through the Background, Text, and Remaining Colors list boxes to view more colors.)

3. Create another dramatic color scheme and apply it to all the slides. Use **Edit, Undo** to compare your two dramatic schemes—which works better?

4. Select the better of the two schemes, and then use **File, Save As** to save the file as **mycolors**.

5. Close the file. Observe that MYPRES1.PPT appears; it was there all the time, hidden away behind COLORS.PPT.

CHANGING INDIVIDUAL COLORS OF A COLOR SCHEME

In the previous section, you learned how to change an entire color scheme (all eight colors). PowerPoint also allows you to change individual color-scheme colors. This handy feature lets you fine-tune a color scheme quickly and easily, without having to recreate the entire scheme. Here's the general procedure for changing individual color-scheme colors:

- Change to Slide view or Slide Sorter view.

- If you are changing the color scheme of a single slide, select this slide.

- Choose Slide, Color Scheme to open the Color Scheme dialog box.

- Double-click on the color that you want to change (Background, Lines & Text, Shadows, and so on) to open the Change A Color dialog box. Use either of the following methods to select your new color:

  - Select the desired color in the color grid.

  - Or, select a color in the color grid that is close to your desired color. Click on the *More Colors button*, and modify this color by manually adjusting the *Hue, Saturation,* and *Luminescence* scales. Click on OK to return to the Change A Color dialog box.

- In the Change A Color dialog box, click on OK to return to the Color Scheme dialog box.

- If necessary, repeat the above steps to change additional color-scheme colors.

- In the Color Scheme dialog box, click on OK.

Let's use this procedure to change the background color of our eagle slide from white to black:

1. In Slide view, display slide 5, the eagle slide.

2. Choose **Slide, Color Scheme** to open the Color Scheme dialog box.

3. Double-click on the current background color (**WT**) to select this color and open the Change A Color dialog box.

4. Select the color **BK** (black) at the bottom of the dialog box.

5. Click on **OK** to return to the Color Scheme dialog box.

6. In the Apply To box, select the **This Slide** option.

7. Click on **OK** to apply your modified color scheme to slide 5—not to the rest of the slides. Observe the results, as shown in Figure 5.14. Your eagle looks even fiercer against a black background.

Figure 5.14   **Changing the eagle-slide background to black**

RECOLORING CLIP ART

As you know, clip-art images are precolored. You do not, however, have to accept these colors. PowerPoint allows you to change a clip-art object's colors, just as it allows you to change a presentation's color scheme. Here's the general procedure for recoloring a clip-art object:

● In Slide view, select the desired clip-art object.

● Choose *Object, Recolor Picture* to open the Recolor Picture dialog box.

- To change the colors of an object's lines, select the *Colors option* in the Change box. To change the colors of the object's fills, select the *Fills option*.

- To change a color, locate it in the From column (you may need to scroll), and then select your new color from the drop-down list box in the corresponding To column.

- Click on the *Preview button* to view your recolored object.

- Repeat the previous three steps for each line and fill color that you want to change.

- To restore an element to its original color, uncheck the Change box in front of the color.

- When you're finished recoloring, click on OK.

Note: As we explained in "Ungrouping Clip Art," once you ungroup a clip-art object into its component subobjects, you cannot recolor these subobjects. So, if you want to recolor a clip-art subobject, recolor the parent object *before* you ungroup it into its subobjects.

Let's fine-tune our cropped eagle's colors. But first we'll explore a limitation of the Recolor Picture command:

1. Display slide 6, the Personal Computer Components slide.

2. Select the monitor object.

3. Click on **Object** to open the drop-down Object menu. Note that the Recolor Picture command is dimmed, meaning that it is unavailable. As you'll recall, the monitor is a subobject of the original personal-computer clip-art object that you ungrouped earlier in this chapter. As mentioned, you cannot recolor an ungrouped subobject; hence the dimmed Recolor Picture command. To change the monitor-screen color, you would have had to make your alterations to the parent clip-art object *before* you ungrouped it into subobjects (monitor, monitor stand, central processing unit, and keyboard).

4. Click on **Object** to close the drop-down Object menu.

5. Repeat steps 2 through 4 for the central-processing unit object and the keyboard object. Note that the Recolor Picture command is dimmed for both of these, since they—like the monitor—are ungrouped subobjects.

Now let's work on our eagle:

1. Display slide 5 and select the eagle object.

2. Click on **Object** to open the drop-down Object menu. Note that the Recolor Picture command is available. Why? Because, although you *cropped* the eagle clip-art object, you did not *ungroup* it.

3. Click on **Recolor Picture** to open the Recolor Picture dialog box. Observe that the entire eagle is displayed in the Preview box. Although you cropped the eagle clip-art object quite severely, PowerPoint still "remembers" the original (uncropped) object. You'll learn how to use this fact to your advantage in the next section, "Uncropping Clip Art."

4. In the Change box, select the **Fills** option. Selecting this option allows you to change the eagle's fill colors—which is what we want to do in this activity—rather than to change the eagle's line colors.

5. Observe the third fill color from the top of the From column, an egg-shell off-white. This is the color of the eagle's head and talons.

6. In the corresponding To column (the third from the top), click on the **down arrow** to display the palette of available colors.

7. Click on **RD8** to change the eagle's off-white color to a red. Note that an *X* appears in the corresponding Change box, indicating that you have changed this color.

8. Click on the **Preview button** to see how your eagle will appear with this color change. Whoa...looks a bit lurid! Let's verify this by viewing the actual slide.

9. Click on **OK** to close the Recolor Picture dialog box. Observe the slide. Our suspicions were correct. RD8 is definitely the wrong color for the head and talons.

10. Select the eagle object, if necessary. Choose **Object, Recolor** to reopen the Recolor Picture dialog box.

11. Select the **Fills** option.

12. Uncheck (remove the *X* from) the Change box of the color you changed in step 7 (the third color from the top).

13. Click on the **Preview button**. By removing the X from the Change box, you've returned the head and talons to their original off-white color.

Let's finish up by changing the color of the eagle's eye:

1. Observe the first color in the list, pure white. This is the color of the eagle's eye.

2. Click on the **down arrow** of the corresponding To box to display the palette of available colors. This time we'll select a color from the Other list.

3. Click on **Other** to open the Other Color dialog box.

4. Select the color **GN8** (bright green) by clicking on the color box at the intersection of the GN column and row 8.

5. Click on **OK** to close the Other Color dialog box.

6. Click on the **Preview button** to see how your eagle will look with its new eye color. Unfortunately, the Preview feature isn't very helpful this time, because the eagle's eye is too small. We'll just have to look at the actual slide.

7. Click on **OK** to apply your color change. Observe the slide. Deselect the eagle to get the full effect. Your bright green eagle eye may be a bit unorthodox, but it definitely works!

8. Save the file.

UNCROPPING CLIP ART

When you crop a clip-art object, PowerPoint hides—but does not delete—the cropped part of the object. That's why the entire eagle appeared in the Recolor Picture dialog box in the last activity, even though you'd severely cropped the eagle earlier in this chapter. Because the entire object remains intact after you crop it, PowerPoint allows you to *uncrop* it; that is, to restore part or all of what you previously cropped. To do so, you follow the same procedure as when cropping a clip-art object. Let's try this out:

1. Select your cropped eagle object.

2. Choose **Object, Crop Picture**.

3. Use the **Cropping tool** to drag the upper-right selection handle as far right as possible. Take care not to change the height of the eagle object.

4. Deselect the eagle object and observe the results. You've uncropped part of the eagle wing, making your slide even more effective.

5. Click on the **Slide Show button** (the third button from the right on the Toolbar, it shows a miniature slide-show screen) to view your eagle slide in its full glory, exactly as it would appear in a slide show. Your screen should match that shown in Figure 5.15.

6. Press **Esc** to return to Slide view.

Figure 5.15   **The uncropped eagle object in slide-show view**

EXITING POWERPOINT WITH AN OPEN, UNSAVED FILE

We've taught you to always save and close a presentation file when you're finished working on it. You may, however, occasionally forget to do this. To prevent accidental data loss if this should happen, PowerPoint will not allow you to exit without first giving you the opportunity to save your open, unsaved files.

MYPRES1.PPT is open and unsaved (you did not save it after uncropping the eagle). Let's issue a File, Exit command and see what happens:

1. Choose **File, Exit** to exit PowerPoint. A dialog box asks whether you want to save the changes you made to MYPRES1.PPT, as shown in Figure 5.16. As mentioned, PowerPoint will not let you exit without first giving you the opportunity to save your open, unsaved files.

Figure 5.16   **Exiting PowerPoint with an open, unsaved file**

2. Click on **Yes** to save your latest version of MYPRES1.PPT and to exit from PowerPoint.

Note: Please don't take this as encouragement to leave your presentation files unsaved and/or unclosed. We strongly recommend that you *always* save and close a file when you're done working on it. However, if you should forget, we want you to know that PowerPoint will catch your oversight when you attempt to exit.

SUMMARY

In this chapter, you completed our two-part series on working with images by exploring clip art and color. You now have a solid repertoire of image creation and enhancement techniques. You learned how to add clip art to a slide, how to resize clip art, how to crop clip art, how to ungroup clip art, and how to scale clip art. You also learned how to change an entire color scheme, how to change individual color-scheme colors, how to recolor clip art, and how to uncrop clip art.

Here's a quick reference for the techniques you learned in this chapter:

Desired Result	How to Do It
Add clip art to a slide	Display the slide in Slide view; choose **File, Open Clip Art**; if necessary, change the current drive and directory; double-click on the desired clip-art file; double-click on the desired slide number; select the clip-art object; choose **Edit, Copy**; close the clip-art file; if necessary, display the target slide (in Slide view); choose **Edit, Paste**
Resize a clip-art object	Select the object; to resize proportionally, press and hold the **Shift key**; to keep the object centered as you resize it, press and hold the **Ctrl key**; to reduce the object, drag a selection handle diagonally toward the object's center; to enlarge the object, drag a handle diagonally away from the center; release the mouse button; if necessary, release the Ctrl key; if necessary, release the Shift key

Desired Result	How to Do It
Crop a clip-art object	Select the object; choose **Object, Crop Picture**; use the **Cropping tool** to drag a selection handle to crop the image as desired; if necessary, repeat the previous step; click on any blank area of the slide to deselect the object and the Cropping tool
Ungroup a clip-art object	Select the object; choose **Arrange, Ungroup**; if a dialog box asks whether you want to convert the imported object to PowerPoint objects, click on **Yes**
Scale a clip-art object	Select the object; choose **Object, Scale**; type your desired scale percentage; repeat the previous step, if necessary; click on **OK**
Change an entire color scheme	Change to Slide view or Slide Sorter view; if you are changing the color scheme of a single slide, select this slide; choose **Slide, Color Scheme**; click on the **Choose A Scheme button**; select a Background color; select a Text (line and text) color; select a set of Remaining Colors (shadow, title-text, fill, and accent colors); click on **OK** to return to the Color Scheme dialog box; select the **This Slide** option or the **All Slides** option; click on **OK**
Change individual color-scheme colors	Change to Slide view or Slide Sorter view; if you are changing the color scheme of a single slide, select this slide; choose **Slide, Color Scheme**; double-click on the color that you want to change; select the desired color in the color grid; or, click on the **More Colors button**, create your new color manually, and then click on **OK** to return to the Change A Color dialog box; click on **OK** to return to the Color Scheme dialog box; if necessary, repeat the above steps to change additional colors; in the Color Scheme dialog box, click on **OK**

Desired Result	**How to Do It**
Recolor a clip-art object	In Slide view, select the object; choose **Object, Recolor Picture**; select the **Colors** option (to change the line colors) or the **Fills** option (to change the fill colors); to change a color, locate it in the From column and select your new color in the corresponding To column; click on the **Preview button** to view your recolored object; repeat the previous three steps for each line and fill color that you want to change; to restore a color back to its original, uncheck the corresponding Change box; click on **OK**

In the next chapter, you'll explore two closely related topics, slide masters and templates. You'll learn how to change the Slide Master's font size, bullet character, and bullet indent; how to enhance the Slide Master; how to apply a template to a presentation; and how to create the default template, DEFAULT.PPT.

IF YOU'RE STOPPING HERE

If you need to break off here, feel free to do so. If you want to proceed directly to the next chapter, please do so now.

CHAPTER 6:
SLIDE MASTERS AND TEMPLATES

Working with Slide
Masters

Working with
Templates

In the first five chapters of this book, you learned how to create, edit, and enhance *individual* slides within a presentation. In this chapter, you'll learn how to edit and enhance *all* the presentation's slides at once. We'll explore two closely related features, slide masters and templates, and show you how to use these features to unify the overall appearance of your presentation. At the end of the chapter, you'll complete the nine-slide presentation that you previewed in Chapter 2.

When you're done working through this chapter, you will know

- How to change the Slide Master's font size, bullet character, and bullet indent
- How to enhance the Slide Master
- How to apply a template to a presentation
- How to create the default template, DEFAULT.PPT

WORKING WITH SLIDE MASTERS

As you learned in Chapter 2, the format of a presentation's title text and body text is determined by the format settings in the presentation's *Slide Master*. For example, when you enter title text on a slide, it is automatically formatted as 36-point bold centered because the title text in the Slide Master is formatted this way.

In addition to the format of the title text and body text, the Slide Master sets the presentation's color scheme; the background graphics (such as borders, lines, and logos); and automatic page numbering and date and time stamping. In doing this, the Slide Master ensures that all your presentation's slides will have a similar appearance; for example, the same color scheme, background logo, and title-text/body-text fonts. This helps to unify the overall presentation and increase its clarity and effectiveness.

 ## CHANGING THE SLIDE MASTER

The Slide Master's Title object and Body object are called the *Master Title object* and the *Master Body object*. The Master Title object determines the font, size, color, style, and alignment of the text in all your presentation's Title objects. The Master Body object determines the font, size, color, style, and alignment of the text; the bullet size and bullet character; and the first-line and trailing-line indents for each of the five levels of text in all your presentation's Body objects.

Over the next few sections, you'll learn how to change the font size of your Master Title and Master Body text and how to change the bullet character and indents of your Master Body bulleted text. In Chapter 10, you'll learn how to change other Slide Master elements, including border, lines, logos, and date/time/page-number stamps.

Changing the Font Size

Here's the general procedure for changing the font size of your Master Title and Master Body text:

- Choose *View, Slide Master* to display the Slide Master.

- To resize all the title or body text, select the Master Title object or Master Body object. To resize part of the body text (for example, levels 4 and 5 only), select this text.

- Use either of the following methods to change the font size of the selected text:

  - Click on the Font Size Plus (+) button or Font Size Minus (–) button to increase or decrease the font size.

  - Or, choose Text, Size and select your desired font size. (As explained below, you should not use this method to resize an entire Master Body object, unless you want all five levels of your body text to be the same size.)

The Master Body object contains five levels of text. In your current PowerPoint setup, these five levels are divided into three progressively smaller font sizes: Level-1 text is 24 points; level-2 and level-3 text are both 18 points; and level-4 and level-5 text are both 14 points.

When you select the entire Master Body object and use the Font Size buttons to resize its text, PowerPoint maintains this size differential. For example, if you resize the entire Master Body object text by clicking once on the Font Size Plus (+) button, the level-1 text is increased to 28 points, the level-2 and level-3 text to 20 points, and the level-4 and level-5 text to 16 points.

If, however, you select the entire Master Body object and use the Text, Size command to resize its text, PowerPoint sets all five levels of text to the same size. For example, if you resize the entire Master Body text by selecting 28 points from the Text, Size submenu, all five text levels are set to 28 points.

The moral is this: Don't use the Text, Size command to resize an entire Master Body object, unless you want all five levels of your presentation's body text to be the same size. (This is normally *not* desirable.)

If you are not running PowerPoint, please start it now. Close all open presentations except for the start-up presentation. Let's open MYPRES1.PPT and use both methods for changing the size of its Master Title and Master Body text:

1. Open **MYPRES1.PPT** from your POWERWRK directory.

2. Display slide 3, the Special Services slide. Observe its title text and body text to get a sense of their font sizes.

3. Choose **View, Slide Master** to display the Slide Master, shown in Figure 6.1. Observe the Master Title object, which contains the title text, and the Master Body object, which contains the five levels of body text.

Figure 6.1   **MYPRES1.PPT's Slide Master**

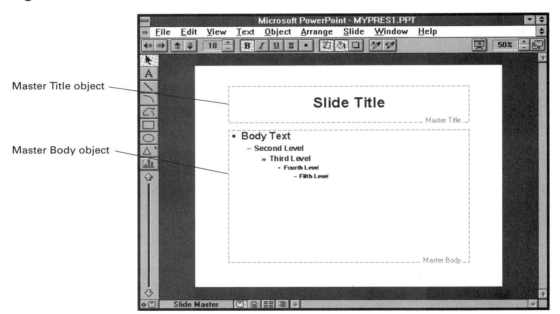

4. Select the **Master Title object**. Observe the Font Size list box on the Toolbar. The Master Title text size is set to 36 points.

5. Click repeatedly on the **Font Size Plus (+) button** to increase the font size to 80 points.

6. Change to Slide view. Observe slide 3's title. Your modified, 80-point font is so large that it forced the title text to break into two lines.

7. Display slide 2 and observe its 80-point title. As mentioned, when you change the Slide Master, you change all the slides in your presentation.

Let's undo our font-size change:

1. Choose **View, Slide Master** to redisplay the Slide Master.

2. Attempt to choose **Edit, Undo**. Can't? Note that the Undo command is dimmed. As mentioned in Chapter 4, in order to undo your last action, you must choose Edit, Undo *immediately* after performing the action. In this case, you performed three actions *after* increasing the font size: You changed to Slide view, you displayed slide 2, and then you displayed the Slide Master. Remember this: If you want to undo your last action, choose Edit, Undo before performing any subsequent actions, no matter how trivial they may seem.

3. Use the procedure outlined in steps 4 and 5 of the previous activity to change the Master Title text's size back to 36 points.

Now let's practice resizing the Master Body text:

1. Select the **Master Body object**.

2. As mentioned, the five levels of your Master Body text are divided into three progressively smaller font sizes: 24 points for level-1 text, 18 points for levels 2 and 3, and 14 points for levels 4 and 5. Verify this by placing the insertion point in each of the five levels and observing the Font Size list box.

3. Deselect the **Master Body object** to remove the insertion point, and then reselect the **Master Body object** to select the entire object. Observe the Font Size list box. It displays ≥ 14, which means that the Master Body object contains two or more font sizes, all greater than or equal to 14 points.

4. Click on the **Font Size Plus (+) button** to increase the Master Body's font sizes to ≥ 16 points (16 points or larger.) Verify this by using the procedure outlined in step 2.

5. Deselect the **Master Body object** to remove the insertion point, and then reselect the **Master Body object**.

6. Click on the **Font Size Minus (–) button** to return the font sizes to their original ≥ 14 points.

Now let's use the Text, Size command to resize the Master Body text:

1. Choose **Text, Size, 18** to change all five levels of the Master Body text to 18 points. Verify this visually, without using the insertion-point technique.

2. Choose **Edit, Undo** to return the font sizes to their original ≥ 14 points. This time Edit, Undo worked, because you used it immediately after performing the action you wanted to undo.

PRACTICE YOUR SKILLS

1. Change the font size of the Master Body level-2 text to 20 points. (Hint: Select the level-2 text and then use the **Text, Size, Other** command.)

2. Save the file.

Changing the Bullet Character

By default, your Master Body object uses three different characters for its bullets: the level-1 and level-4 bullets use the • character; the level-2 and level-5 bullets use the – character; and the level-3 bullet uses the » character. PowerPoint allows you to change the bullet character for each of these five text levels. Here's the general procedure for doing this:

• Display the Slide Master.

• Select the Master Body object.

• Place the insertion point in the text level whose bullet character you want to change.

• Choose *Text, Bullet* to open the Bullet dialog box.

• Proceed as follows:

• To change the font from which you select the bullet character, select a new font in the Bullets From drop-down list box.

• To select the bullet character, click on any of the characters in the character grid.

- To increase or decrease the size of the bullet character, increase or decrease the percentage value in the Size box.

- To change the color of the bullet character, check the *Special Color* option, and then choose your desired new color from the drop-down list box.

- Click on OK.

Let's change the level-1 bullet character in our Master Body object:

1. Place the insertion point anywhere within the Master Body level-1 text (*Body Text*).

2. Choose **Text, Bullet** to open the Bullet dialog box.

3. Observe the character that is selected in the character grid (•). This is your current level-1 bullet character.

4. Click on the Bullets From **down arrow** to display the drop-down list of available fonts.

5. Click on **Monotype Sorts** to select this font. The character grid fills with a new set of characters.

6. Click on the shadowed square character to select it, as shown in Figure 6.2.

7. Still pointing to the shadowed square, press and hold the **left mouse button** to display a magnified view of the character. Release the left mouse button to return to normal view. You can use this technique to get a better look at any of the characters in the grid.

8. Click on **OK** to apply your new level-1 bullet character to the Master Body object. Observe the results. Very nice, except for one thing: The bullet's a bit too large. Let's reduce it.

9. If necessary, place the insertion point within the level-1 text.

10. Choose **Text, Bullet** to reopen the Bullet dialog box.

11. Click twice on the Size box **down arrow** to decrease the bullet character's font size to 90 percent of the level-1 text's font size.

12. Click on **OK** to apply your change to the Master Body object. Well done! The bullet looks much better now.

Figure 6.2   **Selecting a new level-1 bullet character**

The new level-1
bullet character

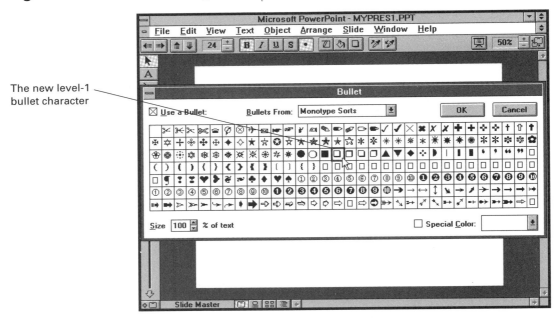

PRACTICE YOUR SKILLS

1. Change the Master Body level-2 bullet character to the Monotype Sorts diamond-shaped character shown in Figure 6.3.
   Specify a size of 100 percent.

2. Change to Slide view. Display slide 3 and observe your two
   new bullets, as shown in Figure 6.4. Looks good, yes?

3. Save the file.

Changing the Bullet Indent

In Chapter 3, you learned how to change your body-text indents
by dragging the indent triangles on the text ruler. You can use this
same technique to adjust the amount of space between a bullet
and its accompanying text. Here's the general procedure:

• In the Slide Master, select the Master Body object.

• Choose *Text, Show Ruler* (or press *Ctrl+r*) to display the ruler.

Figure 6.3   **Selecting a new level-2 bullet character**

The new level-2
bullet character

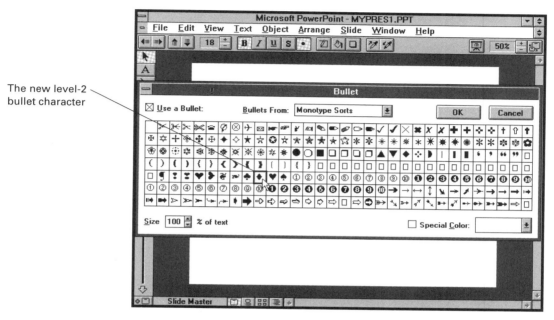

Figure 6.4   **Changing the level-1 and level-2 bullet characters**

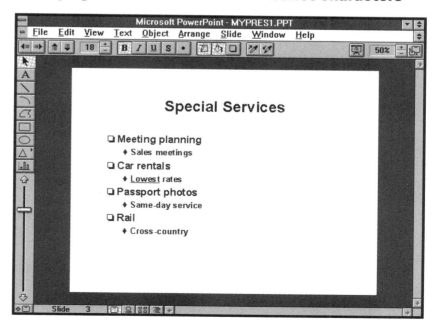

- Locate the pair of indent triangles for the level whose bullet indent you want to change. Drag the trailing-line indent triangle (the lower triangle) to your desired new position on the ruler.

- Click on a blank area of the slide to remove the ruler.

Let's use this simple procedure to fine-tune our level-1 and level-2 bullet indents:

1. Display the Slide Master, and select the **Master Body object**.

2. Press **Ctrl+r** (the keyboard shortcut for choosing Text, Show Ruler) to display the ruler.

3. Observe the ruler. It displays the first-line and trailing-line indent triangles for all five levels of Master Body text.

4. Drag the level-1 **trailing-line indent triangle** (the leftmost lower indent triangle) until its vertical edge is at .4375 inches (halfway between the third and fourth tick marks from the left end of the ruler).

5. Drag the level-2 **trailing-line indent triangle** until its vertical edge is at the .875-inch tick mark (the last tick mark before the 1-inch mark).

6. Click on a blank area of the Slide Master to deselect the Master Body object and remove the ruler.

7. Change to Slide view and observe your fine-tuned bullet indents on slide 3, shown in Figure 6.5. A subtle, but effective change, as you can see by comparing Figures 6.4 and 6.5.

8. Save the file.

ENHANCING THE SLIDE MASTER

By enhancing the appearance of your presentation's Slide Master, you enhance the appearance of the entire presentation. You can enhance many different aspects of a Slide Master, including its color scheme; its Master Title and Master Body fonts, sizes, styles, and colors; the locations, sizes, and borders of its Master Title and Master Body object boxes; and its background graphics (clip art).

Figure 6.5   **Changing the level-1 and level-2 bullet indents**

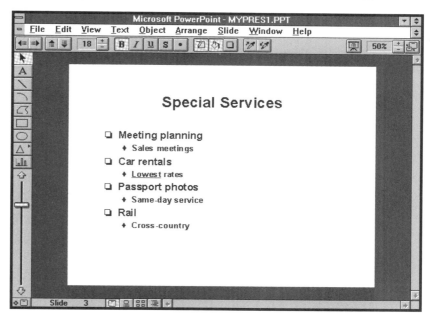

Let's create a new presentation and enhance its Slide Master. We'll begin by changing the background color. (**Note:** This group of activities is unusually long and involved. Figure on spending an uninterrupted hour working through it.)

1. Choose **File, New**.

2. In the New dialog box, select the **Use Default Format** option and click on **OK**. Slide 1 of a new, blank presentation appears.

3. Display the Slide Master of your new presentation.

4. Choose **Slide, Color Scheme** to open the Color Scheme dialog box.

5. Double-click on the current Background color (white) to open the Change A Color dialog box.

6. Click on **BK** (at the bottom of the dialog box) to change the background color to black, and then click on **OK** to return to the Color Scheme dialog box.

7. Click on **OK** to apply your black background to the Slide Master.

8. Use **File, Save** to name your new presentation file **mymaster**.

Now we'll change the fill colors of the Master Title and Master Body objects:

1. Select both the **Master Title object** and the **Master Body object**. You'll have to work by feel, since the black background makes the object boxes invisible.

2. Choose **Object, Fill, GY6** to change both objects' fill colors to light gray.

Let's add our eagle clip-art object to the Slide Master. This object is in MYPRES1.PPT, which is hidden behind MYMASTER.PPT:

1. Choose **Window, 1 MYPRES1.PPT** to make MYPRES1.PPT the active presentation.

2. Display slide 5, the eagle slide.

3. Select the eagle object, and then choose **Edit, Copy** to copy it to the Clipboard.

4. Choose **Window, 2 MYMASTER.PPT** to make this the active presentation.

5. Choose **Edit, Paste** to paste the eagle object from the Clipboard onto the Slide Master.

6. Drag the lower-right selection handle to proportionally reduce the eagle to the size shown in Figure 6.6.

Now let's move and resize the Master Title and Master Body object boxes to dovetail with the eagle:

1. Press **Ctrl+y** to display the guides.

2. Resize the Master Title and Master Body object boxes to align their edges as shown below. Positive (+) numbers indicate positions above the slide center (for the horizontal guide) or to the right of the slide center (for the vertical guide). Negative (–) numbers indicate positions below or to the left of the center. For help, refer to Figure 6.7.

Figure 6.6   **MYMASTER.PPT, after resizing the eagle**

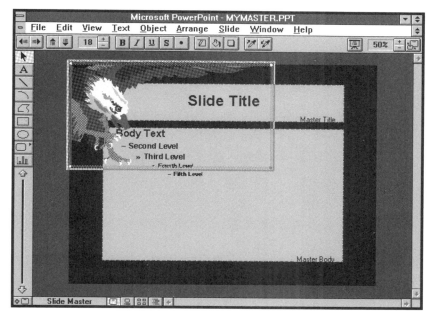

	Master Title	Master Body
Top Edge	+2.50	0.00
Bottom Edge	+1.25	–2.75
Left Edge	–2.50	–4.25
Right Edge	+4.25	+4.25

3. Press **Ctrl+y** to remove the guides. Your Slide Master should match that shown in Figure 6.7. If necessary, proportionally resize the eagle object to fine-tune its fit with the Master Title and Master Body objects.

Now let's change the format of the Master Body object text:

1. Select the **Master Body object**.

2. Choose **Text, Size, 18** to change the size of all five levels of the Master Body object text to 18 points.

Figure 6.7    **MYMASTER.PPT, after resizing the object boxes**

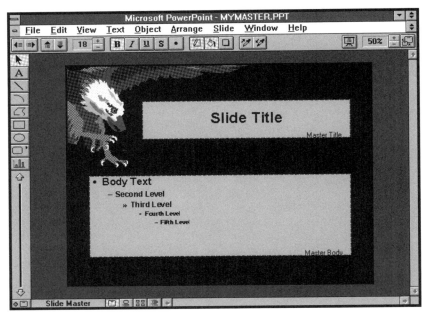

3. Choose **Text, Alignment, Center** to center the Master Body object text.

4. Select all the Master Body object's level-2 through level-5 text. Do not select the level-1 text (*Body Text*).

5. Press **Del** to delete the level-2 through level-5 text. All that should remain is *Body Text* followed by the level-2 bullet.

6. Press **Backspace** to delete the level-2 bullet. All that should remain now is *Body Text*.

7. Click on the **Add Bullet button** on the Toolbar to remove the Body Text bullet.

8. Press **Ctrl+r** to display the text ruler.

9. Drag the **trailing-line indent triangle** (the lower triangle) as far to the left as possible. The two indent triangles should now both be set to 0.

10. Click on a blank area of the Slide Master to deselect the Master Body object and remove the ruler.

Now let's enter a title for slide 1 of MYMASTER.PPT and then copy some body text from MYPRES1.PPT:

1. Change to Slide view. Observe your modified slide 1. As expected, its appearance matches that of the Slide Master.

2. Enter the title **Competitors Beware!**

3. Choose **Window, 1 - MYPRES1.PPT** to activate this presentation.

4. Display slide 10, the slide containing the two text objects you created in Chapter 4.

5. Drag over all the text in the lower text object to select it. Do not select the entire object; we want to copy the text, not the text-object box.

6. Choose **Edit, Copy** to copy the selected text to the Clipboard.

7. Choose **Window, 2 - MYMASTER.PPT** to activate this presentation.

8. Select the **Body object**.

9. Choose **Edit, Paste** to paste the contents of the Clipboard to the Body object. Observe the results.

Your pasted text extends all the way to the top and side edges of the Body-object box, resulting in a somewhat cramped and unbalanced appearance. Let's fix things up by increasing the *box margins*, the spaces between the box edges and the text:

1. Display the Slide Master, and select the **Master Body object**.

2. Choose **Text, Fit Text** to open the Fit Text dialog box. You use this command to change an object box's margins.

3. In the Box Margins box, increase both the left and right margins and the top and bottom margins to .30 inches.

4. Click on **OK** to return to the Slide Master.

5. Change to Slide view. Observe your modified body-text layout, which should match that shown in Figure 6.8. Note how the increased box margins add a sense of balance to the object.

We're almost home! Just one more small refinement. Let's add a border to the Title and Body objects:

1. Display the Slide Master, and select both the **Master Title object** and the **Master Body object**.

Figure 6.8   **MYMASTER.PPT, after adding text and increasing box margins**

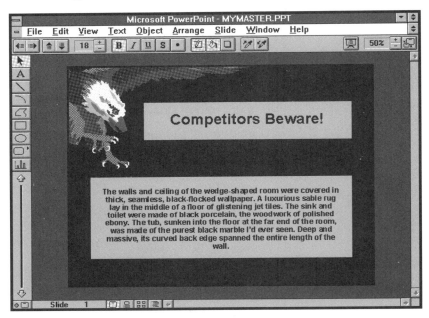

2. Choose **Object, Line, Other Color** to open the Other Color dialog box.

3. In the color grid, click on the color **YG4** (the intersection of the YG column and row 4) to select it.

4. Click on **OK** to apply a yellow-green (YG4) border to your Master Body and Master Body objects.

5. Choose **Object, Line Style** to display the Line Style submenu. Select the third line from the top.

6. Deselect the Master Title object and Master Body object. Note how much stronger they look with their new borders. Note also how nicely the border's green color harmonizes with the eagle's bright green eye.

7. Change to Slide view. Click on the **Slide Show button** to view slide 1 as it would appear in a slide show. Your screen should match that shown in Figure 6.9.

8. Press **Esc** to return to Slide view.

Figure 6.9   **MYMASTER.PPT, completed**

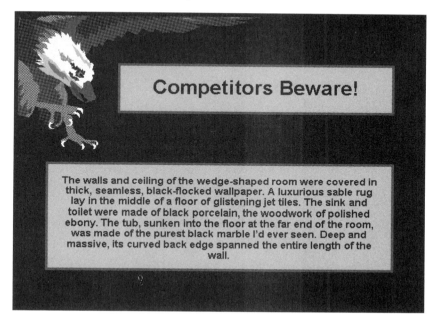

9. Click on the **New Slide button** to create a new slide (slide 2). Observe that its appearance matches that of the Slide Master, as will the appearance of every slide you add to this presentation.

10. Save the file and then close it.

Congratulations on completing this gargantuan, 53-step group of activities! Pat yourself on the back several times, take a deep breath, shake the kinks out of your mousing hand, and take a nice long break before diving into the next section.

WORKING WITH TEMPLATES

As you learned in the previous activity, creating a sophisticated Slide Master can be a long and arduous task. To simplify this task, PowerPoint provides you with a library of 160 *templates*.

When you apply a template to a presentation, the presentation's Slide Master is replaced with the template's Slide Master. Thus, the presentation takes on all the characteristics of the template's

Slide Master: the format of the title text and body text, the color scheme, the background graphics (such as borders, lines, and logos), and automatic page numbering and date and time stamping.

In effect, when you apply a template to a presentation, you create a new, sophisticated Slide Master for the presentation. Only you do it in one step instead of 53.

 APPLYING A TEMPLATE TO A PRESENTATION

Here's the general procedure to apply a template to a presentation:

- Open the presentation to which you want to apply the template. If the presentation does not already exist, open a new presentation.

- Choose *File, Apply Template* to open the Apply Template dialog box.

- If necessary, change the current drive and directory to the drive and directory in which the template is stored.

- In the File Name list box, select your desired template.

- Click on OK.

Note: You can use any PowerPoint presentation as a template. For example, you could use the File, Apply Template command to apply MYMASTER.PPT—the presentation that you created in the previous activity—to another presentation. The target presentation would then have the same black-background, eagle-clip-art Slide Master as MYMASTER.PPT.

Let's apply a template to MYPRES1.PPT, the active presentation:

1. Use the Slide Changer to display slide 1 of MYPRES1.PPT.

2. Choose **File, Apply Template** to open the Apply Template dialog box.

3. Observe the Directories list box. You need to make TEMPLATE the current directory to get at PowerPoint's template files. If TEMPLATE is already the current directory—that is, if the miniature folder icon to the left of the word *template* is darkened—skip directly to step 6.

4. If you see *template* in your Directories list box, double-click on it to make it current, and then skip directly to step 6.

5. If you do not see *template* in your Directories list box, double-click on **c:**. Then, locate and double-click on **powerpnt**, your PowerPoint directory. Finally, double-click on **template** to make it the current directory.

6. Observe the four directories listed under TEMPLATE: 35MSLIDE, B&WOVRHD, CLROVRHD, and VIDSCREN. It is in these directories that PowerPoint's vast library of templates is stored. The 160 templates in these four directories are designed, respectively, for 35mm slide output, black-and-white overhead output, color overhead output, and on-screen slide shows. Since we're preparing a slide show in this activity, we'll concern ourselves with the VIDSCREN directory.

7. Double-click on **vidscren** to make it the current directory.

8. In the File Name list box, select (click once on) the template file **bevelv.ppt**. Observe the preview of this template, which appears on the right side of the dialog box.

9. Click on **OK** to apply the BEVELV.PPT template to MYPRES1-.PPT, as shown in Figure 6.10. Take a look at slides 1 through 4. Note the shadowed title text and the classy, beveled slide borders. Note also that applying this template to your presentation did not change any of its slide text or layout, but instead added background graphics, color, and text enhancements.

10. Display the Slide Master. When you applied the BEVELV.PPT template to your MYPRES1.PPT presentation, you replaced MYPRES1.PPT's Slide Master with BEVELV.PPT's Slide Master, which is what you see right now on your screen.

11. Change to Slide view.

PRACTICE YOUR SKILLS

1. Use the **File, Apply Template** command to apply a new template of your choice to MYPRES1.PPT. Observe slides 1 through 4. Repeat this step for as many different templates as you wish to apply. Note how powerful the File, Apply Template command is; with a few mouse clicks, you can create an entirely different, professional-looking visual world for your presentation!

2. Save the file and then close it.

Figure 6.10   **Applying the template file BEVELV.PPT**

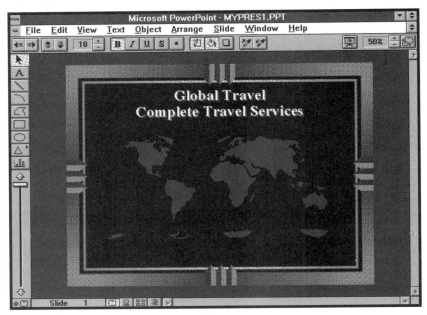

CREATING THE DEFAULT TEMPLATE, DEFAULT.PPT

In Chapter 1, we introduced you to DEFAULT.PPT, the file in which PowerPoint's default settings are stored. DEFAULT.PPT is actually a template; in fact, it is PowerPoint's *default template*. Whenever you open a new presentation file—by choosing File, New and selecting the Use Default Format option in the New dialog box, or by simply starting the PowerPoint program—PowerPoint automatically applies the DEFAULT.PPT template to your new presentation.

As you'll recall, in Chapter 1 we had you copy your DEFAULT.PPT to a file named DEFORIG.PPT and then delete DEFAULT.PPT. Here's why we did this:

- DEFAULT.PPT is a customizable template. You (or, perhaps, a colleague) may have modified your DEFAULT.PPT before you began this book. Your PowerPoint defaults, therefore, may not have matched our defaults, which would have caused you countless problems while working through this book.

- You copied DEFAULT.PPT to DEFORIG.PPT so that you could preserve (and later restore, if you wanted to) your original DEFAULT.PPT settings.

- You then deleted DEFAULT.PPT in order to match our defaults. If PowerPoint finds no DEFAULT.PPT at start-up, it applies its built-in default settings to all your new presentations. Since neither you nor we have a DEFAULT.PPT (we deleted ours also before beginning this book), our PowerPoint defaults match.

Although you do not technically need a DEFAULT.PPT to run Power-Point, it is good to have one, especially when you get around to wanting to customize your default settings. For example, let's say that you preferred working on your new presentations in Outline view, rather than in the current default, Slide view. You could either open each new presentation and then change from Slide to Outline view, or you could customize your DEFAULT.PPT to open new presentations in Outline view.

Let's create a DEFAULT.PPT for your system. In order to match your DEFAULT.PPT settings with ours, you'll exit PowerPoint, and then restart it. Our defaults will match upon start-up, so you can then safely create your DEFAULT.PPT:

1. Choose **File, Exit** to exit PowerPoint.

2. Restart PowerPoint.

3. Choose **File, Save As** to open the Save As dialog box.

4. The current directory, as reported in the directory line (the line beneath the heading *Directories*), should be c:\powerpnt (or d:\powerpnt, and so on), your PowerPoint directory. If you wrote down a different PowerPoint directory name in Chapter 1—remember that piece of paper we told you to save at the beginning of Chapter 1?—the directory line should report this directory instead (for example, c:\winapps\powerpnt).

5. If the current directory is not your PowerPoint directory, change it to your PowerPoint directory now.

6. Type **default.ppt** in the File Name text box.

7. Click on **OK**.

Congratulations! You now have a DEFAULT.PPT template file in your PowerPoint directory (as do we). For now, we'll just let our

DEFAULT.PPT files sit there and be innocuous, well-behaved default templates. In Chapter 10, you'll learn how to modify your DEFAULT.PPT.

PRACTICE YOUR SKILLS

In this activity, you will make some final changes to MYPRES1.PPT and then run a slide show of the presentation:

1. Open **MYPRES1.PPT** from your POWERWRK directory (Chapter 1).

2. Apply the template **BLUEBOXV.PPT** (in the VIDSCREN directory) to MYPRES1.PPT (Chapter 6). Your screen should match that shown in Figure 6.11.

Figure 6.11   **Applying the template file BLUEBOXV.PPT**

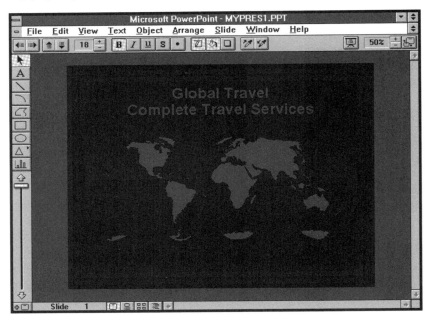

3. Display slides 1 through 4, the Global Travel slides. Note the shaded background (dark blue to light blue), the bright red

title text, and the elegant three-dimensional frame. All in all, a great-looking template!

4. Display slide 5, your eagle slide. Note that it does not look like the other slides. Why? Because you changed its color scheme in Chapter 5, and this change overrides any template that you apply to the presentation.

5. Display slide 6, the Personal Computer Component slide. Very nice.

6. Display slide 7, the enlarged monitor slide. Oops. The monitor is too big for our new slide border. Let's fix this.

7. Use the **Object, Scale** command to scale both the monitor and the text within it down to 80 percent of their original size (Chapter 5). Deselect the two objects. A very nice fit.

8. Display slide 8, the slide you created in Chapter 4 by drawing predefined objects and then using the Object, Change Shape command to change their shapes. Unfortunately, your objects no longer fit within the slide frame. You'll just have to reduce the whole lot of them.

9. Select all the objects. (Hint: Instead of selecting the objects one by one, choose **Edit, Select All** to select them all at once.)

10. Choose **Object, Scale** and type **80** (do not press Enter) to scale all the objects down to 80 percent of their original size. Oops again. Each object is reduced around its own center point, which leaves our frame-overlap problem unresolved.

11. Click on **Cancel** to remove the Scale dialog box without performing the 80 percent reduction. Let's try a different tack.

12. Verify that all the objects are still selected. Choose **Arrange, Group** to *group* all the objects together as a single unit. Note that the numerous individual selection boxes disappear, and that one large selection box appears around the entire group of objects.

13. Scale this large object down to 80 percent of its original size (Chapter 5). Eureka! It fits within the slide frame.

14. Display slide 9, the slide you created in Chapter 4 by drawing free-form objects and then shadowing some of them. Follow the procedure outlined in steps 12 and 13 to group the

objects as a single unit and then scale this unit down to 80 percent of its original size.

15. Display slide 10, your text-object slide. Note that it doesn't really fit in with this presentation. Let's get rid of it.

16. Choose **Slide, Delete Slide** to delete the current slide (slide 10). Slide 9 appears; it is the new current slide.

And there you have it: the nine slides that you previewed at the beginning of Chapter 2. You've come a long way in these last five chapters! Let's end this activity by running a slide show of your entire presentation:

1. Display slide 1 and run a slide show. Advance through all nine slides. Make sure to admire your handiwork—and then return to Slide view (Chapter 2).

2. Save the file, and then close it (Chapter 1).

SUMMARY

In this chapter, you explored two closely related topics, slide masters and templates. You now know how to change the Slide Master's font size, bullet character, and bullet indent; how to enhance the Slide Master; how to apply a template to a presentation; and how to create the default template, DEFAULT.PPT.

Here's a quick reference for the techniques you learned in this chapter:

Desired Result	How to Do It
Display the Slide Master	Choose **View, Slide Master**
Change the Master Title and Master Body font size	In the Slide Master, select the Master Title and/or Master Body text you want to resize; use the **Font Size Plus (+) button** or **Font Size Minus (–) button** to increase or decrease the font size, or choose **Text, Size** and select your desired font size

Desired Result	How to Do It
Change a Master Body bullet character	In the Slide Master, select the **Master Body object**; place the insertion point in the desired text level; choose **Text, Bullet** to open the Bullet dialog box; to change the bullet-character font, select a new font in the Bullets From drop-down list box; to select the bullet character, click on any of the characters in the character grid; to resize the bullet character, increase or decrease the percentage value in the Size box; to change the color of the bullet character, check the **Special Color** option and choose your new color from the drop-down list box; click on **OK**
Change a Master Body bullet indent	In the Slide Master, select the **Master Body object**; choose **Text, Show Ruler** (or press **Ctrl+r**) to display the ruler; drag the desired **trailing-line indent triangle** to your desired new position; click on a blank area of the slide to remove the ruler
Apply a template to a presentation	Open the presentation; choose **File, Apply Template**; if necessary, change the current drive and directory; select your desired template; click on **OK**

In the next chapter, you'll find out how to use the techniques you have learned so far to create and enhance an organization chart. You will learn how to duplicate objects, how to add text to objects, how to add lines to a slide, and how to change the magnification of your view. You will also learn how to align objects, how to change the stacking order of objects, how to work with styles in your organization charts, how to use a Time Saver file to create an organization chart, and how to ungroup and modify a Time Saver organization chart.

IF YOU'RE STOPPING HERE

If you need to break off here, please exit PowerPoint. If you want to proceed directly to the next chapter, please do so now.

CHAPTER 7: WORKING WITH ORGANIZATION CHARTS

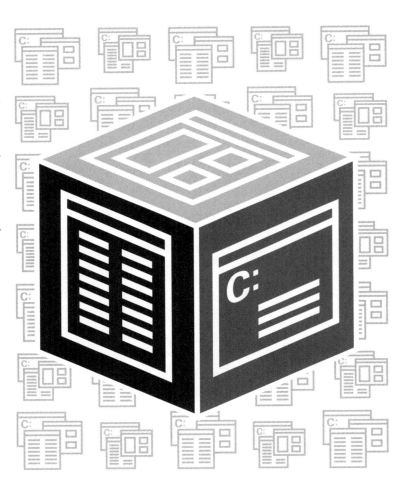

In Chapters 2 through 6, you learned the basics of working with slides. Now you're ready to use those basics to tackle some real-world presentation challenges. Over the next several chapters, you will create a sophisticated presentation that makes use of several new PowerPoint features. In this chapter, you will learn how to use text and objects to create, edit, and enhance an *organization chart*, a diagram depicting the structure of a hierarchical organization, such as a company.

When you're done working through this chapter, you will know

- How to duplicate objects
- How to add text to objects
- How to add lines to a slide
- How to change the magnification of your view
- How to align objects
- How to change the stacking order of objects
- How to work with styles in your organization charts
- How to use a Time Saver file to create an organization chart
- How to ungroup the Time Saver organization chart
- How to modify the Time Saver organization chart

SNEAK PREVIEW, PART 2

Over the course of Chapters 7 though 12, you will create a ten-slide presentation that makes use of many of PowerPoint's advanced slide creation and editing features. We'll begin this chapter by showing you a sneak preview of this presentation. As you observe these ten slides, remember that you'll soon possess the technical mastery to create them yourself!

If you are not running PowerPoint on your computer, please start it now. Close all of the open presentations except the start-up presentation.

Let's run a slide show of PREVIEW2.PPT, a presentation that contains copies of the ten slides you'll create in this and the next five chapters:

1. Open **PREVIEW2.PPT** from your POWERWRK directory.

2. Maximize your presentation window, if necessary.

3. Click on the **Slide Show button** (located on the Toolbar, it displays a miniature screen) to run the slide show with the default settings. You'll learn more about running a slide show in Chapter 12.

4. Choose **File, Close** to close PREVIEW2.PPT.

CREATING AN ORGANIZATION CHART

An *organization chart* is a diagram that depicts the structure of a hierarchical organization. You can also use an organization chart to show structures that don't include people; for example, a diagram might show the relationship of a main office to its branch offices.

Figure 7.1 shows a simplified version of the Global Travel organization chart that you'll create over the course of this chapter. As you can see from this figure, organization charts identify the names and functions of an organization's members, the hierarchical relationships among its upper-level and lower-level positions, and the relationships among its various departments.

Figure 7.1   **Global Travel organization chart, simplified**

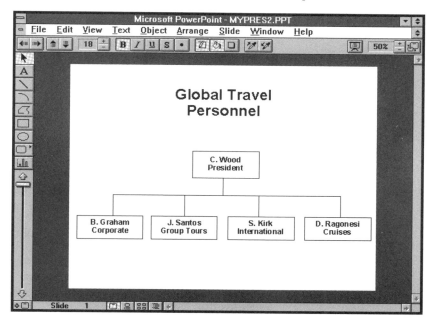

Each box on this chart represents a person and a position in the organization. The lines connecting the boxes indicate the reporting relationship (who reports to whom). For example, the person on the second level reports to the person on the first level.

The Global Travel organization chart that you are going to create in the first part of this chapter has two levels: president and division manager. However, you can create as many levels as you need; later in the chapter, we will create a three-level organization chart.

CREATING AND DUPLICATING BOXES

The first step in creating an organization chart is to create the boxes. We want all the boxes to be the same size and shape; instead of drawing each box separately and estimating, it's faster and easier to draw one box and use the *Edit, Duplicate* command to make as many exact copies as you need.

When you duplicate an object, the copies are stacked on top of the original object. If you duplicate an object several times, you wind up with a stack of objects that looks like a fan.

Here's the general procedure for duplicating objects:

- Select the object you want to duplicate.

- Choose Edit, Duplicate as many times as necessary to create the number of boxes you need for your organization chart.

Let's begin work on the organization chart depicted in Figure 7.1. First, we'll create a new presentation file, MYPRES2.PPT, that will hold the slides you just previewed:

1. If your screen displays the start-up presentation window, then skip this step and go on to step 2. If your screen displays an empty application window (with no presentations open), then choose **File, New** to open a new presentation. (If you have a presentation open that you do not want to close, then choose **File, New**; click on **Use Default Format** to open a presentation based on the DEFAULT.PPT; and click on **OK**.) If necessary, maximize the presentation window.

2. Choose **File, Save As** and type **mypres2** to name the new presentation.

3. Make the POWERWRK directory the current directory and click on **OK** to close the Save As dialog box and save the presentation.

4. Select the **Body object** on the first slide and press **Del**. The Body object is not necessary for an organization chart and would only clutter your screen.

5. Select the **Title object** and type the title **Global Travel**.

6. Press **Enter** to create a new line for the title.

7. Type **Personnel**.

8. Select the **Rectangle tool** and draw a rectangle of the size and at the position of the top box in Figure 7.2.

Figure 7.2 **The positioned organization-chart boxes**

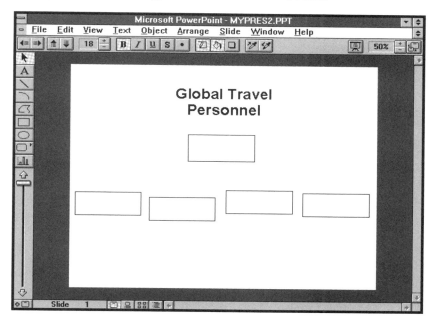

9. Choose **Edit, Duplicate** to place an exact copy of the rectangle on top of the original. The duplicate is selected.

You now have two boxes on your screen; you need three more to complete the organization chart. You could choose Edit, Duplicate three more times to create exact copies of the rectangle, but there is an easier way:

1. Click on **Edit** and observe the Duplicate command. A short-cut key is listed next to the command. Instead of choosing Edit, Duplicate every time you want to duplicate an object, you can press Ctrl+d.

2. Close the Edit menu (click on **Edit** again, or press **Esc**).

3. Press **Ctrl+d** three times to create three more exact copies of the selected box. The duplicates are stacked on top of each other.

4. Select the top box, if necessary, and move it to match the position of the first box in the bottom row of Figure 7.2.

PRACTICE YOUR SKILLS

Let's move the rest of the boxes you just created:

1. Adjust the position of the next duplicate box to match the position of the second bottom-row box shown in Figure 7.2. (Hint: The bottom row of boxes does not need to be horizontally aligned.)

2. Position the remaining two duplicates in the bottom row.

ADDING TEXT TO THE BOXES

Now that we've created and positioned the boxes for the organization chart, it is time to add the names and positions of the people who are part of the organization. In order to add text to an object, you need only select the object and then start typing.

Let's add text to our organization chart:

1. Observe Figure 7.3, which shows the organization chart after text has been added to the boxes.

2. Click on the top box to select it.

3. Type **C. Wood**. When you select an object and type text, the text is automatically placed inside the selected object and attached to it. If you move the object, the text will move with it.

4. Press **Enter** and type **President**. Because the box is still selected, pressing Enter creates a new line that is also attached to the box.

5. Select the leftmost box in the bottom row.

6. Type **B. Graham**, press **Enter**, and type **Corporate** to add the text to the selected box.

7. Select the next box to the right.

8. Type **J. Santos**, press **Enter**, and type **Group Tours**.

Figure 7.3 **The slide with text added to the boxes**

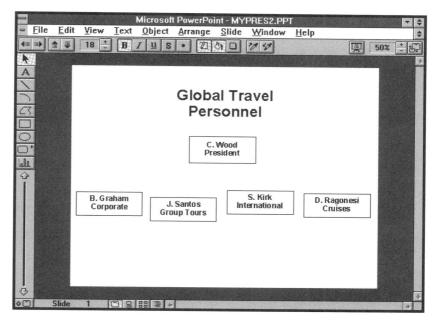

PRACTICE YOUR SKILLS

Let's complete the organization chart text:

1. Using Figure 7.3 as a guide, complete the text in the remaining boxes:

S. Kirk	**D. Ragonesi**
International	**Cruises**

2. Save the file.

ADDING LINES TO THE ORGANIZATION CHART

Next, we need to add lines illustrating the relationships among employees and departments in the company. For example, in the Global Travel organization chart, all four of the division managers (B. Graham, J. Santos, S. Kirk, and D. Ragonesi) report directly to the president. This is indicated in your organization chart by uninterrupted lines connecting the president's box to each of the other four boxes. By *uninterrupted*, we mean that the lines from the president's box do not pass through any other boxes before reaching the boxes of each of the division managers. At the end of this chapter, you will create an organization chart that includes three *levels* (subordinate, manager, and president). In that chart, the line from each subordinate is connected to the president through one of the managers. In Chapter 4, you learned how to draw a straight line on a slide by pressing the Shift key as you drew. Let's use this technique to add lines to the organization chart:

1. Select the **Line tool** (located on the Tool Palette, it displays a slanted line) and move the mouse pointer onto the slide workspace. When you select the Line tool, the mouse pointer becomes a cross hair.

2. Press **Shift** and draw a vertical line that begins inside the top box and matches that shown in Figure 7.4. As you know, pressing Shift while you draw constrains movement so that you draw a straight line.

Figure 7.4   **Adding lines to the organization chart**

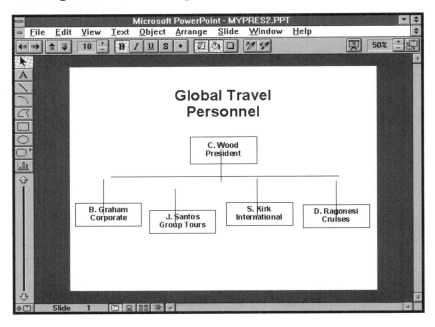

3. Press **Shift** and draw a horizontal line above the bottom row of the boxes to match that shown in Figure 7.4.

PRACTICE YOUR SKILLS

Let's complete the lines for the organization chart:

1. Refer to Figure 7.4 to add the vertical lines that lead from the bottom boxes to the horizontal line. (Hint: Make sure the lines overlap the boxes, but don't worry about making them meet the horizontal line.)

2. Save the file.

CHANGING THE MAGNIFICATION OF YOUR VIEW

Very often when creating drawings such as an organization chart, you will need to zoom in on a particular object or objects to fine-tune your drawing. You can use the *View Scale button* on the Toolbar to change the magnification of the view in which you are working. The View Scale button consists of a *Zoom In button (+)*, which increases the magnification, and a *Zoom Out button (–)*, which decreases the magnification. There are seven view sizes available, ranging from 25 percent to 400 percent.

The *Home View* button, which is located next to the View Scale button, toggles between the last view and the view size that best fits in the window (in our case, 50 percent).

Here's the general procedure for changing the magnification of a view:

• Click on either the Zoom In (+) or the Zoom Out (–) button.

• To return to the view that fits in the window, click on the Home View button.

Let's increase the magnification of Slide view to make it easier to adjust the position of the lines:

1. Observe the View Scale button (located on the Toolbar, it displays plus and minus signs).

2. Select the horizontal line.

3. Click on the **Zoom In button (+)** to increase the view of the selected object to 66 percent. This should make the object large enough to work with easily.

4. Move the horizontal line to meet the vertical line extending from the *C. Wood* box in the organization chart.

5. Select the line extending from the *B. Graham* box.

6. Click on the **Zoom In button (+)** to increase the view size to 100 percent.

7. Move the vertical line extending from the *B. Graham* box to meet the horizontal line.

8. Click on the **Home View button** (the last button on the Toolbar, it displays a small slide and a large slide) to return the view to 50 percent.

PRACTICE YOUR SKILLS

Let's make our organization chart match the one in Figure 7.5:

1. Adjust the location of the other vertical lines as necessary to make them match Figure 7.5. (Hint: Use the **View Scale button** when you need to zoom in and zoom out.)

2. Return the view scale to 50 percent.

3. Save the file.

ALIGNING OBJECTS

Now that we have the basic chart completed, we should clean it up. We want all the boxes in the organization chart to be perfectly aligned; to help you accomplish this, PowerPoint offers several alignment options. You can align objects along their left, right, top, or bottom edges. In addition, you can align objects horizontally or vertically along their center points.

Here's the general procedure for aligning objects:

• Select the objects you want to align.

• Choose *Arrange, Align*.

• Select one of the options from the submenu.

Figure 7.5   **The lines at 100-percent view**

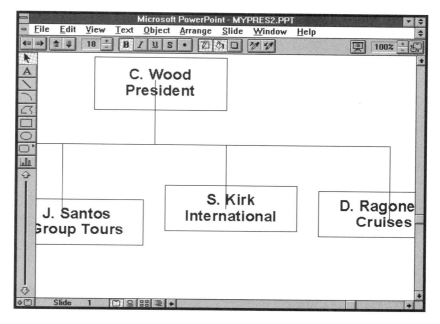

Let's align the boxes in our organization chart:

1. Select the **B. Graham box**.

2. Press and hold **Shift**, and select the other boxes in the row. As you know, pressing Shift while selecting objects allows you to select more than one object.

3. Observe your screen. It should look like that shown in Figure 7.6. Because you selected more than one object, a gray selection bar outlines each selected object.

4. Choose **Arrange, Align, Tops**. This command horizontally aligns the tops of the boxes.

5. Click anywhere on the slide workspace to deselect the boxes.

6. Observe the slide. The boxes in the second level should now be aligned.

Figure 7.6   **The four selected boxes**

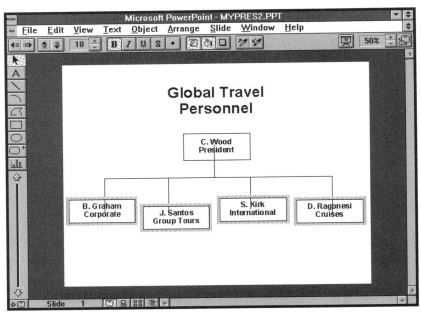

CHANGING OBJECTS' STACKING ORDER

When you add or draw objects on your slide, you can stack them on top of each other, oldest to newest. As you saw at the beginning of this chapter, when you duplicated boxes for the organization chart, they were placed one on top of the other. Because there were several boxes on top of it, you could see only part of the bottom box. Likewise, when you draw lines to connect the boxes in an organization chart, the ends of the lines can be drawn on top of the boxes. If you want to hide the ends of the lines, you need to change the *stacking order* of the objects so that the lines are on the bottom and partially covered by the boxes.

You can change the stacking order by using the *Bring To Front* and *Send To Back* commands or by using the *Bring Forward* and *Send Backward* commands.

Here's the general procedure for changing the stacking order of an object:

• Select the object.

- Choose Arrange and select the appropriate option: Bring To Front and Send To Back will move the selected object to the top or bottom of the stack, respectively; Bring Forward and Send Backward will move a selected object up or down one level in the stack.

Let's change the stacking order of the boxes in the organization chart:

1. Observe your screen. The lines were created after the boxes, so they appear to be on top of the boxes.

2. Press **Shift** and select the four second-level boxes in the organization chart. (Hint: If you accidentally select an extra object, just press **Shift** and click on the object again to deselect it without deselecting everything else.)

3. Choose **Arrange, Bring To Front** to change the stacking order, placing the boxes on top of the lines.

4. Click anywhere on the slide workspace to deselect the boxes and observe the slide. Although the entire line is still there, you can see only the part that is not covered by the box.

5. Select the vertical line extending from the *C. Wood* box.

6. Choose **Arrange, Send To Back** to send the line behind the box.

7. Deselect the line and observe the slide. It should match that shown in Figure 7.7.

ENHANCING THE ORGANIZATION CHART

As you learned in Chapter 4, you can enhance the appearance of a drawn object by changing its attributes, such as the fill color, shadow, and line style. You can apply these techniques to the boxes in your organization chart. Right now the boxes in your organization chart are beautifully aligned and stacked, but they blend into the woodwork. You can enhance them by adding shadows and fill, and changing the line style and color.

Let's change the attributes of the boxes in the organization chart:

1. Select the **C. Wood box**.

2. Choose **Object, Fill** to open the Fill submenu. As mentioned earlier, the Fill submenu provides options for filling the selected object. You can fill the box with a solid color or a pattern or with shading.

Figure 7.7   **The organization chart, after changing the stacking order**

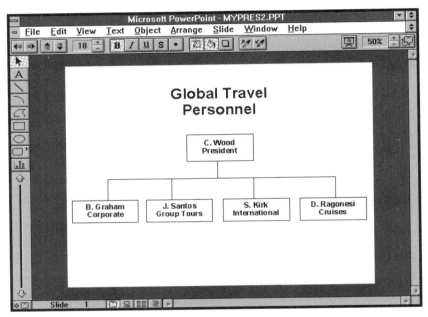

3. Select **GY6** to fill the box with gray.

4. Choose **Object, Shadow** to open the Shadow submenu and view the options available for adding a shadow to the box.

5. Select **BK** to add a black shadow behind the box.

6. Click on the **Line button** (located on the Toolbar, it displays a pencil drawing a box) to remove the black line border from the box.

7. Deselect and observe the *C. Wood* box. Changing the attributes of the box causes it to stand out more, as you can see in Figure 7.8.

PICKING UP AND APPLYING STYLES

All the attributes you apply to an object are called the *style*. Once you have a style you like for one box in your organization chart, you can "pick up" that style and apply it to the other boxes in the chart. When you pick up a style, PowerPoint includes all the attributes associated with the object you select, such as line style and shadow. If the object contains text, text styles are picked up as well.

Figure 7.8 **The formatted box**

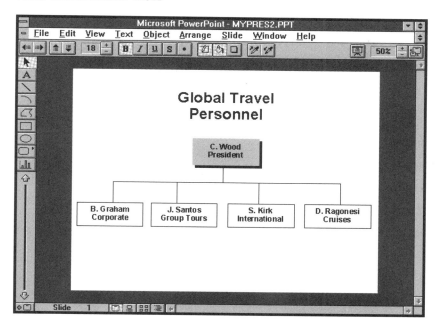

Here's the general procedure for picking up and applying styles:

- Select the object whose style you want to use.
- Click on the *Pick Up Style button* on the Toolbar.
- Select the object or objects whose style you want to change.
- Click on the *Apply Style button* on the Toolbar.

Note: You can pick up and apply styles on the same slide, between slides, between views, and between presentations.

Let's apply the same style to all the boxes in the organization chart:

1. Select the **C. Wood box**.

2. Click on the **Pick Up Style button** (located on the Toolbar, it is the first eye dropper from the left). The Pick Up Style button allows you to pick up all the attributes that have been applied to a selected object. These attributes are held in limbo, ready to be applied to any other object you choose.

3. Select all the boxes in the second level. (Once again, pressing Shift while selecting allows you to select more than one object.)

4. Click on the **Apply Style button** (located on the Toolbar, it shows an eye dropper with a down-pointing arrow). The attributes from the top box are applied to the remaining boxes.

5. Click on a blank area of the slide to deselect the boxes.

6. Observe the slide. It should closely resemble that shown in Figure 7.9. All the boxes are formatted alike and are more interesting.

7. Save the file.

Figure 7.9   **The formatted organization-chart boxes**

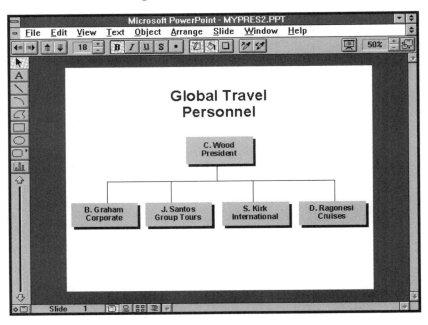

GROUPING OBJECTS

As you know, an organization chart is actually a number of lines and boxes combined to form a single object. Sometimes it is helpful to be able to treat these individual objects as one giant object. You can accomplish this by selecting every object that is part of the organization chart and grouping them together as one object.

Note: You can create groups within groups. For example, you might want to group each box in the organization chart with its line. Then, you could combine these smaller groups into a large group. That way, if you had to edit any part of the chart, you could ungroup just that part without disturbing the rest of the chart.

You already know how to select multiple objects by holding down the Shift key and clicking on each individual object. However, if the objects you want to select are next to each other, you can select all of them at once by drawing a selection rectangle around them. A *selection rectangle* is a dotted outline that appears as you drag a box on the slide workspace by using the Selection tool. The trick to using the selection rectangle is to include *every* part of all the desired objects within its boundary. Think of the selection rectangle as a lasso you throw around all the objects you want to select.

Here's the general procedure for grouping objects:

- Select the *Selection tool.*

- Draw a selection rectangle around all the objects you want to group.

- Choose Arrange, Group. The selected objects now react as one object.

Let's group the boxes and lines of the organization chart:

1. Place the mouse pointer on the upper-left edge of the slide (above the *C. Wood* box and to the left of the *B. Graham* box).

2. Press and hold the left mouse button and draw a rectangle that encompasses all the objects in your organization chart. The selection rectangle appears on your screen as a dotted outline and should include every object in your organization chart (it should not include the slide title).

3. Release the mouse button. Gray selection bars appear around each object that was completely within the selection rectangle.

4. Observe the slide. Each object in your organization chart should be selected.

5. If necessary, press **Shift** and select any unselected objects that are part of the organization chart. Your screen should match that shown in Figure 7.10.

Figure 7.10   **The selected objects in the organization chart**

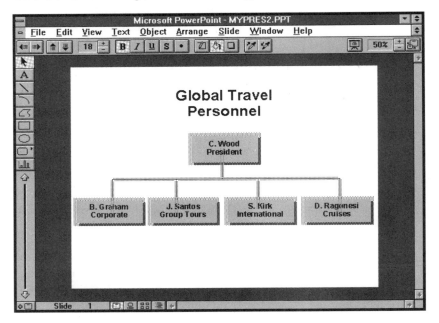

6. Choose **Arrange, Group** to group the objects together. Instead of gray bars indicating that each object is selected, a selection box appears around the entire chart.

7. Place the mouse pointer on one of the boxes and drag the chart to the center of the slide, so that your slide resembles that shown in Figure 7.11. Because the chart is now one object, the entire chart moves together.

Figure 7.11   **The grouped organization chart**

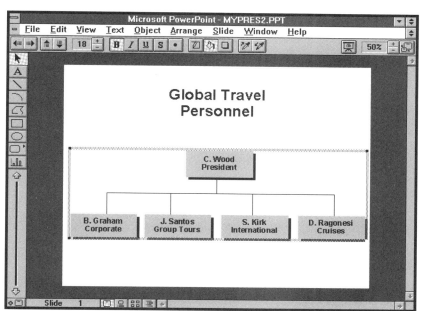

USING TIME SAVERS TO CREATE AN ORGANIZATION CHART

Creating an organization chart from scratch is fine if you have only a few people to chart. However, if you have to create a larger organization chart, you might find this approach too time-consuming. Fortunately, PowerPoint includes files called *Time Savers* that can serve as the basis for special slide formats such as organization charts, calendars, or flow charts.

You can find the Time Saver files in a directory called TIMESAVR, which is located in the POWERPNT directory. Each of the Time Saver files gives you a slide containing instructions for using the Time Saver, as well as several slides containing different images. For example, the organization chart file, ORGCHART.PPT, contains eight slides: one instruction slide and seven slides with at least 11 organization-chart styles. You can choose any of these styles to use as the basis for the organization chart in your presentation.

When you are ready to create a Time Saver organization chart, open the organization-charts file (ORGCHART.PPT). The slides appear in Outline view, and act as a table of contents for the file.

You might want to use the Slide Changer to display all the slides containing images. When you find an image you want to use, you just copy and paste it into your presentation. You can then modify this copy and enter your own text where there are placeholders. The Time Saver files are like clip art; you edit the copies, not the originals. You want the images in the ORGCHART.PPT file itself to remain intact.

Note: There are several other files (such as flow charts, calendars, timelines, tables, and graphs) in this directory. You might want to browse through them to see what other slides you can create with PowerPoint.

Here's the general procedure for creating an organization chart using a Time Saver file:

- Move to the slide on which you want to place the organization chart.

- Choose File, Open and move to the POWERPNT directory.

- Open the TIMESAVR directory.

- Double-click on orgchart.ppt.

- Move to the slide that displays the chart style you want to use.

- Select the chart and choose Edit, Copy.

- Close the ORGCHART.PPT file.

- Choose Edit, Paste to paste a copy of the organization chart onto your slide.

- Choose Arrange, Ungroup to ungroup the organization chart.

- Modify the chart as necessary.

- Select the entire chart and choose Arrange, Group.

Before we begin creating our organization chart, let's take a quick tour of the available Time Saver organization-chart styles:

1. Choose **File, Open**. Do *not* close MYPRES2.PPT. As when working with clip art, you will open the new file on top of the open presentation.

2. From the Drives drop-down list, select the drive that contains the POWERPNT folder, if necessary.

3. In the Directories list box, double-click on **powerpnt**; then double-click on **timesavr** to display the list of Time Saver files. (The left side of Figure 7.12 shows a list of the Time Saver files.)

Figure 7.12   **The Open dialog box**

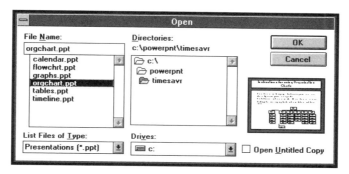

4. Select **orgchart.ppt** and observe the Preview box on the right side of the Open dialog box. It displays the first slide of the ORGCHART.PPT presentation. (Your Open dialog box should match that shown in Figure 7.12.)

5. Click on **OK** to open the ORGCHART.PPT presentation. The presentation opens in Outline view, showing you how many slides there are and what they are called.

6. Observe the outline. There are eight slides with different organization-chart styles. Unfortunately, you can't see what the slides look like in Outline view, so it would be difficult to pick a style at this point.

7. Let's take a look at the slides. Select slide 2 and click on the **Slide view button** to view the organization-chart styles on slide 2. There are five different organization-chart styles on the slide. Each of the styles is for a two-level organization chart. As you learned earlier, this means that everyone on the chart reports to one person.

8. Move to slide 3. Slide 3 shows a three-level organization chart. The two middle columns (representing the second level) report to the top level, and the two outside columns (the third level) report to the second level.

9. Move to slide 4. This slide shows a five-level organization chart. Each person reports to the person above.

10. Move to slide 5. This is another three-level organization chart. Each person in the second level has four people reporting to him or her.

11. Move to slide 6. In this three-level organization chart, the names of third-level workers are not placed in boxes.

12. View the remaining two slides. They are the same style as slides 5 and 6 respectively, except that each has five second-level boxes instead of four.

13. Close the file without saving changes.

Once you have looked at all the slides, you are in a better position to decide which style to use. Let's begin creating a three-level organization chart based on a Time Saver organization chart style:

1. Click on the **New Slide button** to add a new slide for your Time Saver organization chart.

2. Select the **Title object** and type **Global Travel**. Press **Enter** and type **Personnel**.

3. Select the **Body object** and delete it.

Now that the slide is ready, let's open the file for organization charts and copy a style:

1. Open **ORGCHART.PPT**. (Remember, it is located in the TIME-SAVR directory in your POWERPNT directory.)

2. Move to slide 5. You are going to create a three-level organization chart.

3. Select the organization chart and choose **Edit, Copy** to place a copy of the organization chart on the Clipboard, ready to be pasted into another file or application.

4. Close ORGCHART.PPT. If you are prompted to save changes, click on **No**. You do not want to make any changes to the original styles in ORGCHART.PPT.

5. Choose **Edit, Paste** to paste a copy of the organization chart onto your new slide. Your slide should match that shown in Figure 7.13.

Figure 7.13   **The Time Saver organization chart in the presentation**

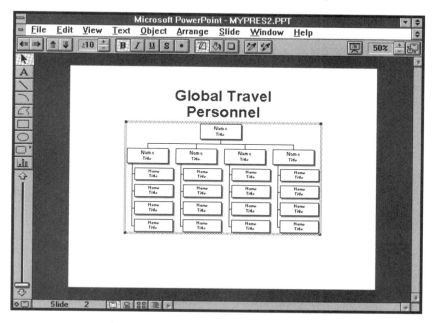

UNGROUPING THE TIME SAVER ORGANIZATION CHART

Well, you have the chart in your presentation, but it still needs to be completed. Currently, the chart is grouped together as one object. In order to make any changes to the chart, we first need to ungroup it.

Let's ungroup the organization chart:

1. Select the organization chart, if necessary.

2. Choose **Arrange, Ungroup** to separate the organization chart into its parts.

3. Click anywhere on the slide workspace to deselect the chart.

4. Click on one of the boxes in the bottom row to select it.

5. Observe the box you just selected. The selection box includes the line leading from the box, as well as the box and text. The box and line have been grouped together.

6. Choose **Arrange, Ungroup** to ungroup the box and line. Both objects are selected.

7. Choose **Arrange, Regroup** to regroup the box and line. *Regroup* will regroup only the last objects that you ungrouped.

8. Select all the boxes in the bottom three rows of the organization chart (refer to Figure 7.14). Because each box in the organization chart is actually a group, you might find it easier to use the Shift key and select the boxes individually.

Figure 7.14   **The selected boxes**

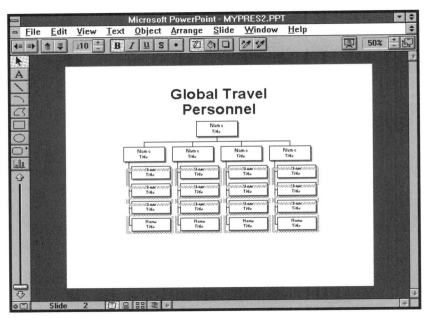

9. Press **Del** to delete the selected boxes. Your organization chart will include only one third-level box.

10. Select the rest of the boxes in the organization chart. (This time, because you want the entire chart, you might want to try using the Selection tool to select the chart.)

11. Choose **Arrange, Ungroup** to ungroup the lines and boxes. You cannot edit the text in the boxes unless the organization chart is completely ungrouped.

MODIFYING THE TIME SAVER ORGANIZATION CHART

Once the chart has been completely ungrouped, you can replace the *text placeholders*, *Name* and *Title*, with your text.

Let's modify the organization chart:

1. Select the top box in the organization chart.

2. Click on the **Zoom In button** twice to increase the magnification to 100 percent.

3. Click on the selected box again to place the insertion point in the text placeholder.

4. Double-click on **Name** in the top box to select the *Name* placeholder, as shown in Figure 7.15.

Figure 7.15   **Selected text**

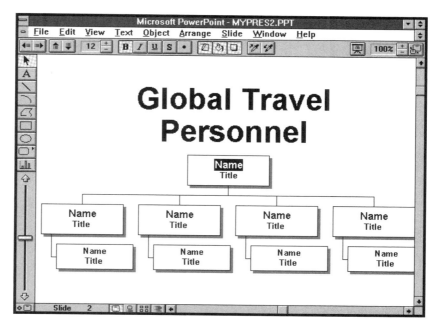

5. Type **C. Wood** to replace *Name* with *C. Wood*.

6. Double-click on **Title** in the top box to select the *Title* placeholder.

7. Type **President** to replace *Title* with *President*.

PRACTICE YOUR SKILLS

Let's complete the Organization chart shown in Figure 7.16:

1. Refer to Figure 7.16 to complete the organization chart with the following text:

B. Graham	J. Santos	S. Kirk	D. Ragonesi
Corporate	Group Tours	International	Cruises
B. Jakat	K. Mack	M. Royal	B. Burrows
Account Rep.	Sales Assistant	Sales Assistant	Sales Assistant

2. Return the magnification to 50 percent. (Hint: Try the **Home View button**.)

3. Save the file.

Figure 7.16   **The completed organization chart at 100-percent view**

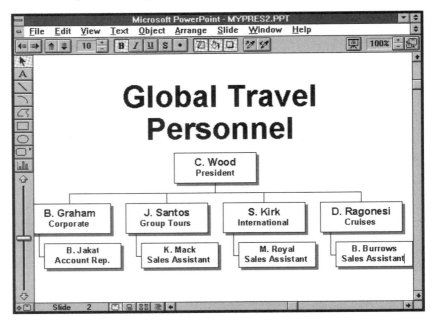

Now that the basic chart is done, let's add the finishing touches:

1. Select all the objects in the organization chart.

2. Choose **Arrange, Group** to group the objects together.

3. Observe the organization chart. Because you deleted several rows of the chart, it now looks too small for the slide. Let's fix that.

4. With the organization chart still selected, choose **Object, Scale**. As you learned in Chapter 5, the Scale command allows you to resize an object while keeping its aspect ratio (proportion of height to width).

5. Type **150** and press **Enter** to enlarge the organization chart to 150 percent of its original size.

6. Drag the organization chart to the center of the slide.

7. Observe the slide, which should match that shown in Figure 7.17.

8. Save the file.

9. Close the file.

Figure 7.17   **The completed slide**

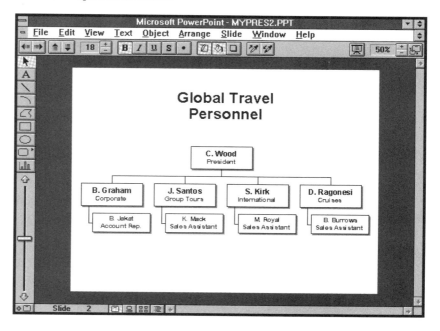

Although using a Time Saver file allows you to save time on formatting, creating a new organization chart using a Time Saver can't be done without a certain amount of effort. Therefore, if you have to create a particular style of organization chart on a regular basis, you might want to place a copy of it on a new slide in the ORGCHART.PPT Time Saver file. Then, you would not have to re-create the organization chart from scratch each time you needed to use it.

SUMMARY

In this chapter, you explored the techniques involved in creating organization charts. You now know how to duplicate objects, how to add text to the chart boxes, how to add lines to the organization chart, how to change the magnification of your view, how to align objects, how to change the stacking order, and how to pick up and apply styles. You also learned how to use a Time Saver file to create an organization chart, how to ungroup the Time Saver organization chart, how to modify the Time Saver organization chart, and how to edit the Time Saver organization chart.

Desired Result	How to Do It
Duplicate objects	Select the object you want to duplicate; choose **Edit, Duplicate** as many times as necessary to create the number of boxes you need for your organization chart
Changing the magnification of a view	Click on either the **Zoom In (+)** or the **Zoom Out (–) button**; to return to the view that fits in the window, click on the **Home View button**
Align objects	Select the objects you want to align; choose **Arrange, Align**; select one of the options from the submenu
Change the stacking order of an object	Select the object; choose **Arrange** and select **Bring To Front** or **Send To Back** to move the selected object to the top or bottom of the stack, respectively, or **Bring Forward** or **Send Backward** to move a selected object up or down one level in the stack

Desired Result	How to Do It
Pick up and apply styles	Select the object whose style you want to use, click on the **Pick Up Style button** on the Toolbar, select the object or objects whose style you want to change, click on the **Apply Style button** on the Toolbar
Group objects	Select the **Selection tool**; draw a selection rectangle around all the objects you want to group; choose **Arrange, Group**
Create an organization chart by using a Time Saver file	Move to the slide on which you want to place the organization chart; choose **File, Open** and move to the POWERPNT directory; open the **TIMESAVR** directory; double-click on **orgchart-.ppt**; move to the slide that displays the chart style you want to use; select the chart and choose **Edit, Copy**; close the ORGCHART.PPT file; choose **Edit, Paste** to paste a copy of the organization chart on your slide; choose **Arrange, Ungroup** to ungroup the organization chart; modify the chart as necessary; select the entire chart and choose **Arrange, Group**

In the next chapter, you'll find out how to use Microsoft Graph to create column charts for your presentation. You will learn how to open Microsoft Graph, how to enter data in the datasheet, how to exclude a row or column of data from the chart, how to edit a cell, how to change the width of a column in the datasheet, and how to delete a row or column from the datasheet. You will also learn how to place a chart on the slide, how to change the placement of the legend, how to format numbers along the y-axis of the chart, and how to add a text label to the chart.

IF YOU'RE STOPPING HERE

If you need to break off here, please exit PowerPoint. If you want to proceed directly to the next chapter, please do so now.

CHAPTER 8: WORKING WITH COLUMN CHARTS

Using Microsoft
Graph

Creating a Column
Chart

Enhancing a
Column Chart

In this chapter, you'll add to your repertoire of chart types by learning how to create, edit, and enhance a *column chart*, a chart in which items of data (such as quarterly sales figures) are displayed as rectangular columns. Column charts are among the most popular and easy-to-understand charts for displaying data trends (growth, decline, and so on) and for comparing related data.

When you're done working through this chapter, you will know

- How to open Microsoft Graph
- How to enter data in the datasheet
- How to exclude a row or column of data from the chart
- How to edit a cell
- How to change the width of a column in the datasheet
- How to delete a row or column from the datasheet
- How to place a chart on the slide
- How to change the placement of the legend
- How to format numbers along the y-axis of the chart
- How to add a text label to the chart

USING MICROSOFT GRAPH

Microsoft Graph is an embedded application that allows you to create charts for your presentations. You can choose from seven two-dimensional chart types (area, bar, column, line, pie, scatter, and combination) and five three-dimensional chart types (area, bar, column, line, and pie), each of which is available in several variations. In total, you can format your chart 84 different ways. By default, Graph plots your data as a column chart. However, you can change this default (we'll show you how in Chapter 9).

The Graph window consists of two windows: the *Chart window* and the *Datasheet window*. When you first open Microsoft Graph, the Datasheet window displays sample data and the Chart window contains a sample chart plotted from that data.

Note: PowerPoint uses the terms *chart* and *graph* interchangeably. In this book, we will use *Graph* to refer to the Microsoft Graph application window and *chart* to refer to anything we create in the Chart window.

Here's the general procedure for starting Graph from the Presentation window:

- Change to Slide view.
- Click on the *Graphing tool*.

- On your slide, drag to create a box that is the approximate size you want your chart to be. Graph will open and display a sample datasheet and chart (see Figure 8.1).

Figure 8.1   **The Microsoft Graph window**

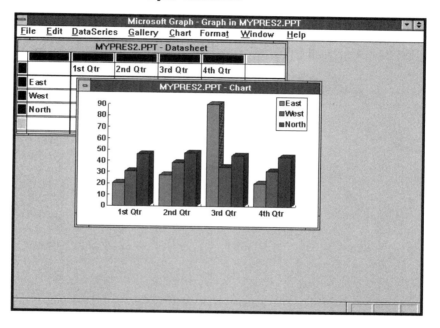

If you are not running PowerPoint on your computer, please start it now. Close all open presentations except the start-up presentation. Let's start Microsoft Graph and take a look at the Graph window:

1. Open **MYPRES2.PPT** and maximize the presentation window, if necessary.

2. Display the last slide in the presentation (slide 2), and click on the **New Slide button** to add a slide to the end of the presentation.

3. Select the **Title object** and type the title **Airline Ticket Sales**.

Let's delete the Body object to eliminate clutter on the screen before we open Graph:

1. Click on the **Body object** and press **Del** to delete it.

2. Select the **Graph tool** (located at the bottom of the Tool Palette, it shows a miniature chart). Move to the slide workspace and note that the mouse pointer changes to a cross hair.

3. Draw a box on the slide, of the size and at the position shown in Figure 8.2. When you release the mouse button, the Microsoft Graph window opens.

Figure 8.2   **Drawing a box with the Graph tool**

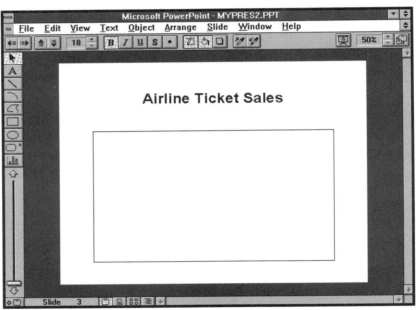

Now that Microsoft Graph is running, let's take a look at the Graph window.

1. Maximize the Graph window and observe the menu options. File, Edit, Window, and Help are standard menu options available in most Windows programs. DataSeries, Gallery, Chart, and Format are Microsoft Graph-specific menus.

2. Click on **DataSeries** and observe the drop-down DataSeries menu. You use this menu to set up the options on your data sheet. For example, if you create a bar chart, you need the data in your datasheet to be set up in columns instead of rows.

3. Click on **Gallery** and observe the drop-down Gallery menu (do not select any of the commands in the Gallery menu). This menu includes one command for each of Graph's basic chart types. Choosing any of the commands opens the Chart Gallery dialog box, which shows several formatting options for the basic chart type you chose. Figure 8.3 shows the chart options available for a 3-D column chart.

Figure 8.3   **The Chart Gallery dialog box**

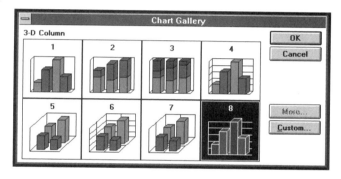

4. Open the **Chart** menu. With this menu, you can add titles, data labels, arrows, a legend, axes labels, and grid lines to your chart.

5. Open the **Format** menu. This menu gives formatting options for the text and axes of the chart.

6. Press **Esc** to close the Format menu.

THE DATASHEET WINDOW

As mentioned earlier, the Graph window consists of the Datasheet window and the Chart window. You enter and edit your data in the Datasheet window, and it is formatted as a chart in the Chart window.

The datasheet itself is divided into 4,000 rows and 256 columns in which you can enter numbers and labels. You might think that because the datasheet looks like a spreadsheet it therefore must be one. Don't be fooled. You cannot enter formulas into the datasheet, as you can into a spreadsheet.

You enter labels for your data in the first row and leftmost column of the datasheet. The first row and column are always visible in the Datasheet window. No matter how much data is in your datasheet, you can always see your labels while scrolling through the datasheet.

Table 8.1 defines the elements of the Microsoft Graph Datasheet window. Figure 8.4 illustrates where each of these elements is located.

Figure 8.4   **The Datasheet window**

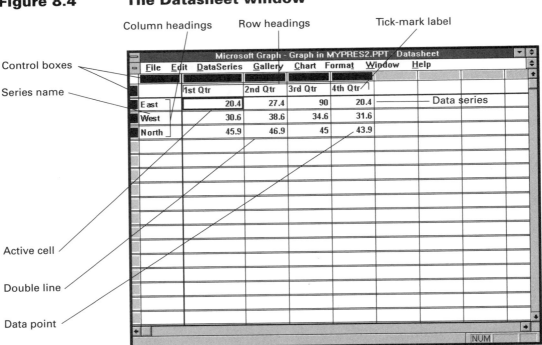

Table 8.1   **The Elements of the Datasheet Window**

Term	Definition
Row and column headings	The top row and the left column of cells on the datasheet. This is where your labels are entered.
Row and column control boxes	Located above row headings and to the left of column headings, you use these to select and deselect rows and columns or to exclude rows and columns from your chart. A control box appears black when the row or column is included, and gray when it is not.
Cell	An intersection of a row and a column on the datasheet. You enter data into cells.
Active cell	The currently selected cell, indicated by a heavy border.
Data series	A row or column of data used to plot one set of bars or columns, or one line or pie.
Data point	A single cell value, representing a single item in a data series.
Series name	A name that identifies a row or column of data. These names appear in the legend.
Tick-mark labels	The names that appear along the horizontal axis of an area, column, or line chart, and along the vertical axis of a bar chart. When data series are in rows, the tick-mark labels identify the columns. When data series are in columns, the tick-mark labels identify rows.
Double lines	The breaks that indicate separate data series. A double line between rows indicates that the data in each row is a separate data series. A double line between columns indicates that each column is a separate data series.

Now let's explore the Datasheet window:

1. Observe the screen. The Graph window is displayed, showing the Datasheet and Chart windows.

2. Click on the **Maximize button** for the Microsoft PowerPoint Graph window. When you maximize the Graph window, you eliminate the possibility of accidentally clicking outside the window.

3. Place the mouse pointer on the chart title and drag the **Chart window** down so that both the datasheet and the chart are visible.

4. Click on the **Datasheet window** to activate it. The datasheet displays rows and columns that intersect to form cells.

5. Observe the cells. Each cell contains a data point (one piece of information that will be plotted on the chart).

6. Observe the column and row headings. The top row of the datasheet contains the column headings, while the first column displays the row headings. These headings appear as labels in the chart.

7. Observe the row and column control boxes. These are the boxes above the row headings and to the left of the column headings. They are used to select and deselect columns and rows of the datasheet. If a control box is black, the information in that column or row is currently selected to be included in the chart. If a control box is gray, any information in that column or row will be excluded from the chart.

8. Open the **DataSeries** menu. The *Series In Rows* option is checked, indicating that the information on the datasheet is read row by row, each row forming a separate data series. This is reflected on the datasheet by the double lines separating the rows.

9. Choose **Series In Columns** and observe the datasheet. The double lines now separate the columns, indicating that each column is a separate data series.

10. Observe the chart. When the Series In Columns option is checked, the row headings in the datasheet become the x-axis labels in the chart. The column headings become the legend.

11. Choose **DataSeries, Series In Rows**. The datasheet and chart change back.

THE CHART WINDOW

The Chart window shows you the graphic representation of the data you enter in the datasheet. After entering data in the datasheet, you can change the look of the chart in the Chart window.

Table 8.2 defines the elements of the Microsoft Graph chart. Figure 8.5 illustrates where some of these elements are located.

Figure 8.5   **The Chart window**

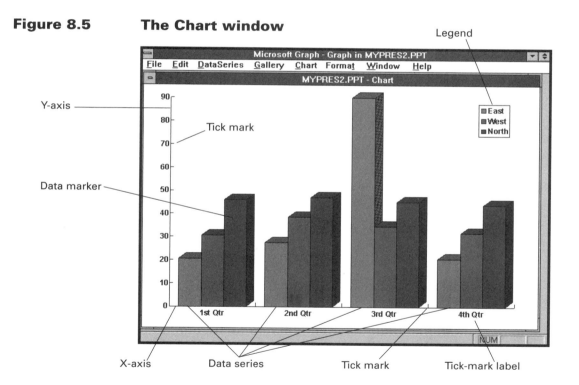

Table 8.2   **The Elements of a Chart**

Term	Definition
Data marker	A bar (in column and bar charts), shape (in area and pie charts), or dot or symbol (in line and xy (scatter) charts) that marks a single data point or value. Related markers in a chart make up a data series.
Data series	A group of related data points. For example, one region's airline-ticket sales figures for all four quarters make up a data series. In the sample chart, each region (East, West, and North) is a data series. A chart can have one or more data series.
Axis	A line that serves as a major reference for plotting data in a chart.
X-axis	The horizontal or category axis.
Y-axis	The vertical or value axis.
Tick mark	A short line that crosses an axis and marks off a category, scale, or data series.
Tick-mark label	Text that appears beside or below a major tick mark to identify it.
Plot area	The area in which Graph plots your data. It includes the axes and all markers that represent data points.
Grid lines	Optional lines that extend from the tick marks on an axis across the plot area to make it easier to view data values. (The grid lines are not turned on in Figure 8.5.)
Chart text	Text that describes data or items in a chart. Text can be attached or unattached.
Attached text	Any label linked to a chart object such as an axis or a data marker. Attached text moves with the item when it is repositioned, but cannot be moved independently of the chart object.

Table 8.2   **The Elements of a Chart (Continued)**

Term	Definition
Unattached text	Text you add by just typing whenever the chart is active and then pressing Esc. You can move unattached text anywhere on the chart.
Legend	A key that identifies a data-series name and the patterns, colors, or symbols associated with that data series.

Let's take a quick tour of the Chart:

1. Activate the **Chart window** (click on it).

2. Observe the x-axis (the horizontal axis). It displays the category—in this case, periods of time—being graphed.

3. Observe the y-axis (the vertical axis). This shows the values being graphed; in our example, the number of sales.

4. Observe the legend. Located in the upper-right corner of the Chart window, it serves as a key identifying the different data series in the chart.

5. Observe the data series. Each data series consists of all the columns that have the same color or pattern. For example, the first column in each quarter is the data series for East.

CREATING A COLUMN CHART

A column chart depicts data graphed against an x-axis (horizontal axis) and a y-axis (vertical axis). The x-axis shows the *category* being graphed, such as products, regions, or periods of time. The y-axis shows the *values* being graphed, such as dollars or numbers of products sold.

Figure 8.6 shows a simplified version of the Airline Ticket Sales column chart that you'll create over the course of this chapter. In this figure, the x-axis categories are regions (North America, Europe, and Far East), and the y-axis values are thousands of dollars.

Column charts are useful for showing variation over a period of time. Each number in the datasheet is represented by a column in the chart. Data is entered into the datasheet by row. This means that the information in the first column of your datasheet appears in your chart as the legend, and the contents of the first row become the labels along the horizontal axis.

Figure 8.6   **Airline Ticket Sales column chart, simplified**

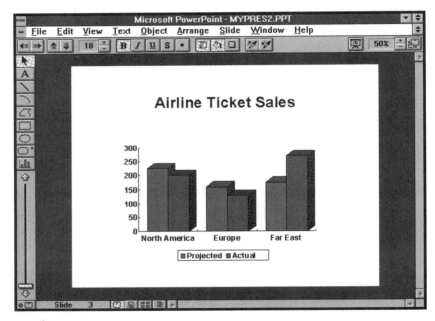

SELECTING CELLS AND ENTERING DATA

To enter data on the datasheet, you first need to make the cell active by selecting it. The cell surrounded by a darkened border is the active cell. You can use the mouse or the keyboard to select a cell. Then, simply type the data. If there is any data in the cell you selected, the new data you type will replace it. If you are going to be entering a row or column of numbers, you can select all the cells in that row or column and then enter your data.

Here's the general procedure for entering data into a selected row or column:

• Click on the Datasheet window to make it active.

- Drag to select the cells in which you want to enter information.

- Type the data, and press Enter to advance to the next selected cell.

- Repeat the previous step until data has been completely entered.

Let's begin creating our column chart:

1. Click on the **Datasheet window** to activate it.

2. Drag from the **1st Qtr** to the **3rd Qtr** cell to select three cells.

3. Observe the selected cells. The active cell always has a darkened border. Any data you type will be entered in the active cell.

4. Type **Canada**. The text you type replaces the contents of the first selected cell.

5. Press **Enter** to make 2nd Qtr the active cell.

6. Observe the Chart window. The first tick-mark label along the horizontal axis reflects the change made on the datasheet.

7. Type **Europe** and press **Enter** to replace *2nd Qtr* with *Europe* and to make *3rd Qtr* the active cell.

8. Type **Far East** to replace *3rd Qtr*.

9. Press **Enter**. Canada becomes the active cell (see Figure 8.7). Because you selected only three cells, pressing Enter toggles you through those cells only.

EXCLUDING A DATASHEET ROW OR COLUMN FROM THE CHART

Excluding a row or column from the datasheet will remove that data from the chart without actually deleting the data from the datasheet.

Here's the general procedure for excluding a row or column of data in the datasheet from the chart:

- Double-click on the control box for the row or column you want to exclude from the chart.

Figure 8.7   **The completed column headings**

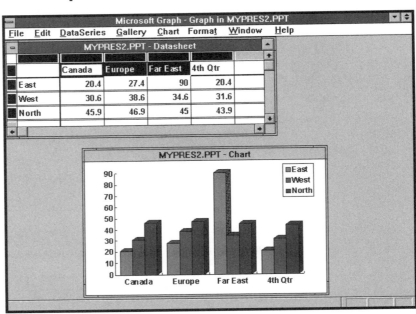

Because we want our chart to include only three data series, we need to exclude the fourth sample data series from the datasheet. Let's do that now:

1. Observe the Chart window. The 4th Qtr data series should be excluded from the chart data.

2. Double-click on the **control box** above the 4th Qtr cell to exclude the 4th Qtr column. Clicking once will only select the column or row, not mark it for exclusion.

3. Observe the chart. The modified column chart has three regions displayed along the horizontal axis. The data in the 4th Qtr column is still on the datasheet, but it does not appear in the current chart (see Figure 8.8).

EDITING A CELL

It is not necessary for you to retype all the information in a cell every time you want to change it. If you would like to modify the data in a cell instead of replace it, you can edit the cell.

Figure 8.8   **The datasheet and chart with the 4th Qtr data excluded**

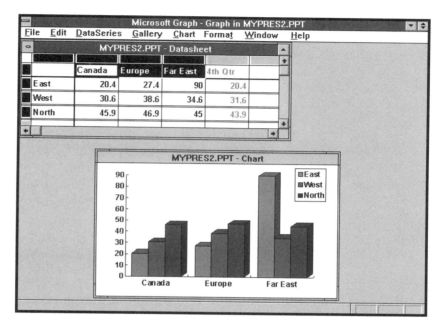

Here's the general procedure for editing a cell in the datasheet:

- In the Datasheet window, double-click on the cell that you want to edit. The *Cell Data dialog box* is displayed.

- Place the insertion point and enter the new text, or press the Backspace and Del keys to edit the text.

- Click on OK. The edited text is placed in the selected cell.

Now let's edit a cell in the datasheet:

1. Click on the **Canada** cell to select it.

2. Type **America** and press **Enter** to replace *Canada* with *America*.

3. Double-click on the **America** cell to open the Cell Data dialog box (see Figure 8.9). In this dialog box, you can edit a cell without retyping all the text.

Figure 8.9   **The Cell Data dialog box**

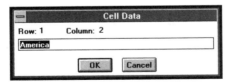

4. Place the insertion point at the beginning of *America*.

5. Type **North** and press **Spacebar**. Now the region covered by the chart will include both Canada and the United States.

6. Press **Enter** to register the change.

CHANGING THE COLUMN WIDTH

Your datasheet has default column widths. If you enter a number that is longer than the cell is wide, Graph will solve the difficulty by expressing the number exponentially. For example, if you enter the number 1,000,000,000 in a narrow cell, the number will be expressed as *1E + 09* (1 + nine zeros). When you enter *text* that is wider than the cell, only the characters that fit in the cell will be displayed; however, all the text characters will be displayed on your chart.

You can increase or decrease the column width as needed to make it easier for you to work with your data on the datasheet. Datasheet columns may be as narrow as the width of one character or wide enough to hold 255 characters. Keep in mind, however, that the width of the column in your datasheet has nothing to do with how the data will be displayed on your chart.

Here's the general procedure for changing column widths:

• Click on the control box for the column whose width you want to change.

• Choose *Format, Column Width* to open the Column Width dialog box.

• Type a number between 1 and 255 that represents the new character width for the selected column.

- Click on OK to change the column width and return to the datasheet.

Let's widen column 1 to view all the text in each cell:

1. Observe the North America cell. You cannot see all of that cell's text on the datasheet.

2. Click on the **control box** above the North America cell to select the column.

3. Choose **Format, Column Width** to open the Column Width dialog box. The standard width for columns is nine characters.

4. Type **13** to widen the column to 13 characters, as shown in Figure 8.10.

Figure 8.10　　　**The Column Width dialog box**

5. Press **Enter** to register the new column width and close the dialog box.

6. Observe the datasheet. It is now possible to see all the text in the North America cell. Note that in order to change the width of one cell, it is necessary to change the width of the entire column.

7. Observe the chart. Changing the column width on the datasheet has no effect on the Chart window.

DELETING A ROW OR COLUMN FROM THE DATASHEET

To delete a row or column from the datasheet, you can use the *Delete Row/Col* command.

You can also delete one cell or a range of cells. Of course, deleted data is not displayed on the chart.

Here's the general procedure for deleting a row or column:

- Select the entire row or column (click on the control box).

- Choose Edit, Delete Row/Col.

Note: If you select only a cell or range of cells in a row or column, then the Delete Row/Col dialog box appears. Make the appropriate choice in the dialog box and then click on OK.

Let's continue working on the datasheet:

1. If necessary, activate the **Datasheet window**.

2. Drag down from the **East cell** to the **West cell** to select the East and West cells. The East cell is active.

3. Type **Projected** and press **Enter** to replace *East* with *Projected* and to move to the West cell.

4. Type **Actual** and press **Enter** to replace *West* with *Actual*.

5. Observe the Chart window. The label for the first set of bars in the legend has changed from *East* to *Projected*, and *Actual* has replaced *West*.

6. Observe the Datasheet window. Projected and Actual are the only two series of numbers we need for the modified chart. Therefore, we should eliminate the North series.

7. Click on the **control box** to the left of the North cell to select the row containing the North data.

8. Choose **Edit, Delete Row/Col** to delete the row from the datasheet and to remove the North column of data from the current chart.

9. Observe your chart and datasheet. They should match those shown in Figure 8.11.

PRACTICE YOUR SKILLS

Now let's complete the datasheet so that it matches that shown in Figure 8.12:

1. Select all the cells from **20.4** in the Projected row through **34.6** in the Actual row. (Hint: Drag to select the cells.)

Figure 8.11   **The Graph window, after deleting a row**

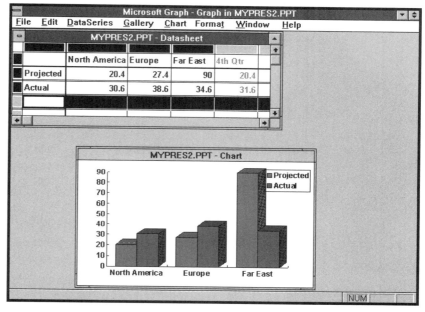

Figure 8.12   **The completed datasheet**

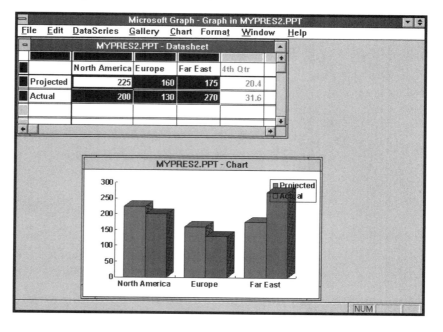

2. Enter the following Projected and Actual values for the North America, Europe, and Far East columns so that your window matches that shown in Figure 8.12:

	North America	Europe	Far East
Projected	225	160	175
Actual	200	130	270

 PLACING A CHART ON A SLIDE

Once you have entered your data and created your chart, you need to exit from the Graph window and place that chart on the slide in your presentation.

Here's the general procedure for exiting the Graph window and placing the chart on the slide:

• Choose *File, Exit And Return*.

• Click on Yes to update your presentation and return to the slide. Or, choose *File, Update* to update any changes on your slide while keeping Graph open.

Let's place our newly created column chart on the slide and see what it looks like:

1. Choose **File, Exit And Return To MYPRES2.PPT**. A message box displaying the prompt *Update Graph in MYPRES2.PPT?* opens.

2. Click on **Yes** to update the chart and to return to the slide. The column chart Airline Ticket Sales that we created in this chapter appears on the slide as an object.

3. Double-click on the chart to reopen Microsoft Graph. The Airline Ticket Sales chart and data are displayed in the Graph window.

ENHANCING A COLUMN CHART

Charts are created with certain defaults, depending on the template you are using for your presentation. However, you are not stuck with these settings. Once you have created a chart, you can enhance it in many ways.

CHANGING THE LEGEND FORMAT

Each group of related data points has a particular pattern, color, or symbol in the chart. The legend is a key that identifies these patterns. By default, the legend appears in the upper-right corner of your chart; however, you can move the legend anywhere on the chart.

Here's the general procedure for changing the placement of the legend:

- Click on the Chart window to make it active.
- Click on the legend.
- Choose *Format, Legend*.
- Select a legend type.
- Click on OK.

Note: You can also move the legend to a new location by dragging it.

Let's change the position of the legend on the chart we created in this chapter:

1. Activate the **Chart window**. The legend appears on top of one of the columns.

2. Click on the legend to select it.

3. Choose **Format, Legend** to open the Legend dialog box, shown in Figure 8.13. You can place the legend at the top or bottom of the screen, as well as to the left, right, or in the corner.

4. Choose **Bottom** and click on **OK** to place the legend at the bottom of the chart.

Figure 8.13   **The Legend dialog box**

FORMATTING Y-AXIS NUMBERS

Your default chart style does not include any formatting for the numbers along the y-axis, so you can't tell if they are supposed to represent currency, percentages, or some other measurements. You can quickly and easily add formatting—such as dollar signs, decimal places, or commas—by formatting the cell at the intersection of the second row and second column of the datasheet.

Here's the general procedure for changing formatting of y-axis numbers:

- Click on the Datasheet window to make it active.
- Click on the cell at the intersection of the second row and second column of the datasheet.
- Choose *Format, Number.*
- Click on the number format desired for the y-axis.
- Click on OK.

Let's add dollar signs to the numbers along the y-axis of our chart:

1. Activate the **Datasheet window**, if necessary.

2. Click on the cell in row 2, column 2. The format of this cell controls the format of the numbers along the vertical axis of the chart.

3. Choose **Format, Number** to open the Number dialog box. This dialog box, shown in Figure 8.14, displays a list of possible formats for numbers.

Figure 8.14   **The Number dialog box**

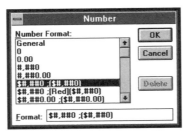

4. Choose **$#,##0;($#,##0)** to format the vertical-axis numbers as currency.

5. Click on **OK** to register the new formatting and close the dialog box.

6. Observe the chart. The numbers along the y-axis are formatted as currency.

7. Choose **File, Exit And Return To MYPRES2.PPT** and click on **Yes** to update the chart and return to the slide.

ADDING A TEXT LABEL ON A SLIDE

As a finishing touch, you can add text labels clarifying or explaining parts of your chart. Here's the general procedure for adding a text label to the chart:

- Return to your slide.

- Select the Text tool.

- Click to place an insertion point on the slide workspace.

- Type the text.

- Select the text and format it as needed.

- Drag the text to the desired location on the slide.

Let's add a text label like the one shown in Figure 8.15:

1. Select the **Text tool** (located on the Tool Palette; it displays the letter *A*).

2. Place the insertion point anywhere on the slide workspace.

3. Type **Sales in thousands**.

4. Select the **Selection tool** from the Tool Palette.

5. Click on **Sales in thousands** to select it.

6. Move the text label to the location shown in Figure 8.15.

7. Save the file.

8. Close the file.

Figure 8.15   **The completed column chart**

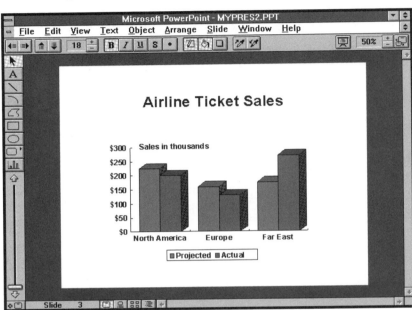

SUMMARY

In this chapter, you explored column charts. You now know how to open Microsoft Graph, how to create a column chart, how to exclude a row or column of data from the chart, how to edit a cell, how to change the width of a column in the datasheet, and how to delete a row or column from the datasheet. You also learned how to place a chart on the slide, how to change the placement of the legend, how to format numbers along the y-axis of the chart, and how to add a text label to the chart.

Here's a quick reference for the techniques you learned in this chapter:

Desired Result	**How to Do It**
Open Microsoft Graph	Change to Slide view; click on the **Graphing tool**; on your slide, drag to create a box that is the approximate size you want your chart to be

Desired Result	How to Do It
Enter data into the datasheet	Click on the **Datasheet window** to make it active, drag to select the cells in which you want to enter information, type the data and press **Enter** to advance to the next selected cell, repeat the previous step until all the data has been entered
Exclude a row or column of data	Double-click on the **control box** for the row or column you want to exclude from the chart
Edit a cell	In the Datasheet window, double-click on the cell that you want to edit; enter the new text in the Cell Data dialog box, or press the **Backspace** and **Del** keys to edit the text; click on **OK**
Changing column width	Click on the **control box** for the column whose width you want to change; choose **Format, Column Width** to open the Column Width dialog box; type a number between 1 and 255 that represents the new character width for the selected column; click on **OK**
Delete a row or column	Select the entire row or column (click on the **control box**); choose **Edit, Delete Row/Col**
Place the chart on the slide	Choose **File, Exit And Return**; click on **Yes** to update your presentation and return to the slide; or, choose **File, Update** to update your slide while keeping Graph open
Change the placement of the legend	Click on the **Chart window** to make it active; click on the legend; choose **Format, Legend**; select a legend type; click on **OK**

Desired Result	How to Do It
Change the format of y-axis numbers	Click on the **Datasheet window** to make it active; click on the cell at the intersection of the second row and second column of the datasheet; choose **Format, Number**; click on the desired number format for the y-axis; click on **OK**
Add a text label to the chart	Return to the slide, select **Text tool**, click to place an insertion point on the slide workspace, type the label text, select the text and format it as needed, drag the text to the desired location on the slide

In the next chapter, you'll find out how to modify Microsoft Graph to suit your needs and how to create and edit pie charts on your slides. You will learn how to clear the datasheet, how to set Microsoft Graph defaults, how to change the chart type, how to change the data series, and how to change legend options. You will also learn how to explode a pie chart, how to create a double-exploded pie chart, how to copy a chart, how to resize a chart, and how to recolor a chart.

IF YOU'RE STOPPING HERE

If you need to break off here, please exit PowerPoint. If you want to proceed directly to the next chapter, please do so now.

CHAPTER 9: WORKING WITH PIE CHARTS

Creating a Pie
Chart

Enhancing a Pie
Chart

*C*harts can be an integral part of any presentation. Power-Point provides you with the tools to create several different kinds of charts. In Chapter 8, you learned how to create column charts for your presentation. In this chapter, you'll learn how to create, edit, and enhance a *pie chart*, a circular diagram that depicts numerical as well as textual information. Both kinds of chart can make your presentation more interesting.

When you're done working through this chapter, you will know

- How to create a pie chart
- How to clear the datasheet
- How to set Microsoft Graph defaults
- How to change the chart type
- How to change the data series
- How to change legend options
- How to explode a pie chart
- How to create a double-exploded pie chart
- How to copy a chart
- How to resize a chart
- How to recolor a pie slice

CREATING A PIE CHART

A pie chart is a circular diagram that depicts that relationship between a whole and its parts. Figure 9.1 shows a simplified version of the Global Travel pie chart that you'll create over the course of this chapter. As you can see from this figure, each slice of the pie represents one part of the whole pie. The percentages indicate the size of each part in relation to the whole; for example, the Europe slice is 41 percent of the whole pie. Pie charts are particularly useful for comparing the relative size of a whole's constituent parts.

Here's the general procedure for creating a pie chart:

- Move to the slide to which you want to add the pie chart.
- Choose the Graph tool from the Tool Palette.
- Draw a box the approximate size you want your chart to be. The Microsoft Graph window opens.
- Choose *Gallery, Pie* to open the Chart Gallery dialog box displaying sample pie-chart formats.
- Choose the pie-chart format you want.
- Click on OK. Any data you enter in the datasheet will be formatted as a pie chart.

Figure 9.1   **Global Travel pie chart, simplified**

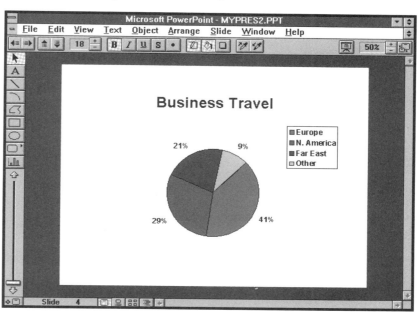

CLEARING DATA FROM THE DATASHEET

As you know, when you create a chart, Microsoft Graph always opens with sample data and a chart based on that data. In Chapter 8, you learned how to edit the sample data to create your own chart. In some cases, you will want to clear all the data from the datasheet and enter your own, instead of editing the sample data.

Here's the general procedure for clearing all data from the datasheet:

- In the datasheet, click on the corner control box to select all the cells in the datasheet.

- Choose *Edit, Clear*. The Clear dialog box is displayed, and the Clear Data option is selected.

- Click on OK. All the data is cleared from the datasheet.

Figure 9.2 shows the Clear dialog box. This dialog box has three options for clearing the datasheet:

- *Clear Data* clears only the data. This is the default option.

- *Clear Format* clears only the number format, leaving the data intact.

- *Clear Both* clears both the data and the number format.

Figure 9.2   **The Clear dialog box**

If you are not running PowerPoint on your computer, please start it now. Close all open presentations except the start-up presentation. Let's clear the data from the datasheet:

1. Open and maximize **MYPRES2.PPT**, if necessary.

2. Add a new slide (slide 4) to the end of the presentation.

3. Add the title **Business Travel**.

4. Delete the Body object.

5. Select the **Graph tool** and drag a box approximately the size of the Body object. The Graph window opens, displaying the sample data and chart.

6. Maximize the Graph window and move the **Chart window** down (place the mouse pointer on the Chart title and drag down).

7. Click on the **Datasheet window** to activate it.

8. Click on the corner **control box** to select all the data. Figure 9.3 shows the corner control box.

9. Choose **Edit, Clear** to open the Clear dialog box. By default, the Clear Data option is checked. If you want to remove only the number format, check Clear Format; to clear both data and number format, check Clear All.

10. Click on **OK** to clear all the data from the datasheet.

11. Click anywhere on the datasheet to deselect it.

12. Observe your datasheet. It should match that shown in Figure 9.4.

Figure 9.3   **The corner control box**

Corner control box

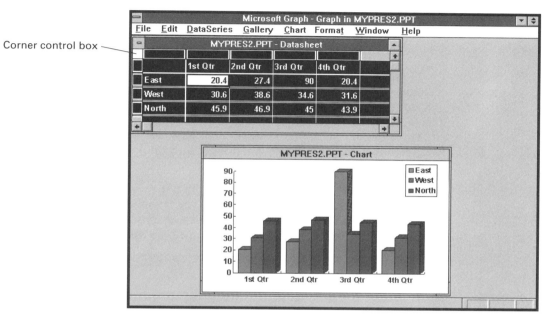

Figure 9.4   **The empty datasheet**

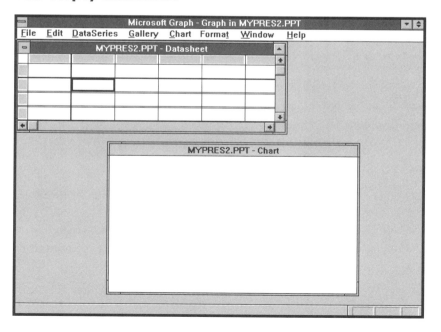

13. Observe the Chart window. When you clear the datasheet, there is no information available for Graph to plot.

CHANGING THE DEFAULTS FOR THE DATASHEET WINDOW

In spite of all your work, Graph will display that sample data again the next time you open the program. This is because the sample data is the default. Unless you are planning to use the sample data and chart in all your presentations, once you have cleared the datasheet, you will probably want to save the empty datasheet as the default. Then, you won't have to clear the datasheet every time you want to create a chart.

In addition to changing the datasheet default, you can also change any of the chart defaults. If you always create a certain type of chart with the legend in a certain position, you might want to save that chart type and legend position as the default.

Here's the general procedure for changing the Microsoft Graph defaults:

• Clear the datasheet, or enter the data you want in the default datasheet.

• Choose a chart type and any formatting options you want for your default chart. For example, if you always create pie charts, you would choose Gallery, Pie and select a pie-chart option.

• Choose *File, Set As Default Graph*. The new defaults are saved in the file DEFAULT.GRA in your Windows directory on your hard drive.

Note: If you ever want the original default settings for the Datasheet and Chart windows, you need only to delete DEFAULT.GRA from your Windows directory. When you delete DEFAULT.GRA, PowerPoint restores the original Microsoft Graph settings—the sample data and chart.

Let's save the empty datasheet as the default:

1. Choose **File, Set As Default Chart**. Microsoft Graph creates a file called DEFAULT.GRA, which is saved in the Windows directory on your hard drive. This file contains the new settings for the Graph window. Even if you were to return to the slide without updating the chart, the next time you created a chart, the Graph window would open with an empty datasheet.

2. Choose **File, Exit And Return To MYPRES2.PPT** and click on **No**. Do not update the chart in your presentation. It may take close to a minute, but the Graph window closes, returning you to the slide, which displays only the slide title.

PRACTICE YOUR SKILLS

Let's redraw the chart object on the slide:

1. Select the **Graph tool**.

2. Drag a box approximately the same size as the one you just removed from the slide.

ENTERING DATA FOR THE PIE CHART

As you learned in Chapter 8, a data series is a group of related values, such as all the sales for a particular region. Each individual piece of data in a series is called a data point. In a pie chart, each data point is represented by a *data marker*, or slice of the pie.

A pie chart always consists of one data series and as many data points as necessary. The pie chart you are creating has one data series with four data points.

Let's enter data for the pie chart:

1. Click on the **Datasheet window** to activate it. By default, you can see four rows of the datasheet. You are going to create a pie chart with four data points, but because you do not enter data in the top row, you need *five* rows of the datasheet.

2. Lengthen the datasheet window so that five rows are visible. (Place the mouse pointer on the bottom border of the window and drag down.) While it is not necessary to lengthen the datasheet, it is easier if you can see all your data.

Now let's enter the data for the pie chart:

1. Select the cells from column 1, row 2 through column 1, row 5 (refer to Figure 9.5). Remember, the first row of the datasheet is reserved for labels. If you accidentally place data there, it will not be plotted in the chart.

Figure 9.5   **The completed labels**

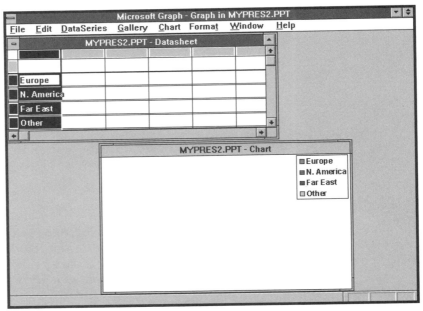

2. Starting in row 2, enter the following data, pressing **Enter** after each label:

   Europe

   N. America

   Far East

   Other

PRACTICE YOUR SKILLS

Let's complete the data for the pie chart:

1. Starting in row 2, enter the following values in the second column:

   551

   406

295

130

(Hint: Select the four cells and press **Enter** after each entry.)

2. Observe your chart. It should match that shown in Figure 9.6. Graph plots the data as a column chart, the default chart type.

Figure 9.6   **The completed datasheet and default chart**

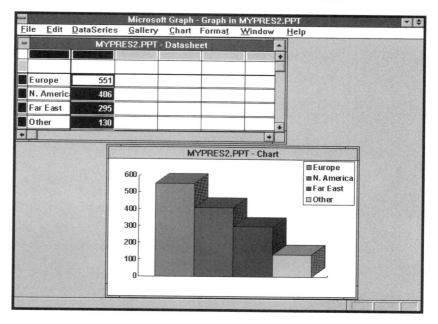

CHANGING THE CHART TYPE

You can change the chart type from the default column chart by choosing a new chart type from the Gallery menu. When you choose a chart type, Graph displays a gallery of chart formats from which to choose.

Figure 9.7 illustrates the pie-chart styles available in the Chart Gallery for pie charts.

Figure 9.7   **The Chart Gallery for pie charts**

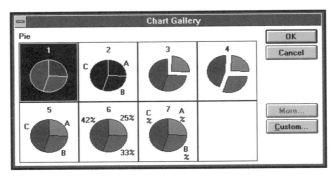

Here's the general procedure for changing the chart type:

- Click on the Chart window.
- Choose *Gallery* and select a chart type. The Chart Gallery is displayed.
- Select the chart format of your choice.
- Click on OK.

Let's change the chart type:

1. Click on the **Chart window** to make it active.

2. Choose **Gallery, Pie**. The Chart Gallery dialog box opens, displaying pie-chart formatting options.

3. Click on pie style **6** (the format for a colored pie chart with labeled percentages) to choose that chart format.

4. Click on **OK**. The bar chart changes to a pie chart.

5. Observe the chart—but don't panic. Your chart should have one visible data marker and match that shown in Figure 9.8. In the next section, you will fix the chart so that you can see all the data markers.

CHANGING THE DATA SERIES

Earlier in this chapter, you learned that a pie chart consists of only one data series and as many data points as necessary. Microsoft Graph provides you with two data-series options: You can enter data series into the datasheet either in rows or in columns.

Figure 9.8   **The pie chart with one data marker**

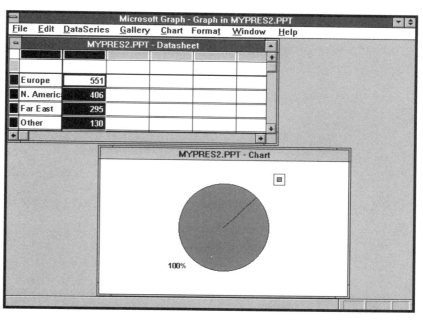

The *DataSeries setting* (rows or columns) affects the way Graph plots your chart. If you enter your data in columns but have the DataSeries option set to rows, then Graph plots the chart using each row as a separate data series. A pie chart can have only one data series, so if you have the DataSeries option incorrectly set, Graph will plot the first data point as the entire series. A pie chart with one pie slice? No thanks. You need to make sure that Graph reads the data series as you intend.

You can create a pie chart by using either DataSeries setting, as long as you understand these rules:

- If the series is set to rows, the first row of the datasheet, starting with the second cell, is reserved for legend labels. The second row, starting with the second cell, starts the data to be plotted.

- If the series is set to columns, the first column of the datasheet, starting with the second cell, is reserved for legend labels. The second column, starting with the second row, starts the data to be plotted.

So, if you create a pie chart and find that only one data point has been plotted, check the DataSeries option before you panic.

Let's change the DataSeries option for your pie chart:

1. Observe the datasheet. The double lines between rows indicate that Graph is set to read each row of the datasheet as a separate data series. Because a pie chart has only one data series, Graph can plot only the data for Europe. This is why our pie chart shows only one data marker (or slice).

2. Choose **DataSeries, Series In Columns** to change the datasheet so that Graph reads each column as a data series.

3. Observe the datasheet. The double lines between columns indicate that the DataSeries In Columns option is selected.

4. Observe the chart. It shows all four data markers and should match that shown in Figure 9.9.

Figure 9.9   **The pie chart with data in columns**

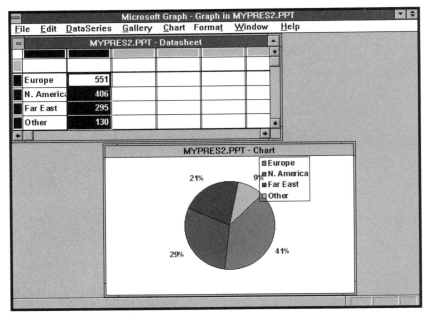

CHANGING LEGEND OPTIONS

The legend works as a key to identify the data markers or slices in your pie chart. By default, when you create a chart, Graph displays the legend somewhere near the upper-left corner of your Chart window. It has a thin line border and the text is 18 point. You can change any of these defaults. In fact, you may *need* to change them; if you change the chart type, chances are that the legend will appear on top of some portion of your chart (as it does in Figure 9.9).

Here's the general procedure for changing the legend options:

- From Microsoft Graph, double-click on the legend in the Chart window. The *Area Patterns* dialog box opens.

- Select the border and area options desired.

- Click on the Font button to change the format of the legend text.

- Click on the Legend button to reposition the legend.

- Click on OK.

Let's change the legend options:

1. Activate the **Chart window**, if necessary.

2. Observe the legend. It is covering a portion of your chart.

3. Double-click on the legend to open the Area Patterns dialog box.

4. Under **Border**, choose **None** to remove the border around the legend.

The Area Pattern, Chart Fonts, and Legend dialog boxes are linked. The Area Pattern dialog box includes buttons that open the Chart Fonts and Legend dialog boxes. The Chart Fonts dialog box includes buttons that open the Area Pattern and Legend dialog boxes. Similarly, the Legend dialog box includes buttons that open the Area Pattern and Chart Fonts dialog boxes. You can make changes to all three dialog boxes before returning to the chart; for our purposes, let's make changes in the Chart Fonts and Legend dialog boxes:

1. Click on **Font** to open the Chart Fonts dialog box.

2. From the Size list box, select **20**.

3. Click on **Legend** to open the Legend dialog box.

4. Select **Bottom** to position the legend at the bottom of the chart.

5. Click on **OK**. The border around the legend is removed, the text is enlarged slightly, and the legend appears at the bottom of the chart. (**Note:** You may need to move the Chart window up to see the changes to the legend.)

6. Return to the presentation to update the chart. (Choose **File, Exit And Return To MYPRES2.PPT** and click on **Yes**.)

7. Deselect the chart and compare your slide to that shown in Figure 9.10.

8. Save the file

Figure 9.10   **The pie chart with formatted legend**

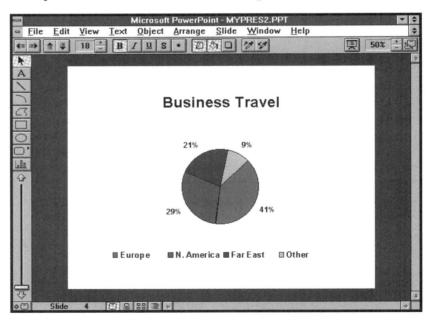

ENHANCING A PIE CHART

If a plain pie chart looks great in a presentation, think how much nicer a customized pie chart will look. As with everything in PowerPoint, there is a lot you can do to enhance your pie chart.

For example, you can add emphasis to certain slices either by separating them from the rest of the chart or by recoloring them.

EXPLODING A PIE CHART

One way to enhance your pie chart is by *exploding,* or dragging away from the pie, one or more sections. If there is a particular piece of data that you want to emphasize, you can explode the pie slice representing that data. For example, if the data representing European sales is the most important part of your pie chart, you can drag the Europe slice away from the pie chart to draw attention to it.

You can explode as many slices as you want to; in fact, you can explode *all* the slices.

Here's the general procedure for exploding a pie-chart slice:

- Activate the Chart window.
- Click on the desired slice of the pie. Handles appear around the slice.
- Place the mouse pointer on the slice.
- Press and hold the mouse button.
- Drag the slice away from the pie.
- Release the mouse button.

Now let's explode the Europe slice in your pie chart:

1. Double-click on the chart to reopen Microsoft Graph.
2. Click on the **Chart window** to activate it, if necessary.
3. Click on the **Europe pie slice** (41%). Handles appear around the pie slice, indicating that it is selected.
4. Place the mouse pointer on the **Europe pie slice** and drag the slice out slightly. Your chart should match that shown in Figure 9.11.
5. Return to the presentation to update the chart (choose **File, Exit And Return To MYPRES2.PPT** and click on **Yes**).
6. Deselect the chart.
7. Save the file.

Figure 9.11   **The exploded pie in the Graph window**

	Microsoft Graph - Graph in MYPRES2.PPT		
File Edit DataSeries Gallery Chart Format Window Help			

MYPRES2.PPT - Datasheet

Europe	551				
N. America	406				
Far East	295				
Other	130				

MYPRES2.PPT - Chart

21%   9%

29%   41%

■ Europe   ■ N. America   ■ Far East   □ Other

CREATING A DOUBLE-EXPLODED PIE CHART

You can fit more than one pie chart on a slide, which can be useful when you want to compare data. For example, in the first part of this chapter, you created a pie chart showing the breakdown of Global Travel business travelers by region and exploded the European region from the pie. You might want to create another pie chart to display detailed information about this European pie slice.

When you create a double-exploded pie chart, you place two charts on one slide. The first chart gives an overview; for example, the number of business travelers by region. The second chart then shows a breakdown of one section of the first pie chart. To continue our example, if Europe accounts for 41 percent of business travelers, then a second pie chart might show the breakdown of the European countries to which business people travel.

COPYING CHARTS

You can create two charts from scratch on the same slide. However, if you have already created one or both of the charts you want to use in the double-exploded pie, why do all that work again? You can copy an existing chart and paste it on another slide.

Here's the general procedure for copying a chart:

- Select the chart you want to copy.

- Choose Edit, Copy to place a copy of the chart on the Clipboard.

- Move to or add the slide on which you want to place the chart.

- Choose Edit, Paste. A copy of the chart is pasted on the new slide.

- Double-click on the chart to edit it, if necessary.

Let's begin creating a double-exploded pie chart:

1. Add a new slide (slide 5) to the end of the presentation.

2. Add the title **European Travel**.

3. Delete the Body object.

4. Move to slide 4. This slide displays the pie chart you just created.

5. Select the pie chart and choose **Edit, Copy** to place a copy of the chart on the Clipboard.

6. Move to slide 5 and choose **Edit, Paste** to paste the pie chart on the new slide.

7. Observe the slide. The pie chart you copied from slide 4 now appears on slide 5. You will use this pie chart as the basis for a double-exploded pie chart.

8. Observe the legend. It stretches across the bottom of the screen and takes up a lot of space. It's a good idea to condense the legend before you add another chart to the slide.

9. Double-click on the chart to open the Microsoft Graph window.

10. Click on the legend to select it.

11. Choose **Format, Legend**.

12. Select **Left** and click on **OK** to move the legend to the left of the chart.

13. Return to the presentation to update the chart.

 RESIZING CHARTS

Right now, the first pie chart is taking up most of the workspace on your slide. In order to fit a second chart on the slide, you need to resize the first chart. There are three ways you can do this:

- *Cropping* changes the frame, but not the chart. In other words, you eliminate the empty white space around the chart without changing the size of the chart itself.

- *Scaling* resizes the entire chart window proportionally.

- *Resizing* changes the size of the chart, but not necessarily proportionally.

If you are trying to place two charts on one slide, it is a good idea to try cropping the charts before you resize them.

Here's the general procedure for cropping a chart:

- Select the chart in Slide view.

- Choose *Object, Crop Picture*. The mouse pointer turns into a Cropping tool.

- Place the Cropping tool over one of the selection handles so that you can see the handle through the hole in the center of the Cropping tool.

- Drag the Cropping tool down and over until you cannot see any extra white space.

- Repeat the above steps as necessary to remove white space from the rest of the chart.

Use this option when you do not want to affect the size of the chart while reducing the white space around it.

Here's the general procedure for scaling the chart:

- Select the chart in Slide view.

- Choose Object, Scale.

- Type the percentage by which you want to resize the chart.

- Click on OK. The chart is scaled by the percentage you indicated.

Scale the chart when you want to resize the chart proportionally.

Here's the general procedure for resizing the chart manually:

- Select the chart in Slide view.
- Place the mouse pointer on one of the selection handles.
- Drag the selection handle to resize the chart.

If you need to resize the chart, but it doesn't matter if you keep the original proportions, use this option.

Let's crop the pie chart:

1. Click on the pie chart to select it.

2. Choose **Object, Crop Picture**. The mouse pointer becomes a Cropping tool, as shown in Figure 9.12.

Figure 9.12   **Cropping the chart**

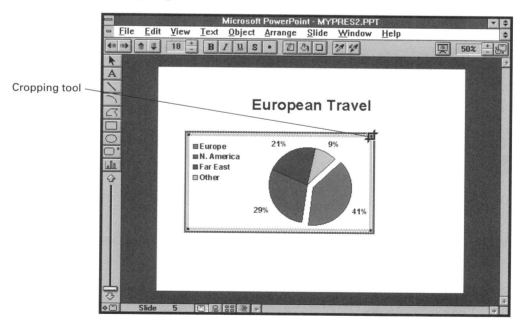

3. Place the center of the Cropping tool over the upper-right selection handle of the chart (refer to Figure 9.12).

4. Press and hold the **left mouse button**. The mouse pointer becomes a 90-degree angle and a dotted line appears around the chart.

5. Drag in and down until the dotted outline is just above and to the right of the chart (refer to Figure 9.12).

6. Release the mouse button. The chart is redrawn with the new, smaller frame.

7. Place the Cropping tool on the lower-left selection handle.

8. Press the **left mouse button** and drag in and up until the dotted outline is just below and to the left of the chart.

9. Release the mouse button and observe the slide. Your chart should match that shown in Figure 9.12.

10. Click anywhere to deselect the chart.

Now let's move the chart to the left edge of the slide:

1. Select the chart.

2. Place the mouse pointer on the chart and drag it to the left edge of the slide. Refer to Figure 9.13 to position the chart.

3. Save the file.

ADDING A SECOND CHART TO THE SLIDE AND DELETING THE LEGEND

You don't have to display the legend as part of your chart. In fact, if you choose one of the pie-chart styles that includes labels for each pie slice, you might not want to have a legend, too.

Here's the general procedure for deleting the legend from your chart:

• Select the legend.

• Choose *Chart, Delete Legend*.

Note: If you decide at a later date that you need the legend, you can display it again by choosing *Chart, Add Legend*.

Figure 9.13   **The chart after resizing and moving**

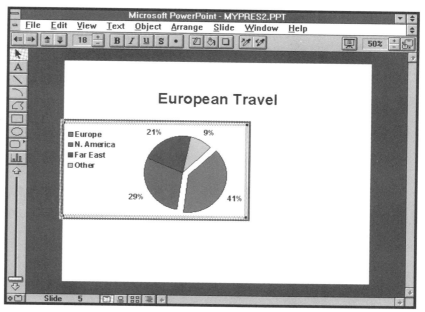

Now you're ready to add a second chart to the slide:

1. Select the **Graph tool** and drag a box of the approximate size and at the position of the one shown in Figure 9.14.

2. Maximize the Graph window and move the **Chart window** down, if necessary.

3. Choose **Gallery, Pie**, select the pie-chart style **5**, and click on **OK** to create a labeled pie chart when you enter data in the datasheet. You don't need to wait until you enter data to select the type of chart you want.

4. Choose **DataSeries, Series In Columns**.

5. Choose **Chart, Delete Legend**. Since you chose a pie style that includes labels for each pie slice, the legend is redundant.

Figure 9.14   **Creating the second chart**

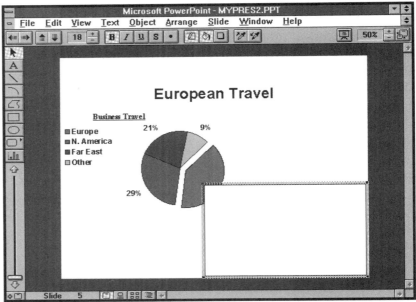

PRACTICE YOUR SKILLS

Let's enter data for the second pie chart:

1. Enter the following data in the datasheet:

Spain	77
Germany	191
England	235
Other	48

2. Compare your slide to that shown in Figure 9.15.

3. Return to the slide to update the chart.

4. Save the file.

Figure 9.15 **The second pie chart**

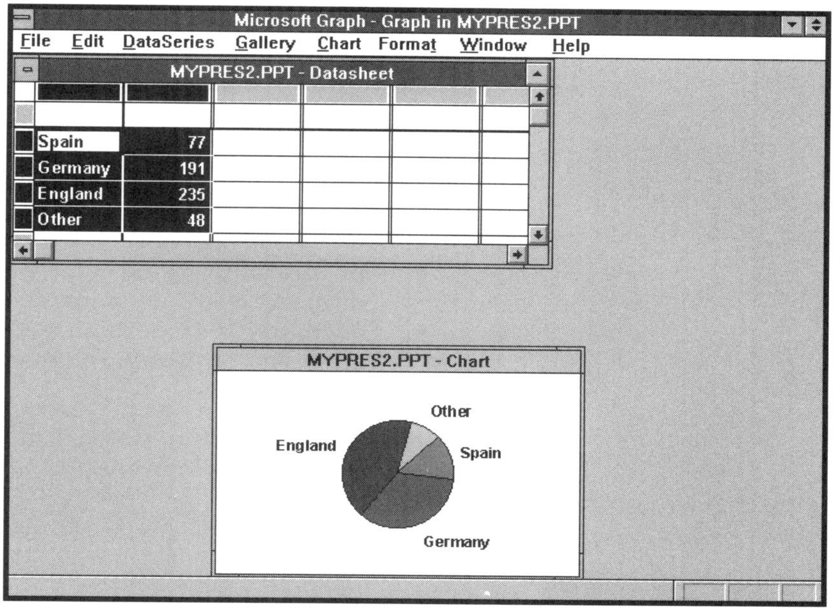
Microsoft Graph - Graph in MYPRES2.PPT
File Edit DataSeries Gallery Chart Format Window Help
MYPRES2.PPT - Datasheet
Spain 77
Germany 191
England 235
Other 48
MYPRES2.PPT - Chart
Other
England
Spain
Germany

RECOLORING A PIE SLICE

You have two pie charts on your slide and they look fine, but both use the default colors, so your audience might find it difficult to distinguish between them. You can recolor the second pie to indicate its relationship to the first pie. For example, if the second pie shows a breakdown by country of the Europe pie slice, you might want to change the color of the second pie so that all the slices are the same color as the first pie's Europe slice. Then, you could change the patterns in the second pie to distinguish between those slices.

Here's the general procedure for recoloring a chart:

- Double-click on the chart to open the Microsoft Graph window.
- Double-click on the pie slice you want to recolor.
- From the Foreground drop-down list, select a color.
- From the Background drop-down list, select a color, if necessary.
- From the Pattern drop-down list, select a pattern.

- Check Apply To All if you want to change the color of all the slices in the pie chart.

- Click on OK.

Let's recolor the second pie chart:

1. Double-click on the second pie chart to open Microsoft Graph and edit that chart.

2. Double-click on the **Spain pie slice** in the Chart window to open the Area Patterns dialog box. This dialog box gives you several options for changing the color and pattern of the selected pie slice, as well as the style, color, and weight of the border. The Pattern, Foreground, and Background options all work together to determine the pattern and color of the selected item.

3. Click on the **Foreground** drop-down list to display the available color options for the foreground of the pie slice.

4. Click on the **Foreground** drop-down list again to close the list. Do not select a new color.

5. Click on the **Background** drop-down list to display the available background color options. Changing the background color will affect the pie only if you choose a pattern other than Solid for your pie slice.

6. Click on the **Pattern** drop-down list to display the available patterns. The patterns are created by mixing the foreground and background colors. For example, if your foreground color is blue and your background color is white, your Pattern choices are blue and white.

7. Check the **Apply To All** option (located below the Cancel button). Selecting this option changes the color for the entire chart.

8. Observe the Area box. The pattern and color are set to Automatic. If you return to the chart now, the chart colors will not change because they are already formatted with the automatic (default) colors.

9. Click on **Custom**. The Spain pie slice is formatted in the default color. If you do not choose Custom, the pie chart will not change—Graph will simply reapply the default color to each slice.

10. Click on **OK** to close the Area Patterns dialog box and format the chart with the new color.

11. Observe the chart. Because you selected the Apply To All and Custom options, each slice of the pie chart is formatted in the same color as the Spain pie slice. Conveniently, this is also the same color as the Europe pie slice. Now it is more obvious that the second pie chart is related to the first pie chart's Europe pie slice.

Because the chart is all the same color, it is difficult to distinguish between the different countries. Let's change the patterns so that each slice of the pie has a unique pattern:

1. Double-click on the **Spain pie slice**.

2. Click on the **Pattern** drop-down list and select a pattern for your pie slice.

3. Click on **OK**.

4. Double-click on another pie slice.

5. From the **Pattern** drop-down list, select a new pattern for the pie slice and click on **OK**.

PRACTICE YOUR SKILLS

Let's finish customizing the pie chart:

1. Change the pattern for each of the other slices in the pie chart. Make sure that you use a different pattern for each pie slice. (Hint: You must select each slice of the pie to change it's pattern.)

2. Return to the slide to update the chart.

3. Save the file.

CREATING TITLES FOR PIE CHARTS

If you have two pie charts on a slide, it helps lessen the confusion if you add a title to each chart. As you know, you can add unattached text labels to charts in Slide view.

Here's the general procedure for adding a title to the chart in Slide view:

- Select the Text tool.
- Place the insertion point on the slide above the chart.
- Type a title for the chart.
- Select the Selection tool.
- Select the title.
- Change the format, if necessary.
- Move the title to center it above the chart, if necessary.

Let's add a title to each of the pie charts:

1. Select the **Text tool**.
2. Place the insertion point on the slide above the first pie chart.
3. Type **Business Travel**.
4. Select the **Selection tool**.
5. Select the text you typed in step 3.
6. Choose **Text, Font** and select **Times New Roman** (or an equivalent font).
7. Click on the **Underline button** (located on the Toolbar, it displays as an underlined *u*) to underline the text.
8. Position the title above the Business Travel chart as shown in Figure 9.16.
9. Save the file.

PRACTICE YOUR SKILLS

Let's create a title for the second chart:

1. Create the 18-point, underlined, Times Roman title **European Travel Breakdown** for the second chart.
2. Refer to Figure 9.16 to position the title above the European Travel chart.
3. Save the file.
4. Close the presentation.

Figure 9.16   **The double-exploded pie chart**

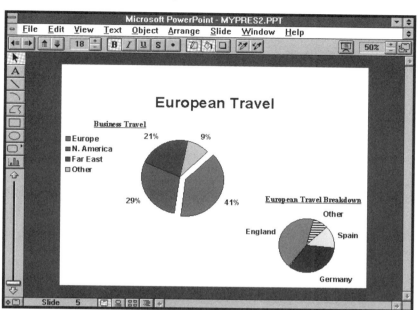

PRACTICE YOUR SKILLS

Wow, now you know everything you've ever wanted to about charts! Congratulations on making it this far. You've learned several important PowerPoint charting techniques in the past three chapters. The following group of activities gives you an opportunity to practice these techniques.

Note: In case you need to refresh your memory about a certain procedure, the relevant chapter number is included in parentheses at the end of each step.

Follow these steps to create the organization chart shown in Figure 9.17:

1. Create a new presentation (Chapter 7).

2. Add the title **Travel Literature** to the new slide (Chapter 7).

3. Delete the Body object (Chapter 7).

4. Draw a rectangle the approximate size of those in Figure 9.17 (Chapter 7).

Figure 9.17   **The completed organization chart**

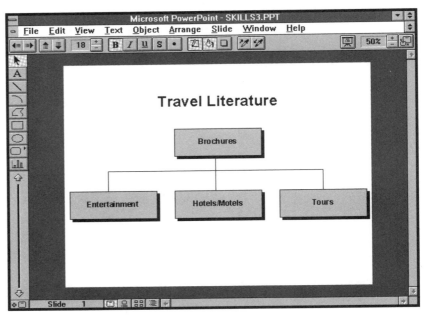

5. Duplicate the rectangle three times (Chapter 7).

6. Arrange the boxes to match Figure 9.17 (Chapter 7).

7. Type the following text into the organization chart (Chapter 7):

top box: **Brochures**

second row, left: **Entertainment**

second row, middle: **Hotels/Motels**

second row, right: **Tours**

8. Using Figure 9.17 as a guide, add lines to the organization chart to connect the boxes (Chapter 7). (Hint: Be sure to draw the lines *into* the boxes.)

9. Select the vertical lines and send them behind the boxes (Chapter 7).

10. Change the fill of the top box to **GY6** and add the shadow effect **BK** (Chapter 7).

11. Apply the fill and shadow you applied in step 10 to the remaining boxes in the organization chart (Chapter 7). (Hint: Use the **Pick Up Style** and **Apply Style buttons**.)

12. Align the tops of the boxes in the bottom row (Chapter 7).

13. Save the presentation as **SKILLS3** (Chapter 7).

14. Compare your slide with Figure 9.17.

15. Group the organization chart as one large object (Chapter 7).

Follow these steps to create the slide shown in Figure 9.18:

1. Add a new slide to the presentation (Chapter 7).

2. Add the title **Sales Report (in thousands)** (Chapter 7).

3. Delete the Body object (Chapter 7).

4. Using the **Graph tool**, draw a box of the size and at the position of the Body object you deleted (Chapter 8).

Figure 9.18   **The completed column chart**

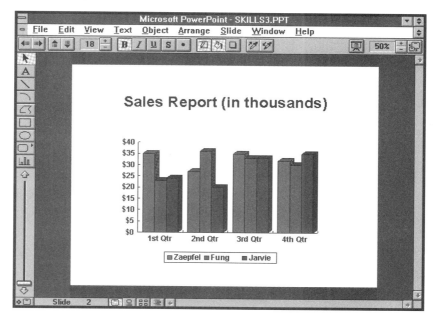

5. Maximize the Graph window and move the **Chart window** down, if necessary (Chapter 8).

6. Enter the following labels in the first column (Chapter 8). (Hint: Begin entering the labels in the second row of the first column.)

Zaepfel

Fung

Jarvie

7. Type in the following new data (Chapter 8):

	1st Qtr	2nd Qtr	3rd Qtr	4th Qtr
Zaepfel	35	27	35	32
Fung	23	36	33	30
Jarvie	24	20	33	35

8. Change the y-axis format to **$#,##0;($#,##0)** (Chapter 8).

9. Place the legend at the bottom of the chart (Chapter 8).

10. Return to the presentation to place the chart on the slide (Chapter 8).

11. Save the presentation (Chapter 2).

12. Compare the slide to Figure 9.18. (The y-axis values displayed will vary, depending on the size of the chart.)

Follow these steps to create the slide shown in Figure 9.19:

1. Add a new slide (slide 3) to the end of the presentation (Chapter 7).

2. Add the title **Computer Spray Sales** (Chapter 7).

3. Delete the Body object (Chapter 7).

4. Using the **Graph tool**, draw a box of the size and at the position of the Body object you deleted (Chapter 9).

5. Change the DataSeries setting to read in columns (Chapter 9).

Figure 9.19   **The completed pie chart**

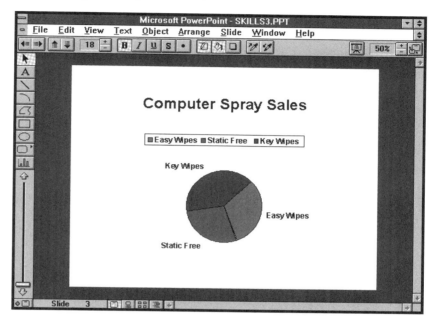

6. In the first column, add the following labels (Chapter 9):

   Easy Wipes

   Static Free

   Key Wipes

7. In the second column, add the following values (Chapter 9):

   82

   73

   101

8. Change the chart type to **Pie** and select style **5** (Chapter 9).

9. Place the legend at the top of the chart (Chapter 9).

10. Return to the presentation to place the chart on the slide (Chapter 8).

11. Save the presentation (Chapter 2).

12. Compare the slide to Figure 9.19.

13. Close the presentation (Chapter 7).

SUMMARY

In this chapter, you explored pie charts. You now know how to create a pie chart, how to clear the datasheet, how to set Microsoft Graph defaults, how to change the chart type, how to change the data series, and how to change legend options. You also learned how to explode a pie chart, how to create a double-exploded pie chart, how to copy a chart, how to resize a chart, and how to recolor a pie slice.

Here's a quick reference for the techniques you learned in this chapter:

Desired Result	How to Do It
Create a pie chart	Move to the slide to which you want to add the pie chart; choose the **Graph tool** from the Tool Palette; draw a box of the approximate size you want your chart to be; choose **Gallery, Pie** to open the Chart Gallery dialog box displaying sample pie-chart styles; choose the pie-chart format you want; click on **OK**
Clear data from the datasheet	In the datasheet, click on the corner **control box** to select all the cells; choose **Edit, Clear**; click on **OK**
Change Microsoft Graph defaults	Clear the datasheet, or enter the data you want in the default datasheet; choose a chart type and any formatting options you want for your default chart; choose **File, Set As Default Graph**
Change the chart type	Click on the **Chart window**, choose **Gallery** and select a chart type, select the chart style you want, click on **OK**

Desired Result	How to Do It
Change the legend options	From Microsoft Graph, double-click on the legend; select the border and area options desired; click on the **Font** button to change the format of the legend text; click on the **Legend** button to reposition the legend; click on **OK**
Explode a slice from the pie chart	Activate the **Chart window**, click on the desired slice of the pie, place the mouse pointer on the slice, press and hold the **mouse button**, drag the slice away from the pie, release the mouse button
Copying a chart	Select the chart you want to copy; choose **Edit, Copy** to place a copy of the chart on the Clipboard; move to or add the slide on which you want to place the chart; choose **Edit, Paste**; double-click on the chart to edit it, if necessary
Crop a chart	Select the chart; choose **Object, Crop Picture**; place the Cropping tool over one of the selection handles so that you can see the handle through the hole in the center of the Cropping tool; drag the Cropping tool down and over until you cannot see any extra white space; repeat the above steps as necessary to remove white space from the rest of the chart
Scale a chart	Select the chart; choose **Object, Scale**; type the percentage by which you want to resize the chart; click on **OK**
Resize a chart manually	Select the chart, place the mouse pointer on one of the selection handles, drag the handle to resize the chart
Delete the legend from a chart	Select the legend and choose **Chart, Delete Legend**

Desired Result	How to Do It
Recolor a chart	Double-click on the chart to open the Microsoft Graph window; double-click on the pie slice you want to recolor; from the **Foreground** drop-down list, select a color; from the **Background** drop-down list, select a color, if necessary; from the **Pattern** drop-down list, select a pattern; check **Apply To All** if you want to change the color of all the slices in the pie chart; click on **OK**
Add a title to the chart in Slide view	Select the **Text tool**; place the insertion point on the slide above the chart; type a title for the chart; select the **Selection tool**; select the title; change the format, if necessary; move the title to center it above the chart, if necessary

In the next chapter, you'll further explore templates and slide masters. You will learn how to apply a template to a presentation, how to change the background color of a template, how to change chart colors in a template, how to create a logo for a template, how to insert slide numbers, how to remove background items from a slide, and how to apply a presentation as a template.

IF YOU'RE STOPPING HERE

If you need to break off here, please exit PowerPoint. If you want to proceed directly to the next chapter, please do so now.

CHAPTER 10: ADVANCED TEMPLATES AND SLIDE MASTERS

Customizing a
Template

Applying a
Presentation as
a Template

In Chapter 6, you learned that you can apply any one of PowerPoint's 160 templates to your presentation. The *template* is a set of masters and a color scheme that give consistency. In this chapter, you will create your own template by customizing a PowerPoint template.

When you are done working through this chapter, you will know

- How to apply a template to a presentation
- How to change the background color of a template
- How to change chart colors in a template
- How to create a logo for a template
- How to insert slide numbers
- How to remove background items from a slide
- How to apply a presentation as a template

CUSTOMIZING A TEMPLATE

As you learned in Chapter 6, a template consists of a set of slide masters and their color scheme. It includes all the basic elements—colors and formatting—that you need to create a presentation. You can use any of the 160 templates that come with PowerPoint as a basis for creating your own template.

 ### APPLYING A TEMPLATE TO THE PRESENTATION

Before you can customize a PowerPoint template, you have to apply one to your presentation. As you know, PowerPoint's templates are stored in the TEMPLATE directory on your hard drive. (The TEMPLATE directory is located in the POWERPNT directory.)

Here's the general procedure for adding a template to your presentation:

- Choose File, Apply Template.
- Move to the directory that holds the template you want to apply.
- Select the template you want to apply to your presentation.
- Click on OK.

If you are not running PowerPoint on your computer, please start it now. Close all open presentations except the start-up presentation. Let's apply a template to your presentation:

1. Open and maximize **MYPRES2.PPT**, if necessary.

2. Save the file. It is a good idea to save your presentation before you apply a template. Then, if something goes wrong, you lose nothing but time.

3. Choose **File, Apply Template**.

4. Move to the **POWERPNT** directory, if necessary.

5. Double-click on the **TEMPLATE** directory. You should choose a template that is appropriate for the type of presentation you are creating. For example, MYPRES2.PPT is intended to be run as an on-screen slide show, so you should choose a template that was created specifically for slide shows. As you learned in Chapter 6, these templates are stored in the VIDSCREN directory.

6. Double-click on the **VIDSCREN** directory.

7. Scroll down and select **metlbarv.ppt**.

8. Observe the preview box. Your screen should match that shown in Figure 10.1.

Figure 10.1   **The Apply Template dialog box with METLBARV.PPT selected**

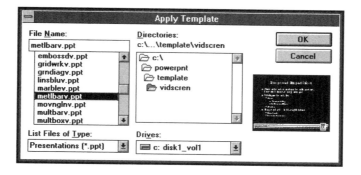

9. Click on **OK** to apply the template METLBARV.PPT to MYPRES2-.PPT. The Slide Master, Notes Master, Outline Master, and Handout Master from the template become the masters for MYPRES2.PPT. At this point, you need to be concerned only with the Slide Master. You will learn more about the other masters in Chapter 12.

10. Observe the screen message: *Updating graphs with new color scheme.* Depending on the speed of your computer, this might take quite a while, so relax and enjoy a cup of coffee. If after five minutes the color scheme still has not been updated, you might need to turn off your computer and start again.

Note: Your computer might freeze up if you have several charts in the presentation to which you are applying a template. If you reboot your computer and still are unable to apply a template to the presentation, you may have to apply templates to your presentations before you create charts.

11. Observe the screen. The slides are formatted with the color scheme and design of the METLBARV.PPT template.

 MODIFYING THE TEMPLATE

PowerPoint formats your presentation based on the formats saved in the Slide Master of the template you apply. You can change any or all of the template formats once you have applied the template.

For example, if you like the look of a certain template, but not its colors, you can apply the template and then change the colors to ones that you find more appealing.

Here's the general procedure for changing a color in a template:

- Apply the template you want to the presentation.

- Choose Slide, Color Scheme.

- From the Scheme list, select the color you want to change.

- Click on Change A Color to open the Change A Color dialog box.

- Select a new color. You can choose a color from the grid or the Scheme Colors list, or you can click on More Colors to create your own color.

- Click on OK to return to the Color Scheme dialog box. (If you created your own color, you must click on OK twice to return to the Color Scheme dialog box.)

- Click on OK to return to your presentation and register the color change.

Let's change the color of the Title object:

1. Choose **Slide, Color Scheme** to open the Color Scheme dialog box. Any changes that you make here will affect the entire presentation unless you specify otherwise.

2. Click on the title-text color (**YW8**) to select the color that you want to change.

3. Click on **Change A Color** to open the Change A Color dialog box.

4. Observe the dialog box, shown in Figure 10.2. As you learned in Chapter 5, the Change A Color dialog box displays a grid of available colors, a list of the colors in the current color scheme, and the current color of the selected item.

Figure 10.2　**The Change A Color dialog box with BG5 selected**

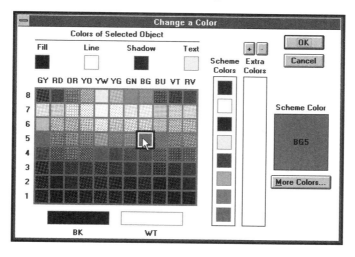

5. In the color grid, click on the color located at the intersection of column BG and row 5 (refer to Figure 10.2).

6. Click on **OK** to return to the Color Scheme dialog box. BG5 replaces YW8 as the scheme color for title text.

7. Observe the Apply To box in the bottom-left corner of the dialog box. The All Slides option is selected. This means PowerPoint is set to recolor the title text for all the slides in

your presentation with BG5. (By default, any changes you make to the color scheme are applied to all the slides in your presentation. If you want to change a color for one slide only, you select the This Slide option in the Apply To box.)

8. Click on **OK** to close the Color Scheme dialog box and return to the presentation.

9. Observe the slide. The title color is blue-green instead of yellow.

10. Save the file.

CHANGING THE DEFAULT CHART COLORS

In the last chapter, you learned that you can change colors for any or all of the data markers on a particular chart without affecting the default colors for the rest of the charts in your presentation. You can also change default colors for the all charts in a presentation. If there is a particular color that you hate, this is the perfect opportunity to change that color in the Color Scheme dialog box so you will never be bothered by it again.

Data markers for charts are formatted using the bottom four colors in the Scheme list (beginning with Fills). The first data marker uses the fill color, the second data marker uses the first accent color, the third data marker uses the second accent color, and so on. To change default chart colors, you need only change any or all of these colors.

Here's the general procedure for changing the chart color scheme:

• Choose Slide, Color Scheme to open the Color Scheme dialog box. Charts are formatted using the bottom four colors in the Scheme list.

• Select the color you want to change. It must be one of the bottom four colors in the Scheme list.

• Click on Change A Color.

• Select the color you want from either the color grid or the Scheme Colors list. If you want, you can also create your own color by clicking on the More Colors button.

• Click on OK.

- Repeat the above steps as necessary until you are satisfied with the chart colors.

Let's change the color scheme for the charts:

1. Move to slide 3 and observe the column chart. The second data marker is now nearly the same color as the slide title. You want your chart to stand out, so it would be a good idea to change the color of that second data marker.

2. Choose **Slide, Color Scheme**.

3. Move the **Color Scheme dialog box** to the left side of the screen until the Far East data series is visible.

4. Observe the chart. The first data marker is red. This corresponds with the color in the Fills box. The second data marker is blue-green. This corresponds with the first accent color in the scheme.

5. In the Color Scheme dialog box, select the first accent color (**C**). This color is nearly the same as the title-text color. Let's change it.

6. Click on **Change A Color**.

You want to select a color that will work well with the background and the other chart colors. Red and yellow provide a good contrast, so let's change the second data marker to yellow:

1. In the color grid, select the color at the intersection of column YW and row 8.

2. Click on **OK** and observe the new accent color.

3. Click on **OK**. Using this method to change the chart colors changes the color on every chart in the presentation.

4. Observe the slide. The column chart now looks like a hot dog stand.

 INSERTING SLIDE NUMBERS

You can add a code to your Slide Master that will automatically number your slides. Then you can reference the slides in your presentation by number. When you insert the code, it will appear as two number symbols (##) in all views. To see the actual page numbers on the slide, you need to either view the slide in a slide show or print it.

Here's the general procedure for inserting page numbers on slides:

- Go to the Slide Master.
- Select the Text tool.
- Place your insertion point where you want to insert the code.
- Choose *Edit, Insert, Page Number*.
- Return to Slide View.
- Run the slide show to view the numbers.

Let's insert page numbers on the slides:

1. Choose **View, Slide Master**.
2. Select the **Text tool**.
3. Place the insertion point below the gray bar in the lower-left corner of the slide (refer to Figure 10.3).

Figure 10.3   **Inserting page numbers**

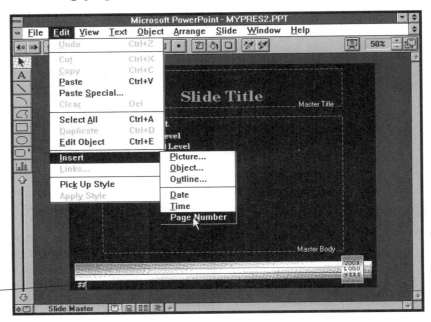

Insertion point

4. Choose **Edit, Insert, Page Number**. A number symbol appears at the insertion point.

5. Go to Slide view (click on the **Slide View button**). The page number still appears as a code.

6. Click on the **Slide Show button** (located on the Toolbar, it displays a miniature movie screen) to view the slide show.

7. Observe the page number. You can see page numbers when you run a slide show or print the slides.

8. Press **Esc** to stop the slide show and return to Slide view without viewing the rest of the slides.

 CREATING A LOGO

You can further enhance the appearance of your presentation by adding a logo to the slides. One effective way of customizing your presentations is to combine clip art, text, and drawn objects to create your own logos. You can create the logo directly on the Slide Master so that it appears in the same position on every slide.

Here's the general procedure for adding a logo to your presentation:

- Choose View, Slide Master.
- Choose File, Open Clip Art.
- Double-click on the clip-art file that contains the graphic you want to use as part of your logo.
- Double-click on the clip-art slide you want to use.
- Select the graphic and choose Edit, Copy to place a copy of it on the Clipboard.
- Choose File, Close to close the clip-art file. Do not save any changes.
- Choose Edit, Paste to place the graphic on your slide master.
- Choose Object, Scale to resize the graphic.
- Move the graphic to the appropriate place on your slide.
- Select the Text tool.
- Type the text for your logo.
- Select the Selection tool.

- Select and format the logo text, if necessary.

- Move the logo text to the appropriate place on your slide, if necessary.

- Move to Slide view to see the logo on the slide.

Let's create a logo to add to the Slide Master. First, we must copy the clip art on which we want to base the logo:

1. Choose **View, Slide Master**. Because you want the logo to appear on every slide, you need to create it on the Slide Master.

2. Choose **File, Open Clip Art**.

3. Double-click on **INTLMAPS.PPT**.

4. Double-click on the slide icon for the **World Globe (Western Hemisphere)** to select the slide and go directly to Slide view.

5. Select the globe.

6. Choose **Edit, Copy** to place a copy of the globe on the Clipboard. You don't want to edit the clip art in the clip-art file itself because you might want to use the original in the future.

7. Choose **File, Close** to close the clip-art file. Do not save any changes.

8. Choose **Edit, Paste**. A copy of the globe appears in the middle of the Slide Master, as shown in Figure 10.4.

The globe that appears on your screen is the same size and in the same position as the one you copied from the clip-art file. It needs to be edited so that it can serve as part of the logo:

1. Select the globe, if necessary, and choose **Object, Scale**.

2. In the Scale dialog box, type **30** and click on **OK** to reduce the globe to 30 percent of its original size.

The globe is now the perfect size to serve as a logo. Now we can prepare the slide master for your logo:

1. Select the gray bar at the bottom of the slide. The horizontal bar and the *logo placeholder*—the rectangle that says "*PLACE LOGO HERE*"—are actually two objects. You need to ungroup them.

Figure 10.4   **The globe before scaling**

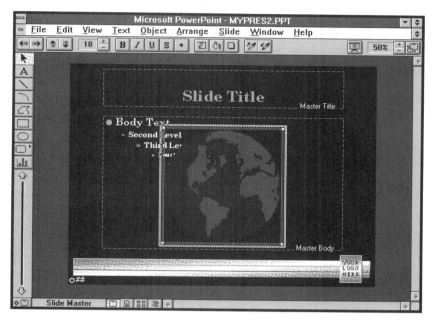

2. Choose **Arrange, Ungroup** to ungroup the horizontal bar and the logo placeholder.

3. Click anywhere on the slide to deselect the bar and placeholder.

4. Select the **logo placeholder** and press **Del** to delete it to make room for your globe logo.

5. Move the globe to the lower-right corner of the window (refer to Figure 10.5).

After you complete the graphic part of your logo, you might want to add text, such as the company name. Let's do that now:

1. Select the **Text tool** and click below the horizontal bar at the bottom of the screen to place the insertion point.

2. Type **Global Travel**.

3. Select the **Selection tool** and click on **Global Travel** (the text you just typed) to select the text.

Figure 10.5   **The globe logo**

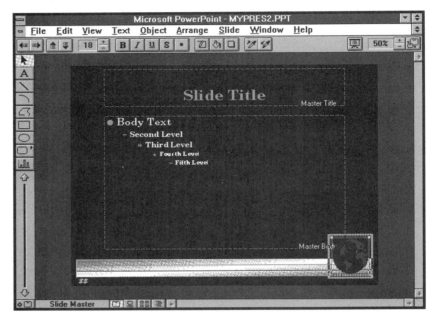

4. Click once on the **Font Size Minus (–) button** (located on the Toolbar, it is the bottom half of the fifth button from the left) to decrease the size to 16 points.

5. Refer to Figure 10.6 to move the text below the globe.

PRACTICE YOUR SKILLS

Let's make the logo match that shown in Figure 10.7:

1. Add a thin line border around the logo text. (Hint: You must select the text in order to change its attributes.)

2. Add a gray fill and gray shadow to the text. (Hint: Use the **Object** menu to add fill and shadow.)

3. Go to Slide view and view the logo on the first slide.

4. Save the file.

Figure 10.6   **The Global Travel logo**

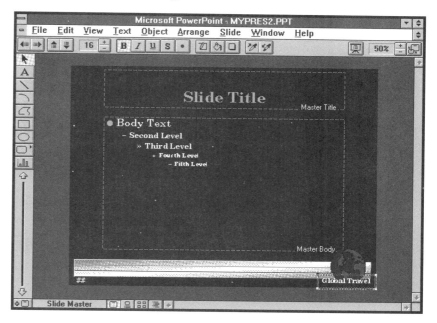

Figure 10.7   **The completed logo**

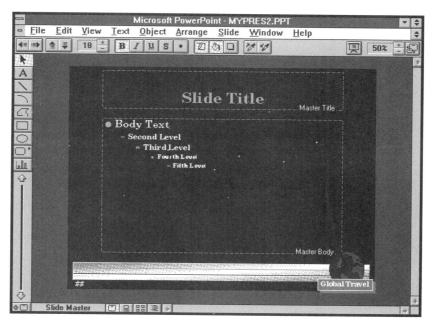

DELETING BACKGROUND ITEMS FROM A SLIDE

There may be times when you do not want background items to appear on an individual slide. For example, you might want to create a title slide to introduce the presentation, or you might create a chart that overlaps several of the background items. In these cases, you don't want the distraction of background items. When you turn off the display of background items on a slide, any objects placed on the Slide Master will be hidden.

Here's the general procedure for turning off the display of background items on a slide:

- Move to the slide on which you want to hide the background items.
- Choose *Slide, Follow Master, Background Items*. The background items disappear from that slide.

Here's the general procedure for returning the background items to the slide:

- Move to the slide on which you want to view the background items.
- Choose Slide, Follow Master, Background Items again. The background items are returned to the slide.

Let's turn off the display of background items on the double-exploded pie chart slide:

1. Move to slide 5 and observe it. You can't see all of the double-exploded pie chart because some of the items on the Slide Master are in the way.

2. Choose **Slide, Follow Master, Background Items**, as shown in Figure 10.8.

3. Observe the slide. The background items disappear from slide 5, allowing you to see both charts in their entirety (see Figure 10.9).

4. Choose **Slide, Follow Master** and observe that there is no check mark in front of Background Items. To display the items once more, you would select Slide, Follow Master, Background Items again.

Figure 10.8   **Turning off the display of background items**

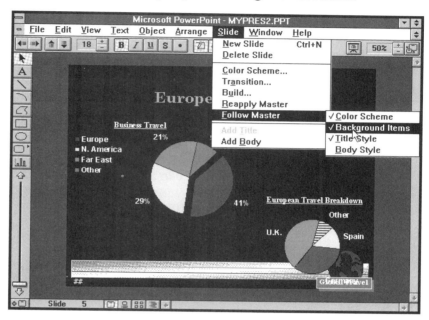

Figure 10.9   **The slide with background items hidden**

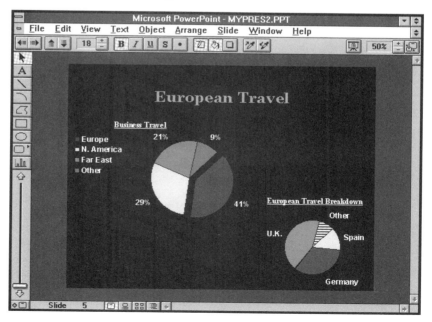

5. Press **Esc** three times to close the Slide menu without making any selections.

6. Move to slide 4. When you turn off the display of background items, it affects only the active slide. Therefore, you can still see the background items on this slide.

7. Move to slide 1.

8. Save the file.

APPLYING A PRESENTATION AS A TEMPLATE

In PowerPoint, you can apply any presentation as a template. When you do so, the open presentation uses the slide masters and color scheme from the presentation you are applying.

Here's the general procedure for applying a presentation as a template:

- Open the file to which you want to apply the template.

- Choose File, Apply Template.

- Move to the directory containing the presentation file you want to use as a template.

- Select the file.

- Click on OK.

Let's apply MYPRES2.PPT as a template:

1. Close **MYPRES2.PPT**.

2. Choose **File, New** to open a new file based on the default presentation.

3. Add the title **Global Travel**.

4. Choose **File, Apply Template** to open the Apply Template dialog box.

5. If necessary, go to the drive that contains your POWERWRK directory.

6. Open the **POWERWRK** directory and double-click on **MYPRES2-.PPT** to apply MYPRES2.PPT as the new presentation's template. The masters and color scheme from MYPRES2.PPT are

applied to the new presentation. You can apply any Power-Point file as a template.

7. Compare the slide to Figure 10.10. The Global Travel logo appears in the lower-right corner of the slide and the page-number code appears in the lower-left corner. The background and title colors are the same as in MYPRES2.PPT.

8. Close the file without saving your changes.

Figure 10.10  **The new file with MYPRES2.PPT template**

SUMMARY

In this chapter, you explored templates and slide masters. You now know how to apply a template to a presentation, how to change the background color of a template, and how to change chart colors in a template. You also learned how to create a logo for a template, how to insert slide numbers, how to remove background items from a slide, and how to apply a presentation as a template.

Here's a quick reference for the techniques you learned in this chapter:

Desired Result	How to Do It
Apply a template to your presentation	Choose **File, Apply Template**; move to the directory that holds the template you want to apply; select the template; click on **OK**
Change a color in a template	Apply the template you want to the presentation; choose **Slide, Color Scheme**; from the Scheme list, select the color you want to change; click on **Change A Color**; select a new color from the grid, from the Scheme Colors list, or by clicking on **More Colors** to create your own color; click on **OK** as many times as necessary to return to the Color Scheme dialog box; click on **OK**
Change the chart color scheme	Choose **Slide, Color Scheme** to open the Color Scheme dialog box; select which of the bottom four colors you want to change; click on **Change A Color**; select the color you want from either the color grid or the Color Scheme box, or click on the **More Colors button** and create your own color; click on **OK** until you return to the Color Scheme dialog box; repeat the above steps as necessary
Insert slide numbers	Go to the Slide Master; select the **Text tool**; place the insertion point where you want the code to be inserted; choose **Edit, Insert, Page Number**; return to Slide view; run the slide show

Desired Result	How to Do It
Add a logo to your presentation	Choose **View, Slide Master**; choose **File, Open Clip Art**; double-click on the clip-art file that contains the graphic you want to use as part of your logo; double-click on the clip-art slide you want to use; select the graphic and choose **Edit, Copy** to place a copy of it on the Clipboard; choose **File, Close** to close the clip-art file (do not save any changes); choose **Edit, Paste** to place the graphic on your Slide Master; choose **Object, Scale** to resize the graphic; move the graphic to the appropriate place on your slide; select the **Text tool**; type the text for your logo; select the **Selection tool**; select and format the logo text, if necessary; move the logo text to the appropriate place on your slide, if necessary; move to Slide view to see the logo on the slide
Turn off the display of background items on a slide	Move to the slide in which you want to hide the background items and choose **Slide, Follow Master, Background** Items
Return the background items to the slide	Move to slide on which you want to view the background items and choose **Slide, Follow Master, Background Items**
Apply a presentation as a template	Open the file you want to apply the template to; choose **File, Apply Template**; move to the directory containing the presentation file you want to use as a template; select the file; click on **OK**

In the next chapter, you'll explore two closely related topics: importing and exporting files. You will learn how to import an outline, how to import data and charts from other applications, how to import a picture, how to export a PowerPoint presentation as an outline, and how to export a PowerPoint slide as a graphic.

IF YOU'RE STOPPING HERE

If you need to break off here, please exit PowerPoint. If you want to proceed directly to the next chapter, please do so now.

CHAPTER 11: IMPORTING AND EXPORTING

Importing Data
and Charts from
Other Applications

Importing an
Outline

Importing a
Picture

Exporting
PowerPoint
Presentations
and Slides

Throughout this book, you learned how to create the different PowerPoint slides that make up a presentation. In this chapter, you will learn how to *import* (use files or objects that were created in another presentation or application) and *export* (use Power-Point slides and presentations in other applications). You can import data, outlines, and pictures from other sources into your presentation, saving you the work of creating them more than once. In addition, you can export PowerPoint slides and presentations to enhance your spreadsheets or word-processing documents.

When you are done working through this chapter, you will know

- How to import data from a Microsoft Excel worksheet
- How to import a chart from Microsoft Excel
- How to import an outline from Word for Windows
- How to import a picture
- How to export a PowerPoint presentation as an outline
- How to export a PowerPoint slide as a Windows metafile

IMPORTING DATA AND CHARTS FROM OTHER APPLICATIONS

Computer software allows you to automate your office. There is an application for every use, and chances are you use another application besides PowerPoint, such as Microsoft Excel or Lotus 1-2-3. If this is the case, you can import data from the other application into Graph. You can either directly import the data, or you can copy and paste the data from another document.

If you have a spreadsheet that shows the monthly sales for a company, for example, and you want to create a chart based on that information for your PowerPoint presentation, you can use the information from your Excel or Lotus spreadsheet to plot the PowerPoint chart. Instead of taking the time to create your Excel or Lotus data all over again in PowerPoint, you import data from the other application directly into a Graph datasheet. You don't even have to run the other application.There are several applications from which you can use data to create PowerPoint charts; they are listed in Table 11.1.

Table 11.1   **File Formats That Can Be Imported into PowerPoint**

Extension	Application(s)
.WKS	Lotus 1-2-3 Release 1A and Microsoft Works
.WK1	Lotus 1-2-3 Release 2.0
.WRI	Symphony

Table 11.1   **File Formats That Can Be Imported into PowerPoint (Continued)**

Extension	Application(s)
.XLS	Microsoft Excel (worksheet)
.SLK	Microsoft Multiplan, Microsoft Excel
.XLC	Microsoft Excel (chart)

IMPORTING DATA FROM MICROSOFT EXCEL

If you have a Microsoft Excel worksheet that contains the information you want to plot in your PowerPoint chart, you can import the data from the worksheet directly into your PowerPoint presentation.

Here's the general procedure for importing data from Microsoft Excel:

- Move to the slide on which you want to create the chart.

- Add a title to the slide and delete the Body object.

- Select the Graph tool and draw a Graph object on the slide.

- Maximize the Graph window and drag the Chart window down, if necessary.

- Activate the Datasheet window, and select the cell where the data will begin (usually this is the first cell of the datasheet).

- Choose *File, Import Data*.

- Select the file name.

- Click on the All button at the bottom of the dialog box to import all the data, or click on the Range button and type the data range in the Range box to import a range of data.

- Click on OK.

If you are not running PowerPoint on your computer, please start it now. Close all open presentations except the start-up presentation. Let's create a PowerPoint chart with data imported from Microsoft Excel:

1. Open and maximize **MYPRES2.PPT**, if necessary.

2. Add a new slide (slide 6) to the end of the presentation.

3. Add the title **Global Travel Package Rates**.

4. Delete the Body object from the slide.

5. Select the **Graph tool** and draw a Graph object approximately the same size as the Body object.

6. Maximize the Graph window and drag the **Chart window** down, if necessary.

7. Click on the **Datasheet window** to activate it.

8. If your datasheet is empty, then skip this step and go on to step 9. Select all the data in the datasheet, choose **Edit, Clear**, and click on **OK** to clear all the data from the datasheet. If you do not clear data from the datasheet before importing data, Graph asks if you want to overwrite the existing data.

9. Select the first cell of the datasheet, as shown in Figure 11.1. Graph will place the imported data in the datasheet beginning with the selected cell.

Figure 11.1   **The first cell of the datasheet**

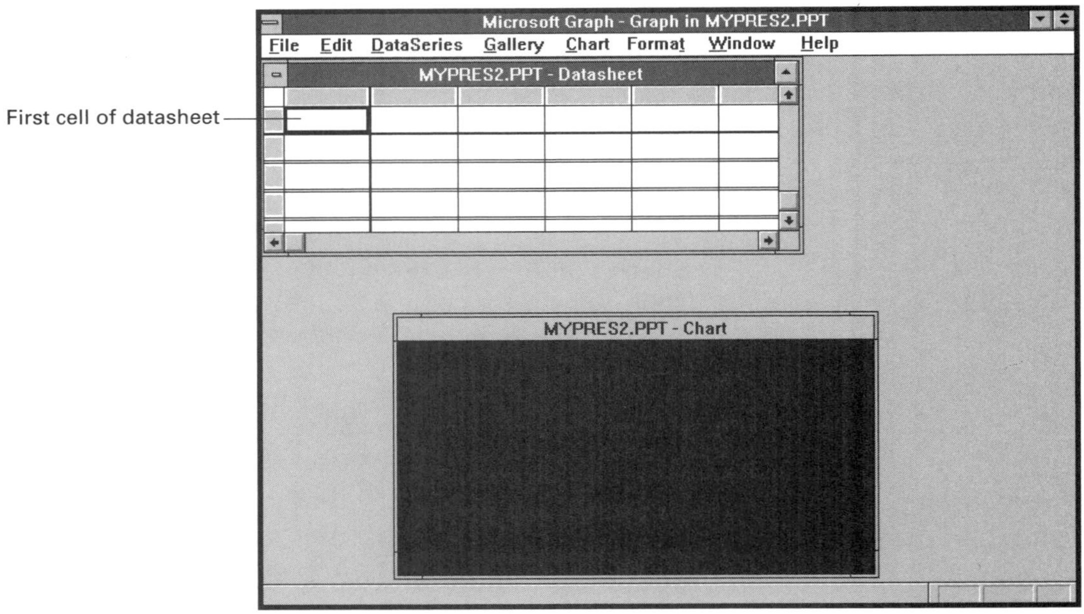

10. Choose **File, Import Data** to open the Import Data dialog box, shown in Figure 11.2.

Figure 11.2 **The Import Data dialog box**

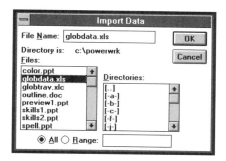

11. If necessary, move to your POWERWRK directory.

12. Select the file name **globdata.xls**. This is the worksheet on whose data we want to base a PowerPoint chart.

13. Click on **All** (at the bottom of the dialog box), if necessary. When you select All, Graph imports all the information in the worksheet. If you wanted to import only a portion of the worksheet, you would click on Range and type in the range you wanted to plot as a chart. For example, to create a chart from a worksheet like the one shown in Figure 11.3, based on the vacation package data without including the extra text, you would select Range and type the range A3:E7. Only the information in cell A3 through cell E7 would be plotted.

14. Click on **OK** to import all the data from GLOBDATA.XLS into the Graph datasheet.

15. Observe the Datasheet window. The Excel data is pasted into the datasheet.

16. Observe the chart. Graph plots a chart based on the Excel data.

17. Choose **File, Exit And Return To MYPRES2.PPT** and click on **Yes** to update the chart.

18. Observe the slide. The legend covers part of the chart.

Figure 11.3   **Sample Excel worksheet**

Microsoft Excel							
File Edit Formula Format Data Options Macro Window Help							

GLOBDATA.XLS

	A	B	C	D	E	F	G	H
1		Global Travel Package rates						
2								
3		2 Days	5 Days	7 Days	9 Days			
4	Ski Resort*	157	300	425	550			
5	Cruise	259	450	675	895			
6	Conference	142	250	335	450			
7	Golf Resort**	200	500	740	950			
8								
9		all rates include hotel accommodations, continental breakfast and dinner						
10		all rates are per person based on double occupancy						
11		* includes ski passes						
12		** includes 18 hole greens fees						
13								
14								
15								
16								
17								
18								

Ready

PRACTICE YOUR SKILLS

Let's move the legend to the bottom of the chart:

1. Use the **Format, Legend** command to move the legend to the bottom of the Chart window. (Hint: You must open the Graph window before you can move the legend.)

2. Return to the slide and update the chart.

3. Save the file. Your chart should match the one in Figure 11.4.

IMPORTING A MICROSOFT EXCEL CHART

You can use Microsoft Excel to create charts as well as worksheets. If you do use Excel to create a chart and then decide you must have that chart in your PowerPoint presentation, you can import the chart itself without importing the Excel data. Once you import the Microsoft Excel chart, the chart is *embedded* in your presentation—the original information is stored in your PowerPoint presentation file, allowing you to edit the object in PowerPoint.

Figure 11.4 **The completed chart**

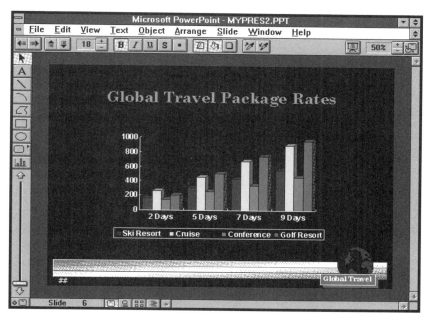

Note: If you want to import files other than Microsoft Excel chart files, you must import the data.

Here's the general procedure for importing an Excel chart into Graph:

- Move to or create the slide on which you want to add the Excel chart.

- Add a title for the chart and delete the Body object.

- Select the Graph tool and draw a Graph object.

- Maximize the Graph window and drag the Chart window down, if necessary.

- Choose *File, Open Microsoft Excel Chart*.

- Select the name of the file containing the chart you want to import.

- Click on OK. The Excel chart opens in Graph, and the data used to create the chart is displayed in the datasheet.

Let's import an Excel chart:

1. Add a new slide (slide 7) to the end of the presentation.

2. Add the title **Package Sales** and delete the Body object.

3. Select the **Graph tool** and draw a Graph object of the approximate size and at the position of the Body object.

4. Maximize the Graph window and move the **Chart window** down, if necessary.

5. Choose **File, Open Microsoft Excel Chart**. You should see the message *Opening a Microsoft Excel chart will overwrite existing data and chart formatting. Continue?* When you import a Microsoft Excel chart, the Excel chart formatting will overwrite any PowerPoint formatting defaults. Even if you cannot see a chart, the PowerPoint default formatting is still there each time you open Graph. So, every time you import an Excel chart, you have to confirm overwriting the existing chart.

6. Click on **OK** to overwrite the PowerPoint chart formatting.

7. Move to your POWERWRK directory, if necessary.

8. Select **GLOBTRAV.XLC**. The .XLC extension indicates that this is an Excel chart file.

9. Click on **OK**. You might see the message *File error: data may have been lost.* Excel charts are linked to worksheets; this message is Graph's way of telling you that you are importing the chart without its source worksheet.

10. Click on **OK**. The Microsoft Excel chart opens in Graph. Its data is included in the Graph datasheet.

11. Return to the slide and update the chart.

12. Observe the slide. The chart is smaller than the Graph object you drew on the slide. Let's enlarge the chart.

13. Select the chart, if necessary.

14. Choose **Object, Scale,** type **130**, and click on **OK** to enlarge the chart to 130 percent of its original size.

15. Compare your chart to that shown in Figure 11.5.

16. Save the file.

Figure 11.5   **The completed slide**

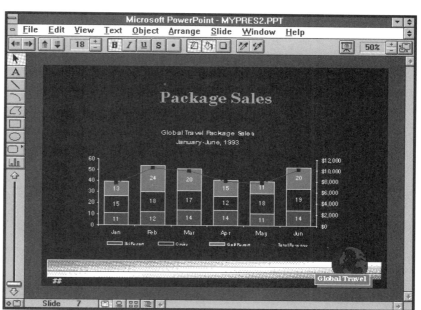

IMPORTING AN OUTLINE

In PowerPoint, you can import an outline to begin a new presentation or to add to an existing presentation. You can import outlines from Microsoft Word or other word-processing applications. PowerPoint can read Microsoft Word files directly, as well as *RTF* (Rich Text Format) and plain text (.TXT) files.

When reading a Microsoft Word or an RTF file, PowerPoint picks up the outline structure from the styles used in the file (a heading 1 in Microsoft Word becomes a title in PowerPoint, a heading 2 becomes the first level of a Body object, and so on). If the file contains no outline styles, PowerPoint uses the paragraph indents or tabs to determine titles and body text levels.

In plain text files, PowerPoint uses tabs at the beginning of paragraphs to determine the outline structure. For example, if there is no tab at the beginning of a line, PowerPoint imports it as a slide title. If there is one tab at the beginning of the line, PowerPoint imports the paragraph as level-1 body text.

Note: Microsoft Word outlines can have up to nine indent levels, but PowerPoint outlines have only six (one for titles and five for body text). When you import a Word for Windows outline, Power-Point discards all text that is not part of a six-level outline.

Figure 11.6 illustrates the Word for Windows outline with outline styles applied. Figure 11.7 shows the same outline delineated with tabs.

Figure 11.6　**A Word for Windows outline formatted with outline styles**

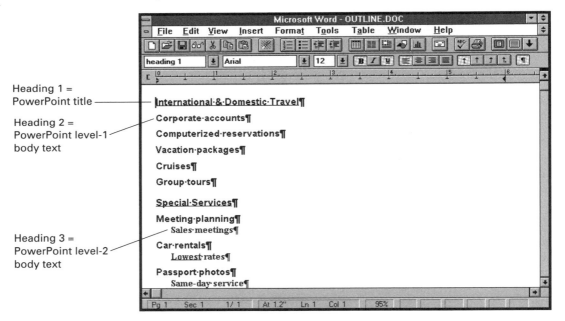

Heading 1 = PowerPoint title

Heading 2 = PowerPoint level-1 body text

Heading 3 = PowerPoint level-2 body text

You can import an outline in any of PowerPoint's views. Power-Point inserts slides after the current slide in Slide view and Outline view, and after the selected slide in Slide Sorter view.

Here's the general procedure for importing an outline into a Power-Point presentation:

● Move to the slide after which you want to insert the outline.

● Choose *Edit, Insert, Outline.*

Figure 11.7   **A Word for Windows outline delineated with tabs**

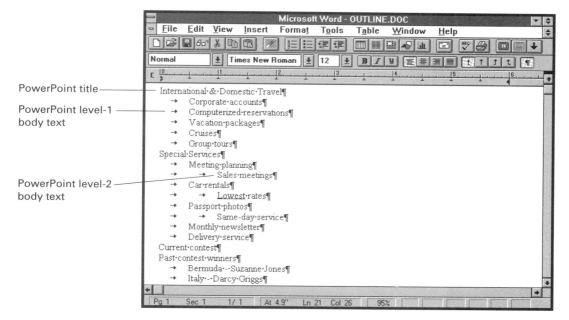

Move to the appropriate drive and directory and select the file that contains the outline you want to import.

- Click on OK. The new slides are added after the current or selected slide and are formatted according to the Microsoft Word outline style applied to them, or the number of tab markers at the beginning of the paragraph.

Let's import an outline to add text slides to MYPRES2.PPT:

1. Move to the last slide in the presentation (slide 7), if necessary.

2. Choose **Edit, Insert, Outline** to open the Insert Outline dialog box, shown in Figure 11.8.

3. Move to the POWERWRK directory, if necessary, and select **OUTLINE.DOC**. This is a Word for Windows file containing text for the new PowerPoint slides.

4. Click on **OK**. PowerPoint imports the file, adding its text to your presentation.

Figure 11.8 **The Insert Outline dialog box**

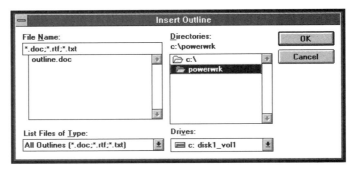

PowerPoint creates a new slide for each level-1 heading and adds the other headings as body text. The slides appear after the current slide in your presentation and follow the format of the template.

Before we do anything to the text slides, let's take a look at the new slides. As you learned in Chapter 1, you can use Slide Sorter view to get an overview of your presentation:

1. Choose **View, Slide Sorter** to view all the slides you imported.

2. Scroll down to view the new slides (slides 8 through 12). All the new slides, except the last, contain text only, as shown in Figure 11.9. The last slide is blank.

3. Save the file.

IMPORTING A PICTURE

As you learned in Chapter 5, PowerPoint comes with several clip-art files containing many graphics you can use in your presentations. However, if you want to use a particular *picture* (a drawing created in another application), you can import it into your presentation. This allows you to create an illustration in Paintbrush or Draw Perfect, for example, and have that illustration placed on a slide in your presentation. You cannot, however, edit an imported picture in PowerPoint, because an imported graphic does not retain any information about the application in which it was created.

Here's the general procedure for importing a picture:

• Move to the slide on which you want to add the picture.

Figure 11.9   **The new slides in Slide Sorter view**

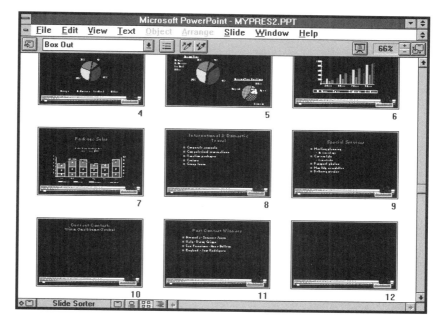

- Choose *Edit, Insert, Picture* to open the Insert Picture dialog box. This dialog box shows a list of available picture files in the current drive and directory.

- Choose the drive and directory that contains the picture file you want to import.

- Choose the picture file you want.

- Click on OK. PowerPoint places the picture on the active slide.

Let's import a picture into MYPRES2.PPT:

1. Double-click on slide 10 (Current Contest). When you double-click on a slide in Slide Sorter view, PowerPoint returns you to Slide view for that slide.

2. Delete the Body object. Because you are placing a picture on the slide, the Body object is not necessary.

3. Choose **Edit, Insert, Picture** to open the Insert Picture dialog box, shown in Figure 11.10.

4. Move to your POWERWRK directory, if necessary.

Figure 11.10   **The Insert Picture dialog box**

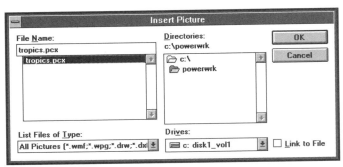

5. Select **TROPICS.PCX** and click on **OK** to import the tropics graphic.

6. Observe the slide. PowerPoint places the tropics graphic in the center of the slide, as shown in Figure 11.11.

7. Select the text **Win a Caribbean Cruise**!

Figure 11.11   **The tropics graphic on the slide**

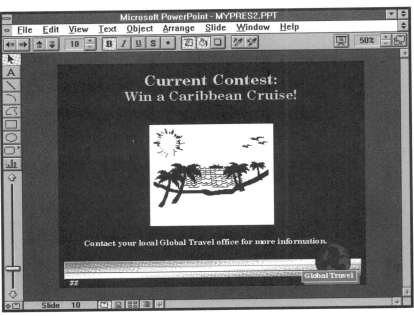

8. Click on the **Font Size Minus (–) button** to decrease the font size of the selected text to 32 points.

9. Select the **Text tool**, place the insertion point on the slide workspace, and type the text **Contact your local Global Travel office for more information**.

10. Move the text so that its position matches that shown in Figure 11.11. (Hint: Select the text and then move it.)

11. With the text still selected, click on the **Font Size Plus (+) button** to change the size to 20 points.

12. Save the file.

EXPORTING POWERPOINT PRESENTATIONS AND SLIDES

Exporting means using PowerPoint presentations or slides in documents created with other applications. You can export a presentation as an outline, or export a slide by attaching it to another document or saving it as a *Windows metafile* (a graphical format with a .WMF extension). You can use PowerPoint and any other applications to make your life easier and your work more consistent.

EXPORTING A PRESENTATION AS AN OUTLINE

If you create a PowerPoint presentation and then decide that you want to create a document explaining the presentation, you can save the PowerPoint presentation as an outline and open it in a word-processing application. Only text is saved when you save a presentation as an outline.

Here's the general procedure for saving a PowerPoint presentation as an outline:

• Choose File, Save As to open the Save As dialog box.

• Type a name for the outline.

• Select the appropriate drive and directory.

• From the Save File Of Type drop-down list, select Outline (RTF).

• Click on OK. The presentation is saved as an outline and you can open it in any word-processing application that will read RTF files.

Let's save your PowerPoint presentation as an outline:

1. Choose **File, Save As** to open the Save As dialog box.

2. From the Save File Of Type drop-down list, select **Outline (RTF)**. In order to save your presentation as an outline, you have to tell PowerPoint that's what you want to do.

3. Click on **OK** to close the Save As dialog box and save the presentation as an outline.

4. Choose **Edit, Insert, Outline** to open the Insert Outline dialog box.

5. Observe that MYPRES2.RTF is available in the File Name list box. You can use it in any application that reads .RTF files.

6. Click on **Cancel** to close the dialog box without inserting the outline.

 EXPORTING THE CURRENT SLIDE AS A WINDOWS METAFILE

If you save a slide as a Windows metafile, you save all graphics and text on the slide. Then, you can use PowerPoint to export the Windows metafile to another document.

Here's the general procedure for saving a slide as a Windows metafile:

- Move to the slide you want to save as a metafile. (You can save only one slide at a time.)

- Choose File, Save As to open the Save As dialog box.

- Type a name for the metafile. Include the .WMF extension in the file name.

- Choose the appropriate drive and directory.

- From the Save File Of Type list, select *Windows Metafile*.

- Click on OK. The current slide is saved as a Windows metafile and can be used in another presentation.

Let's save a slide as a Windows metafile:

1. Move to slide 3 (Airline Ticket Sales). You can save only one slide at a time as a Windows metafile, and you have to move to the slide you want before you can save it.

2. Choose **File, Save As** to open the Save As dialog box.

3. Type **slschart.wmf** to name the Windows metafile. Remember to include the .WMF extension when you name your file.

4. From the **Save File Of Type** list, select **Windows Metafile**.

5. Click on **OK**. Your slide is saved as a Windows metafile, ready to be used in another presentation or application.

6. Close MYPRES2.PPT. Do not save changes.

SUMMARY

In this chapter, you added slides to MYPRES2.PPT by importing objects and files created in other applications. You also learned how to export PowerPoint presentations and slides. Now that you are finished working through this chapter, you know how to import data from Microsoft Excel, how to import a Microsoft Excel chart, how to import an outline from Word for Windows, how to import a picture, how to save a PowerPoint presentation as an outline, and how to save the current slide as a Windows metafile.

Here's a quick reference of the techniques covered in this chapter:

Desired Result	How to Do It
Import data from Microsoft Excel	Move to the slide on which you want to create the chart; select the **Graph tool** and draw a Graph object on the slide; maximize the Graph window and drag the **Chart window** down, if necessary; activate the **Datasheet window** and select the cell where the data will begin (usually this is the first cell of the datasheet); choose **File, Import Data**; select the file name; click on the **All button** at the bottom of the dialog box to import all the data, or click on the **Range button** and type the data range in the Range box to import a range of data; click on **OK**

Desired Result	**How to Do It**
Import an Excel chart into Graph	Move to or create the slide on which you want to add the Excel chart; add a title for the chart and delete the Body object; select the **Graph tool** and draw a Graph object; maximize the Graph window and drag the **Chart window** down, if necessary; choose **File, Open Microsoft Excel Chart**; select the name of the file containing the chart you want to import; click on **OK**
Import a picture	Move to the slide on which you want to add the picture; choose **Edit, Insert, Picture**; choose the drive and directory that contains the picture file you want to import; choose the picture file you want; click on **OK**
Import an outline into a PowerPoint presentation	Move to the slide after which you want to insert the outline; choose **Edit, Insert, Outline**; move to the appropriate drive and directory and select the file that contains the outline you want to import; click on **OK**
Save a PowerPoint presentation as an outline	Choose **File, Save As**; type a name for the outline; select the appropriate drive and directory; from the Save File Of Type drop-down list, select **Outline (RTF)**; click on **OK**
Save a slide as a Windows metafile	Move to the slide you want to save as a metafile (you can save only one slide at a time); choose **File, Save As**; type a name for the metafile, including the .WMF extension; choose the appropriate drive and directory; from the Save File Of Type list, select **Windows Metafile**; click on **OK**

In the next chapter, you'll find out how to add the finishing touches to your presentation. You will learn how to change the order of slides in Outline view and in Slide Sorter view, how to delete slides from your presentation, how to add transition effects to your slides, how to add builds to text slides, how to run the slide show, and how to add notes to your presentation.

IF YOU'RE STOPPING HERE

If you need to break off here, please exit PowerPoint. If you want to proceed directly to the next chapter, please do so now.

CHAPTER 12: PRESENTATION OPTIONS

Rearranging Slides in a Presentation

Adding Transitions and Builds to the Presentation

Running a Slide Show

Adding Notes to a Presentation

So far, you have created and enhanced text slides, graphics slides, and chart slides to create a presentation. In this chapter, you will add the finishing touches to your presentation to prepare it for viewing by the general public.

When you are done working through this chapter, you will know

- How to change the order of slides in Outline view
- How to change the order of slides in Slide Sorter view
- How to delete slides from your presentation
- How to add transition effects to your slides
- How to add builds to text slides
- How to run a slide show
- How to add notes to your presentation

REARRANGING SLIDES IN A PRESENTATION

When you create your slides, you really don't need to worry about placing them in a particular order. Finish all the slides first, and then move them around until you have them in the order that best fits your presentation. You can reorder your slides in either Outline view or Slide Sorter view.

CHANGING THE ORDER OF SLIDES IN OUTLINE VIEW

If you move a slide title, all its subheadings move with it. However, if you move a subheading, only that subheading moves. Therefore, if you want to change the order of your slides in Outline view, it is generally a good idea to first collapse your outline by clicking on the *Titles Only button*. Just the titles of your slides will then be displayed, making it easier to view all the slides and ensure that all the text on each slide moves with that slide.

Here's the general procedure for rearranging slides in Outline view:

- Click on the Titles Only button.
- Select the slide you want to move.
- Click on the Move Up or Move Down button to move the slide up or down in the outline. Or, place the mouse pointer on the slide icon and drag it up or down in the outline.
- Click on the Titles Only button to return body text to the outline.

If you are not running PowerPoint on your computer, please start it now. Close all open presentations except the start-up presentation. Let's move a slide in Outline view:

1. Open and maximize **MYPRES2.PPT**, if necessary.

2. Click on the **Outline View button** (located at the bottom of the screen, it displays a miniature outline) to move to Outline view.

3. Observe the outline. The slides containing graphs and other graphics show only their titles. You can see only title and body text in Outline view.

4. Click on the **Titles Only button** (refer to Figure 12.1) to collapse all text in the outline except the slide titles. You don't have to collapse slides before you rearrange them, but it is easier if you do.

Figure 12.1   **The presentation in Outline view with titles only**

Titles Only button

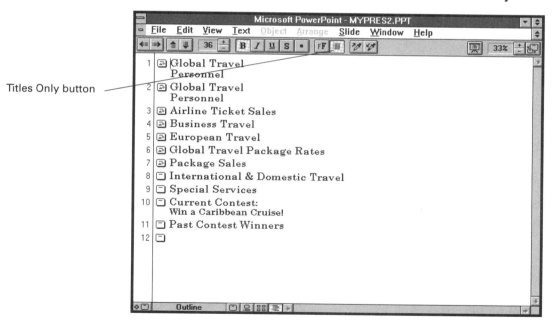

5. Observe the slide icons. On those for slides containing graphs or graphics, shapes are displayed.

6. Select slide 8 (International & Domestic Travel).

7. Click on the **Move Up button** (located on the Toolbar, it displays an upward-pointing arrow) to move the slide above the Package Sales slide.

8. With the International & Domestic Travel slide still selected, click on the **Move Up button** four times to move the slide up to slide 3. Your International & Domestic Travel slide is now slide 3.

9. Click on the **Titles Only button** to return all the text to the outline.

10. Observe slide 3. All the subheadings moved with the slide title.

PRACTICE YOUR SKILLS

Let's make slide 9 (Special Services) the fourth slide in the outline:

1. Display only the slide titles.

2. Move the **Special Services slide** in front of the Airline Ticket Sales slide. (Hint: You must select the slide before you can move it.)

3. Compare your outline to that shown in Figure 12.2.

4. Display all the slide text.

5. Save the file.

CHANGING THE ORDER OF SLIDES IN SLIDE SORTER VIEW

The only disadvantage to moving slides in Outline view is that you can't see what the slide looks like. If you want to see how the presentation actually looks as you rearrange it, you might want to rearrange slides in Slide Sorter view.

Here's the general procedure for changing the order of slides in Slide Sorter view:

• Move to Slide Sorter view.

Figure 12.2   **The outline after rearranging the slides**

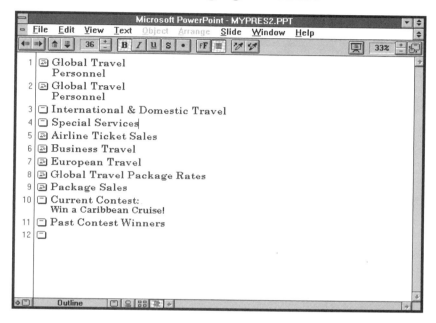

- Select the slide you want to move.
- Start dragging the slide. The mouse pointer becomes a slide icon.
- Drag the slide icon to a new position.

Let's change the order of slides in Slide Sorter:

1. Click on the **Slide Sorter View button** (located at the bottom of the screen, it looks like a miniature waffle).

2. Observe the Slide Sorter. You can see a miniature representation of each slide, and beneath each slide is its slide number.

3. Place the mouse pointer on slide 7. You are going to move the European Travel slide to a new location.

4. Press and hold the **left mouse button** and move the mouse pointer. The pointer changes to a slide icon.

5. Drag the **slide icon** to the right of slide 9 (Package sales).

6. Release the mouse button. The European Travel slide is now the ninth slide in the presentation, as shown in Figure 12.3.

Figure 12.3   **The presentation after moving the European Travel slide**

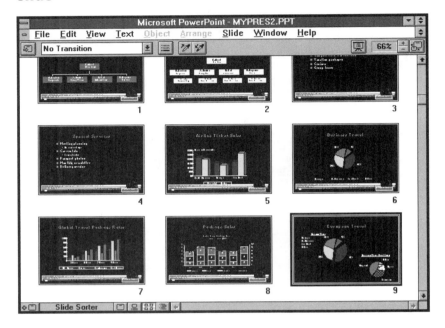

7. Observe the slide numbers. The slides have been automatically renumbered.

8. Select slide 6 (Business Travel).

9. Drag the **slide icon** to a position between slides 8 and 9 to place the Business Travel slide in front of the European Travel slide.

PRACTICE YOUR SKILLS

Let's move another slide in Slide Sorter view, so that your presentation matches that shown in Figure 12.4:

1. Move the Airline Ticket Sales slide (slide 5) in front of the Special Services slide (slide 4).

2. Save the file.

Figure 12.4 **The presentation in Slide Sorter view, after rearranging the slides**

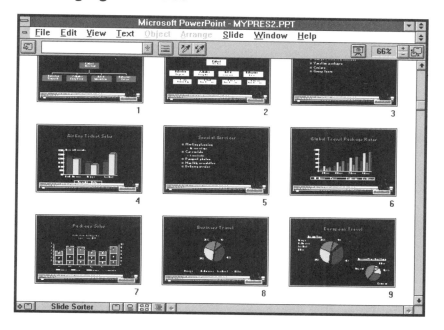

DELETING A SLIDE

As you look at your presentation, you may find that there is a slide you really don't need. PowerPoint allows you to quickly and easily delete any unnecessary slides.

Here's the general procedure for deleting slides in Outline view and Slide Sorter view:

- Select the slide you want to delete.

- Press Del.

Here's the general procedure for deleting slides in Slide view:

- Move to the slide you want to delete.

- Choose *Slide, Delete Slide*.

Let's delete a slide in Slide Sorter view:

1. Observe your presentation. In Chapter 7, you created two flow charts that duplicated information. Only one of the personnel flow charts is necessary, so let's get rid of the other.

2. Select slide 1. This flow chart lists only first-level managers, so we'll delete this one.

3. Press **Del** to delete the slide from the presentation.

4. Observe the presentation. The slide has been removed and the remaining slides have been renumbered.

PRACTICE YOUR SKILLS

Let's delete another slide from your presentation:

1. Follow the steps above to delete slide 11 (the blank slide) from the presentation. Your presentation should now contain 10 slides and look like that shown in Figure 12.5.

Figure 12.5   **The presentation, after deleting slides**

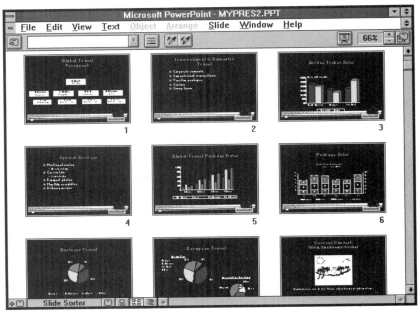

2. Save the file.

ADDING TRANSITIONS AND BUILDS TO THE PRESENTATION

Once you have your presentation in the order in which you want to present it, you can make it more interesting by adding transitions and builds. PowerPoint gives you several options to control how your slides are displayed during a slide show. You can set a *transition effect* (the method by which one slide moves off the screen and the next slide moves on). You can also control whether the slides advance automatically, and set the amount of time each slide is displayed. In addition, you can *build* body text—add a major bullet and its subpoints one by one—on each slide.

TRANSITION EFFECTS

For each slide, you can set a different transition effect, as well as determine how quickly the transition will take place. You can set transition effects in Slide view or in Slide Sorter view. When you set a transition effect in Slide view, the effect applies only to the current slide. So, if you want to set transition effects for more than one slide at a time, select the slides in the Slide Sorter and then apply the effects.

Here's the general procedure for setting transition effects:

- Display the slide in Slide view, or select the slide(s) in Slide Sorter view.

- Choose *Slide, Transition* (or click on the *Transition Dialog button* in Slide Sorter view) to open the Transition dialog box.

- Select the transition effect from the drop-down list box.

- Select the transition speed (*Slow, Medium, Fast*).

- Select whether to advance to the next slide by clicking the mouse or automatically.

- Click on OK.

Let's add transition effects to your presentation:

1. Switch to Slide view.

2. Move to slide 1, if necessary.

3. Choose **Slide, Transition** to open the Transition dialog box, shown in Figure 12.6. Here you can set a transition effect, tell PowerPoint how fast or slow you want the effect to take place, and determine whether the slide will advance automatically or when you click the mouse. (The picture of a dog in the upper-right corner of the dialog box represents a slide graphic.) You can see what a transition effect will look like in your presentation by watching the dog when you choose an effect from the Effect drop-down list box.

Figure 12.6   **The Transition dialog box**

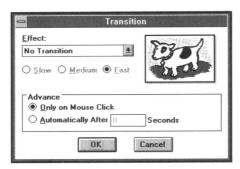

4. Click on the **down arrow** to display the transition options available in the Effect drop-down list box.

5. Select **Box Out**. When you select a transition effect, it is applied to the picture of the dog.

6. Click on **Medium** to set the speed for the transition.

7. In the Advance box, click on **Automatically** to advance to the next slide automatically.

8. Type **3** to display the slide for 3 seconds before advancing to the next slide.

9. Click on **OK**.

10. Switch to Slide Sorter view

11. Observe slide 1. Below it, you see an icon and the number *:03* (refer to Figure 12.7). The slide icon with an arrow indicates that a transition effect has been applied to the slide.

The number :03 indicates that the slide will automatically advance in 3 seconds.

Figure 12.7 **The slide with transition effect in Slide Sorter view**

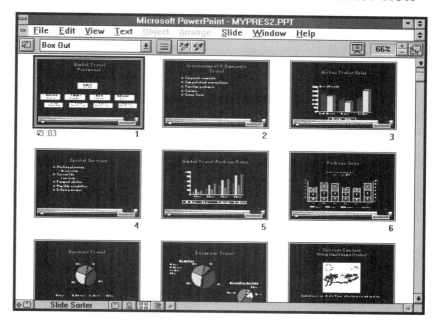

12. Observe slide 2. Because there is no transition effect set for this slide, there are no icons or numbers beneath it. Let's set a transition effect for slide 2.

13. Select slide 2.

14. Click on the **Transition Dialog button** (located on the Toolbar, it displays a slide with an arrow) to open the Transition dialog box.

15. Choose **Box In** from the Effect drop-down list box.

16. Set the speed to **Medium**, if necessary.

17. Set the slide to advance automatically after 3 seconds.

18. Click on **OK**.

19. Select slides 3 through 6 (while holding **Shift**, click on each slide). Your screen should now look like that shown in Figure 12.8. You can apply a transition effect to more than one slide at a time in Slide Sorter view.

Figure 12.8

Selecting multiple slides

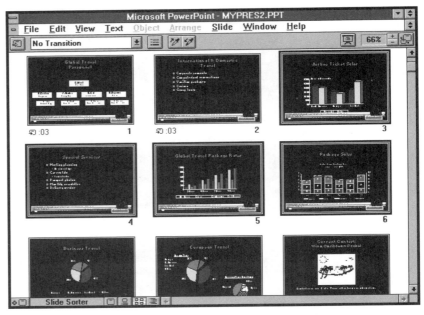

20. Click on the **Transition Dialog button** to open the Transition dialog box, and choose **Dissolve** from the Effect drop-down list box.

21. Set the speed to **Medium**, if necessary.

22. Set the slides to advance automatically after 3 seconds.

23. Click on **OK**.

PRACTICE YOUR SKILLS

1. Set the transition effect and speed of your choice for the remaining slides.

2. Set all the slides to advance automatically after 3 seconds.

3. Save the file.

ADDING BUILDS

Text slides are a necessity for imparting information during your presentation, but they can be boring. You can keep your audience interested in your presentation during text slides if you use the *Build* command to add each major bullet (and its subpoints) to the slide one at a time. You choose the effect you want to see as each new bullet point is added to the slide and presto, your boring old text slides have new life.

If you add a build to a slide and the slide is set to advance automatically, each bulleted item on the slide is displayed for an equal portion of the time set for that slide. For example, if a slide is timed to advance after 8 seconds and there are four bullets, each bullet will be displayed for 2 seconds.

Here's the general procedure for adding builds to slides:

- Move to the slide with the bulleted list.

- Choose *Slide, Build*.

- Check *Build Body Text*.

- If desired, check *Dim Previous Points* and select a color from the drop-down list box.

- Check Effect and select an effect from the drop-down list box.

- Click on OK.

Let's add builds to the text slides in your presentation:

1. Double-click on slide 2 (International & Domestic Travel) to return to Slide view.

2. Choose **Slide, Build** to open the Build dialog box, shown in Figure 12.9.

3. Check **Build Body Text**.

4. Check **Effect**.

5. Display the Effect drop-down list box to view the available build effects.

Figure 12.9   **The Build dialog box**

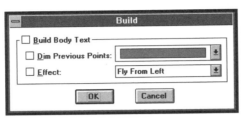

6. Select **Fly From Right**. (You might need to scroll up to see it.)

7. Click on **OK**. Each bulleted item on the International & Domestic Travel slide will "fly" in from the right side of the screen when you run your slide show.

8. Switch to Slide Sorter view.

9. Observe slide 2. The bulleted icon below the slide indicates that when you run the slide show, the body text will build one item at a time. You can add a build only to a text slide.

10. Select slide 4. You can set a build in Slide Sorter view, as well as in Slide view.

11. Click on the **Build button** (located on the Toolbar, it displays a bulleted list with the first two items dimmed) to open the Build dialog box.

12. Check **Build Body Text**.

13. Check **Dim Previous Points**. You can dim earlier bulleted points to draw attention to the current point.

14. Display the Color drop-down list box and select the color of your choice. When a new point is added to the screen, the previous point is dimmed and assumes the color you select.

15. Check **Effect** and select the effect of your choice.

16. Click on **OK**.

PRACTICE YOUR SKILLS

Let's add a build to Past contest winners slide in your presentation:

1. Add the build effect of your choice to slide 10.

2. Save the file.

RUNNING A SLIDE SHOW

As you learned in Chapter 2, you can display a presentation on your computer screen by running a slide show. Running a slide show is an excellent way to rehearse before giving your presentation. You can see the effect each slide has, try different transitions, change the timing to suit your script, and generally design your electronic presentation so that it gets your point across in a clear, professional manner.

If the timing of your slide show is not quite right, you can change it during your rehearsal, or you can wait and change it in the Transition dialog box. Use whichever method is most convenient for you.

Here's the general procedure for running a slide show:

- Choose File, Slide Show to open the Slide Show dialog box.

- Choose either All or From/To, depending on how many of the presentation slides you want in the slide show.

- Choose the method you want to use to advance the slides. Choose *Manual Advance* to change slides by clicking the mouse button. Choose *Use Slide Timings* to advance the slide show automatically, using the timings you set in the Transition dialog box. Choose *Rehearse New Timings* to check timings and adjust them as necessary during the slide show.

- Click on the Show button. Either the first slide in the presentation, or the first slide in the range you specified, appears in slide-show format.

Now that you have added transition and build effects to your slides, let's see how they look in the slide show:

1. Switch to Slide Sorter view, if necessary.

2. Choose **File, Slide Show** to open the Slide Show dialog box.

3. Click on **All**, if necessary, to view all the slides in the presentation.

4. Click on **Use Slide Timings**, if necessary, to run the slide show with the timings you set earlier in this chapter.

5. Click on **Show**. The slide show runs, with each slide advancing automatically after 3 seconds. This means that the slides with text builds are moving too fast to be really effective.

PRACTICE YOUR SKILLS

Obviously, if you want to talk during this presentation, you need to reset the timings. Let's do so:

1. Change the slide timings for the following slides:

slide 2: 12 seconds

slide 4: 12 seconds

slide 10: 10 seconds

(Hint: You can change the timings in the Transition dialog box.)

2. Make any transition or build changes you want.

3. Run a slide show to check the new timings, transitions, and builds.

4. Save the file.

ADDING NOTES TO A PRESENTATION

You can create a *Notes page*, containing a slide image and additional space for your speaker notes, for every slide in your presentation. This can be a helpful reference tool. The Notes page is formatted based on the *Notes Master*.

The Notes Master controls the format and placement of the following items:

- *Background items*. Anything you add to the Notes Master is displayed on each Notes page.

- *Body style attributes*. Like the Slide Master, the Notes Master has a Master Body object with five indent levels that you can format. If you change the format of any master text, that format change affects on every Notes page.

- *Slide image*. You can change the size and position of the slide image.

Here's the general procedure for adding notes to a presentation:

- Move to the slide for which you want to create a Notes page.

- Choose *View, Notes*. The Notes page for the current slide appears.

- Type notes in the Body object.
- Use the Tool Palette to add any graphics you want.
- Click on the Slide Changer to move to the Notes page for the next slide.
- Repeat the above steps until you are finished writing notes.

Let's take a look at the Notes Master page before adding notes to your presentation:

1. Choose **View, Notes Master** to display the Notes Master page.

2. Observe the Notes Master, shown in Figure 12.10. The Notes Master page contains a slide placeholder and a Master Body object for your notes. The bottom-left corner of the screen displays the words *Notes Master*, indicating that anything you change or add here will be displayed on every Notes page.

Figure 12.10   The Notes Master

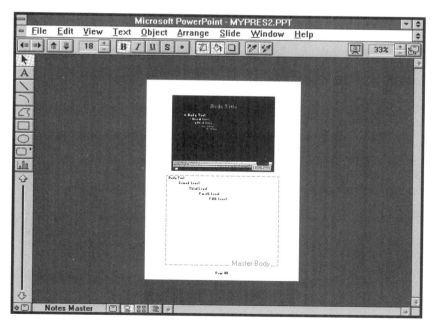

3. Click on the **Master Body object** to select it.

4. Click on the **Zoom In button** twice to increase the view size to 66 percent. The text in the Master Body object is easier to read now, as you can see in Figure 12.11. The Master Body object contains five text levels.

Figure 12.11   **The Master Body object at 66 percent magnification**

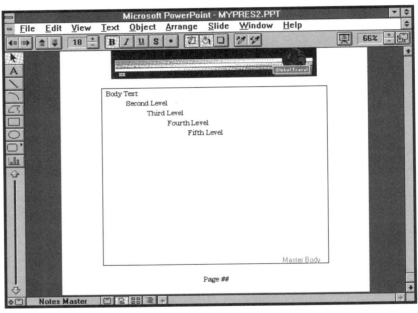

5. Click on the **Line button** (located on the Toolbar, it displays a pencil drawing a box) to add a line around the Notes body text. Because you added a line around the Master Body object, it will appear on every Notes page.

Now, let's add notes to the presentation:

1. Choose **View, Notes** to leave the Notes Master and move to a Notes page.

2. Move to Notes 1, if necessary.

3. Click on the **Body object** for Notes 1 to select it.

4. Type the following:

Global Travel, a full-service travel agency, was founded in 1970. Our office is operated by a team of qualified managers and experienced assistants whose goal is to provide you with quality service at the lowest price.

5. Observe your slide. It should match that shown in Figure 12.12.

Figure 12.12   **The Notes page, after adding text**

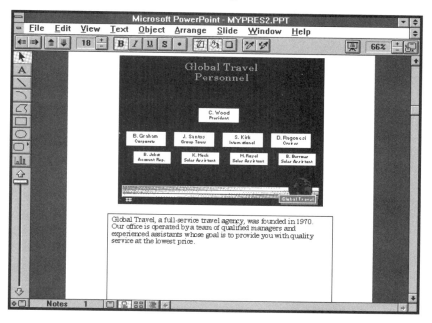

PRACTICE YOUR SKILLS

Let's create a Notes page that matches that shown in Figure 12.13:

1. Move to Notes 9. (Hint: Your Notes 9 should display the Current Contest slide.)

Figure 12.13   **Notes page 9**

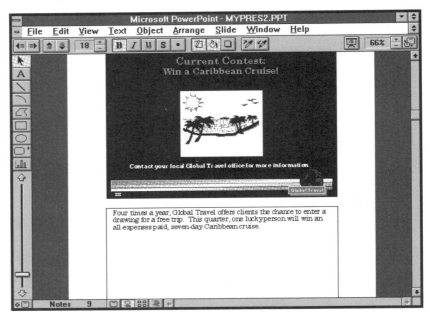

2. Add the following speaker's note:

> **Four times a year, Global Travel offers clients the chance to enter a drawing for a free trip. This quarter, one lucky person will win an all-expenses paid, seven-day Caribbean cruise.**

(Hint: You must select the **Body object** before you can type.)

3. Return to Slide view and save the file.

4. Close the file.

SUMMARY

Congratulations—you've completed your presentation! Doesn't it feel great? In this chapter, you learned how to change the order of slides in Outline view, how to change the order of slides in Slide Sorter view, and how to delete slides from your presentation. You also learned how to add transition effects to your slides, how to add builds to text slides, how to run a slide show, and how to add notes to your presentation.

Here's a quick reference of the techniques you learned in this chapter:

Desired Result	**How to Do It**
Rearrange slides in Outline view	Click on the **Titles Only button** to view slide titles only; select the slide you want to move; click on the **Move Up** or **Move Down button** to move the slide up or down in the outline, or place the mouse pointer on the **slide icon** and drag it up or down in the outline; click on the **Titles Only button** to restore the complete outline
Change the order of slides in Slide Sorter view	Move to Slide Sorter view, select the slide you want to move, start dragging the slide, drag the **slide icon** to a new position
Delete slides in Outline and Slide Sorter views	Select the slide you want to delete and press **Del**
Delete slides in Slide view	Move to the slide you want to delete; choose **Slide, Delete Slide**
Set transition effects	Display the slide in Slide view, or select the slide(s) in Slider Sorter view; choose **Slide, Transition** (or click on the **Transition Dialog button** in Slide Sorter view) to open the Transition dialog box; select the transition effect from the drop-down list box; select the transition speed (**Slow, Medium, Fast**); select whether to advance to the next slide by clicking the mouse or automatically; click on **OK**

Desired Result	How to Do It
Add builds to slides	Move to the slide with the bulleted list; choose **Slide, Build**; check **Build Body Text**; if desired, check **Dim Previous Points** and select a color from the drop-down list box; check **Effect** and select an effect from the drop-down list box; click on **OK**
Run a slide show	Choose **File, Slide Show** to open the Slide Show dialog box; choose either **All** or **From/To**, depending on how many of the presentation slides you want in the slide show; choose **Manual Advance** to change slides by clicking the mouse button, choose **Use Slide Timings** to advance the slide show automatically using the timings you set in the Transition dialog box, or choose **Rehearse New Timings** to check timings and allow you to change them during the slide show; click on the **Show button**
Add notes to a presentation	Move to the slide for which you want to create a Notes page; choose **View, Notes** to display the Notes page for the current slide; type notes in the Body object; use the Tool Palette to add any graphics you want; click on the **Slide Changer** to move to the Notes page for the next slide; repeat the above steps until you are finished writing notes

In the next chapter, you will explore the various options available for printing your presentation. You will learn how to change the slide setup, how to print black-and-white slides, how to set a print range, how to reverse the print order, how to scale your slides to fit your paper size, how to print a presentation, how to print handouts, how to print an outline, and how to print notes.

IF YOU'RE STOPPING HERE

If you need to break off here, please exit PowerPoint. If you want to proceed directly to the next chapter, please do so now.

CHAPTER 13: PRINTING

The Slide Setup
Command

Using Printing
Options

Printing Slides,
Notes, Handouts,
and an Outline

U ntil now, you have viewed all the parts of your presentation only on your screen. Eventually, you will probably need to create and print a complex presentation. This chapter introduces various techniques to help you manage the printing of a presentation (the slides themselves), an outline, notes, and handouts.

When you're done working through this chapter, you will know

- How to change the slide setup
- How to set print options
- How to print slides
- How to print Handout pages
- How to print an outline
- How to print Notes pages

THE SLIDE SETUP COMMAND

When you open a new presentation, PowerPoint creates slides that have a width of 10 inches, a height of 7.5 inches, and *landscape orientation* (the slide is wider than it is tall). However, you can use the *Slide Setup* command to change these settings as well as to set the number with which to begin numbering your slides.

Figure 13.1 shows the Slide Setup dialog box with the default setting, and Table 13.1 describes the elements of the dialog box.

Figure 13.1   **The Slide Setup dialog box with default settings**

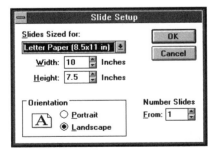

Table 13.1   **Elements of the Slide Setup Dialog Box**

Element	Purpose
Slides Sized For box	Allows you to select a size for your slides. There are four standard slide-size options and a custom option that allows you to specify a nonstandard size.
Width and Height boxes	Located below the Slides Sized For box, these show the width and height of the slide work-space. If you choose one of the standard sizes in the Slides Sized For box, slides have a 1-inch margin. For example, if you choose Letter Paper (8.5×11 in), your slide width is set to 10 inches and the height to 7.5 inches. If you choose the Custom option, then you can set your own slide width and height.
Orientation box	Allows you to set the orientation of the slides. You can choose *Landscape* (wide) or *Portrait* (tall).
Number Slides From box	Allows you to set the number to be assigned to the first slide in the presentation. Usually, it is fine to start numbering your presentation from 1. However, if you have a very long presentation that has been split into two or more files, you might want to start the numbering in the second and following files with something other than 1. As you learned in Chapter 10, you must first insert page numbers on the Slide Master before you can print those numbers.

You can modify the slide setup at any time, but if you change settings *after* creating your slides, PowerPoint must adjust the slides to fit the new size. Everything on the slide will be scaled to reflect the new setting. For example, if you change your slide width from 10 inches to 12 inches, every object on your slide will be made wider.

When you change the settings for existing slides, PowerPoint politely lets you know that you might need to edit your slides. We advise that, if possible, you choose a slide setup *before* you begin creating slides.

Note: If you change the slide setup after creating slides, it is a good idea to take a look at the entire presentation on screen and print a draft copy to make sure it looks okay in the new size or orientation.

Here's the general procedure for changing the slide setup:

- Choose File, Slide Setup.
- Choose the appropriate Slides Sized For option for your presentation output.
- Choose an orientation option.
- Set a number with which to begin numbering the slides.
- Click on OK.
- If you already have slides in your presentation and you change the size setting, you'll see a message saying that you may need to edit your slides to fit. If you decide to go ahead with the change, click on *Change*.
- Look at your presentation on screen and print a draft copy to make sure the old format and content fit appropriately in the new size.
- If necessary, edit the slides or change the size again.

If you are not running PowerPoint on your computer, please start it now. Close all open presentations except the start-up presentation. Let's take a look at the Slide Setup dialog box:

1. Open and maximize **MYPRES2.PPT** and move to Slide view, if necessary.

2. Choose **File, Slide Setup** to open the Slide Setup dialog box. You can change the size and orientation of your slides and choose the page number for the first slide here.

3. Click on the **down arrow** in the Slides Sized For box to display the slide-size options, as shown in Figure 13.2. There are five slide-size options you can choose from. *On-screen Show* is for a presentation that you run on your computer. *Letter Paper (8.5×11 in)* is for a presentation you print on regular-size U.S. paper. *A4 Paper (210×297 mm)* is for slides printed on regular-size International paper. *35mm Slides* is

for slides printed as 35mm color slides. *Custom* allows you to set your own slide size.

Figure 13.2   **The Slide Setup dialog box with slide-size options displayed**

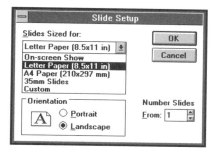

Let's change the slide size and see what happens:

1. Choose **35mm Slides** from the Slides Sized For list to resize the slides, preparing them as 35mm color slides.

2. Observe the Width and Height boxes. The contents of the Width box change to *11.25"*. The Height box setting stays the same.

3. Click on **OK**. PowerPoint gives you the message *You may need to edit all the slides to fit if you make this change to the slide size.*

4. Click on **Change** to go ahead and change the size of the slides.

5. Watch the status bar. PowerPoint swiftly resizes every slide and Notes page, making them wider.

6. Observe the first slide. It should resemble that shown in Figure 13.3. The slide itself, as well as every object on the slide, is slightly wider.

PRACTICE YOUR SKILLS

Let's reset the Slide Setup dialog box to letter-sized paper:

1. Choose **File, Slide Setup**.

Figure 13.3   **The first slide of the presentation resized for 35mm color slides**

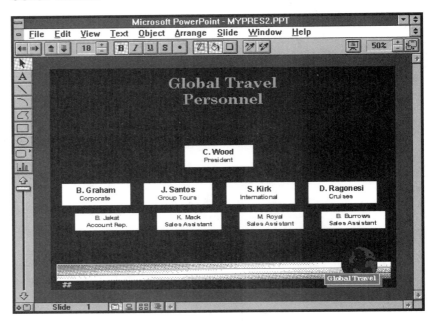

2. From the Slides Sized For list, select **Letter Paper (8.5×11 in)** to reset the slides to print on U.S. letter paper.

3. Click on **OK**.

4. Click on **Change**.

5. Save the file.

USING PRINTING OPTIONS

Once your slides are set up the way you want them, you are ready to print all or part of the presentation. As you know, Power-Point has four views. You can print hard copy for any of these views and customize the printed copy with the print options available in the Print dialog box, shown in Figure 13.4. We will look at a few of these options in the following sections.

Figure 13.4   **The Print dialog box**

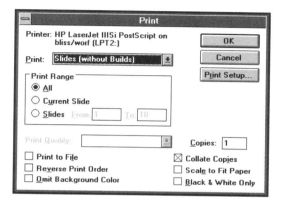

Note: Depending on the printer you have installed, you may have different options available to you in the Print dialog box. For the purpose of this chapter, we are assuming that you are using a laser printer. If you are using a dot-matrix or bubble-jet printer, you may see different options in the Print dialog box. Don't panic. Choose the options that are appropriate for your printout. If you do not have a printer, you can still walk through most of the steps in this chapter.

If you aren't sure whether you have a printer installed, you can open the Print dialog box and check. The installed printer is displayed at the top of the dialog box.

THE PRINT RANGE OPTION

You can choose to print all the slides in your presentation, just the current slide, or a specific range of slides. This is helpful if you have a long presentation and want to see how one of the slides will look when you print it out, or if you want to show someone part of your presentation to give them an idea of what it looks like without giving the whole thing away.

Here's the general procedure for printing all the slides or just the current one:

- Choose *File, Print*.

- Click on the appropriate *Print Range* option.

- Click on OK.

Here's the general procedure for printing a range of slides:

- Choose File, Print.
- Click on *Slides*.
- Type the number of the first slide in the range you want to print.
- Press Tab.
- Type the number of the last slide in the range you want to print.
- Click on OK.

THE BLACK & WHITE ONLY OPTION

If you check the *Black & White Only* option, then all the slides in your presentation will be printed in black ink. The program will interpret all colors and fills as areas that are to be left white, and all text and lines will be converted to black.

This can be particularly useful if you want to quickly print draft copies of color presentations. It is also standard practice to print speaker's notes or handouts (we will discuss Handout pages later in this chapter) in black and white, to make them easier to read.

Figure 13.5 shows a Notes page printed in black and white. Figure 13.6 shows the same Notes page printed with the Black & White Only option turned off.

THE REVERSE PRINT ORDER OPTION

The Reverse Print Order option prints the presentation from last page to first. Particularly if you have a long presentation, this can be a useful feature. If you check this option, then you will not have to shuffle the papers into their proper order after you print them.

With most newer printers, the pages of your presentation will be automatically collated in the proper order, making this option unnecessary. However, some older printers—many of which do not offer this built-in feature—can't support the Reverse Print Order option. If your printer can't print in reverse order, the option won't be available.

Figure 13.5   **The Notes page printed in black and white**

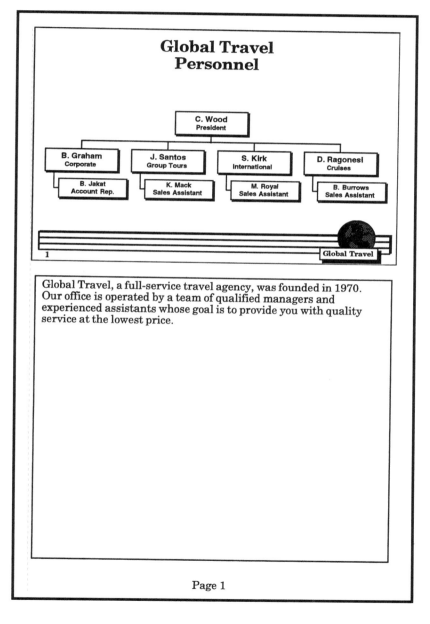

Global Travel, a full-service travel agency, was founded in 1970. Our office is operated by a team of qualified managers and experienced assistants whose goal is to provide you with quality service at the lowest price.

Page 1

Figure 13.6   **The Notes page printed regularly**

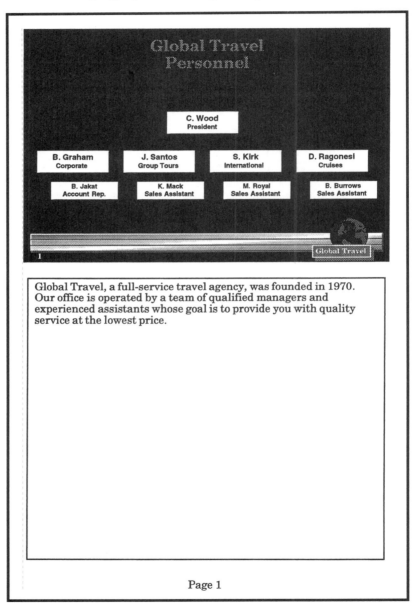

THE SCALE TO FIT PAPER OPTION

The Scale To Fit Paper option automatically sizes slides to fit the paper loaded in the printer. If you are creating a presentation that is to be printed on 5×7 paper or 11×14 paper, all you have to do is put the paper in the printer. This option will then be chosen for you if the paper in the printer doesn't correspond to the slide size and orientation specified in the Slide Setup box.

PRINTING SLIDES, NOTES, HANDOUTS, AND AN OUTLINE

Once you understand some of the print options that you can choose from, you are ready to look at the different output options PowerPoint offers you. Besides choosing a print range and print options in the Print dialog box, you can choose to print any part of your presentation—a slide, a Notes page, a Handout page, or an outline.

PRINTING SLIDES

When you print the slides in your presentation, you have two options:

- *Slides (With Builds)* prints each bulleted item of a build slide as a separate slide, beginning with the slide title. One bulleted item is added on each subsequent printout until all the bulleted items are printed.

- *Slides (Without Builds)* prints one page per slide, with all the bulleted items present, even though the slide builds when you run the Slide Show.

Figure 13.7 shows a printed slide without builds, and Figure 13.8 shows the first printout of the same slide when the Slides (With Build) option is selected.

Here's the general procedure for printing slides:

- Choose File, Print to open the Print dialog box.

- Select the type of slide printout from the Print drop-down list box.

- Select the number of slides to print from the Print Range box. You can print all slides, the current slide, or a range of slides.

Figure 13.7   **Slide 2 without builds**

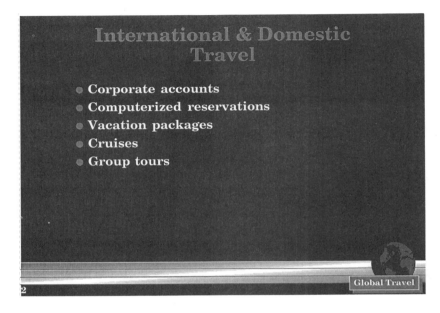

Figure 13.8   **Slide 2 with builds**

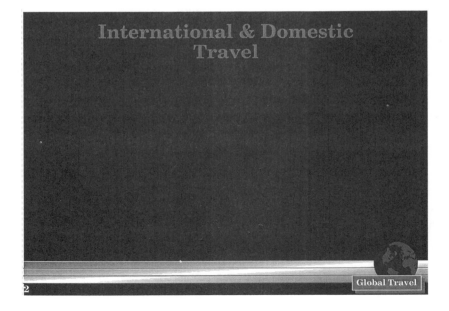

- Set the number of copies you want to print.
- Click on OK.

Let's print a slide from MYPRES2.PPT:

1. Save the file. It is a good idea to save the file before you print. Then, if anything goes wrong, you still have a good copy of the presentation.

2. Move to slide 2.

3. Choose **File, Print** to open the Print dialog box.

4. In the Print box, select **Slides (Without Builds)**, if necessary.

5. In the Print Range box, click on **Current** to print only the current slide (slide 2).

6. Set the number of copies to **1**, if necessary. (It is a good idea, whenever possible, to print out only one copy and then photocopy it as necessary. This is especially true with laser printers, which are sometimes warrantied for a certain number of copies rather than for a given length of time.)

7. Click on **OK** to print slide 2. Your printout should resemble that shown in Figure 13.7.

PRACTICE YOUR SKILLS

Now that you have printed a slide without builds, let's try printing a slide with builds:

1. Print slide 2 with builds. The first page of your output should resemble that shown in Figure 13.8.

2. Save the file.

PRINTING HANDOUTS

If you are giving a presentation, you frequently will find it helpful to have handouts for your audience. PowerPoint allows you to print Handout pages showing your presentation in miniature. This allows your audience to follow along more easily as you give your presentation.

You can choose from three options when printing handouts:

- 2 Slides Per Page
- 3 Slides Per Page
- 6 Slides Per Page

You can see what these options look like in the *Handout Master*. The Handout Master, shown in Figure 13.9, allows you to format and place the text and graphics that you want on each page. It has placeholders showing what two, three, and six slides per page will look like when printed.

Figure 13.9   **The Handout Master**

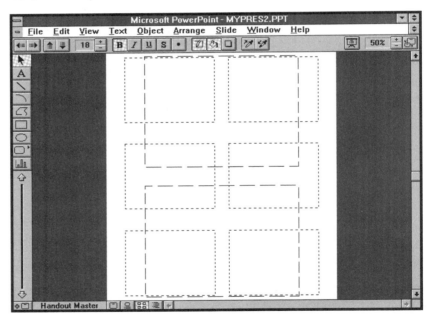

Here's the general procedure for adding text or graphics to the Handout Master:

- Choose *View, Handout Master*.

- Select the Text tool and place the insertion point on the slide workspace.
- Type the text you want to appear on every Handout page.
- Reposition the text, if necessary, so that it is not overlapping the Handout placeholder for the option (2, 3, or 6) that you want to print.
- Add any clip art or drawings that you want on each Handout page.

Here's the general procedure for printing audience handouts:

- Add the text and graphics you want on each Handout page to the Handout Master.
- Choose File, Print.
- From the Print box, select the appropriate Handout option.
- From the Print Range box, select the range you want to print.
- If necessary, set the number of copies you want to print.
- Check the Black & White Only print option.
- Click on OK.

Let's print Handout pages for MYPRES2.PPT. We'll begin by adding the company name to the Handout Master:

1. Choose **View, Handout Master** to move to the Handout Master.
2. Select the **Text tool** and place the insertion point anywhere on the slide workspace.
3. Type **Global Travel Sales Presentation**.
4. Select the text you typed in step 3 and move it to the upper-right corner of your Handout Master.
5. Save the file.

Now that you've added the company name to your Handout pages, let's print them and see how they look:

1. Choose **File, Print** to open the Print dialog box.
2. From the Print box, select **Handouts (3 Slides Per Page)** to print three slide images per page.

3. In the Print Range box, click on **All** to print all the slides on Handout pages. You can choose to print a range of slides, too.

4. Check the **Black & White Only** option. Because handouts are easier to read if they are black and white, we suggest that you always check this option when printing them.

5. Click on **OK**. PowerPoint prints Handout pages that should resemble those shown in Figure 13.10.

PRINTING AN OUTLINE

PowerPoint prints an outline just as it appears on your screen. To add background items to the printed outline, you use the *Outline Master*. The Outline Master, like the Handout Master, contains a placeholder. You can add text, dates, or borders that you want to appear on every page of your outline.

Figure 13.11 shows the Outline Master with a title and date added.

Your outline prints according to the way you format it in Outline view. For example, if you display only the slide titles and increase the view to 50 percent, then your printed outline will show only slide titles at a text size comparable to a 50 percent view.

Here's the general procedure for printing an outline:

• Choose *View, Outline Master* and add any elements that you want on every page.

• In Outline view, format your outline: collapse or expand the titles and body text, and choose an appropriate view scale and font.

• Choose File, Print.

• From the Print drop-down list, select *Outline View*.

• Click on OK.

Let's print an outline that resembles that shown in Figure 13.11:

1. Choose **View, Outline Master** to move to the Outline Master.

2. Observe the Outline Master. There is only an outline place-holder on it. However, you can add any text or graphics that you want to show up on each page of your outline.

Figure 13.10   **The Handout pages**

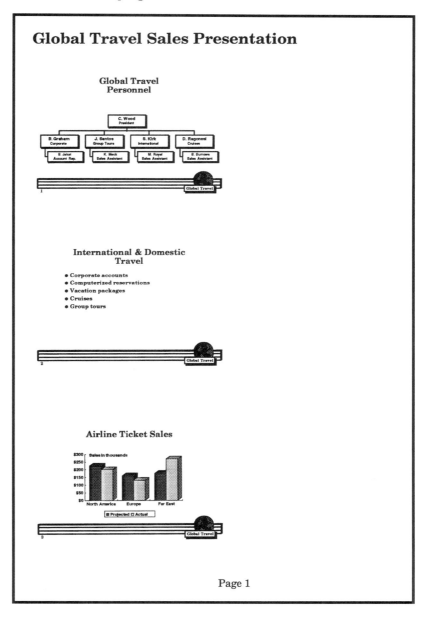

Figure 13.10   **The Handout pages (Continued)**

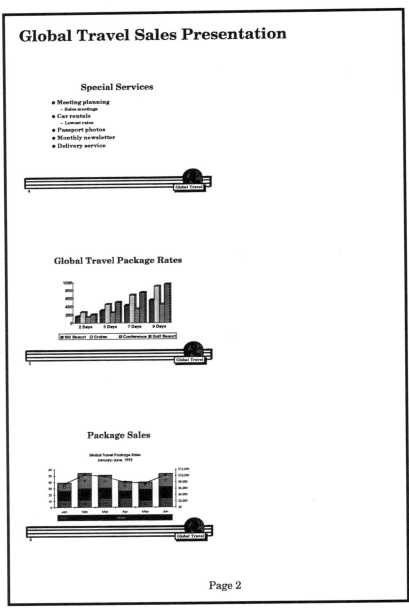

Figure 13.10   The Handout pages (Continued)

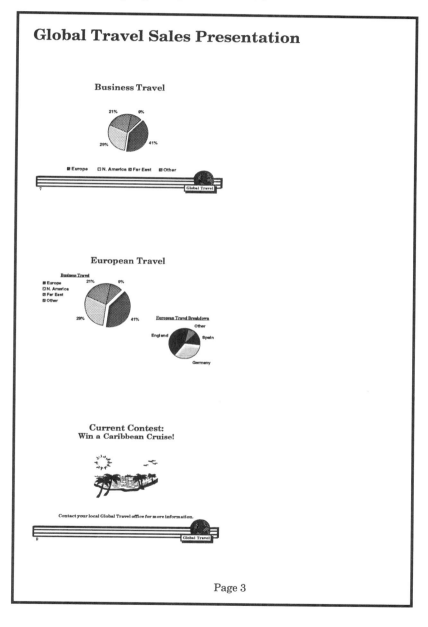

Figure 13.10   **The Handout pages (Continued)**

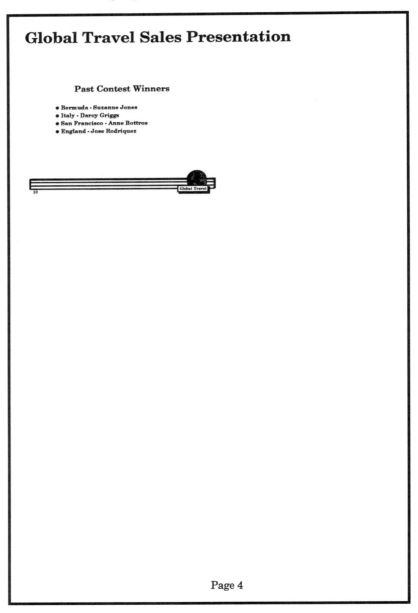

Figure 13.11   **The outline with title and page numbers**

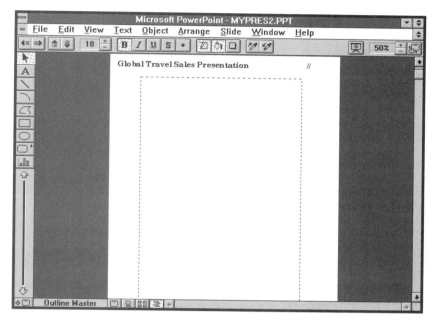

Let's add a title and date to the outline. We'll start with the title:

1. Click on the **Zoom In button** to increase the magnification to 50 percent, if necessary. With the higher magnification, it is easier to see what you type.

2. Select the **Text tool** and place the insertion point in the upper-left corner of the Outline Master. (Refer to Figure 13.11 if you aren't certain where the title should be.)

3. Type **Global Travel Sales Presentation**. This is the title for your outline.

4. If necessary, select the title and move it until its placement matches that shown in Figure 13.11.

5. Select the **Text tool** and place the insertion point in the upper-right corner of the Outline Master in preparation for adding a date to the outline. (Once again, refer to Figure 13.11, if necessary.)

6. Choose **Edit, Insert, Date** to add the date code (//) to the outline. When you print the outline, the current date is inserted at the date code's location.

When you are finished with the Outline Master, return to Outline view to format the outline.

1. Choose **View, Outline**. You want to print an outline that contains only slide titles.

2. Click on the **Titles Only button** to collapse the body text. Printing titles only gives you a list of your slides and their slide numbers. You can then use this list to keep track of slides as you run your presentation.

3. Click on the **Zoom In button** to increase the magnification to 50 percent, if necessary.

Now that your outline is formatted the way you want it, you're ready to print:

1. Save the file. Remember, it is a good idea to save your presentation before you print it.

2. Choose **File, Print**.

3. From the Print drop-down list box, select **Outline View**.

4. From the Print Range box, select **All**, if necessary, to print the entire outline.

5. Click on **OK**.

6. Compare your printout to that shown in Figure 13.12.

 PRINTING NOTES

In addition to slides, handouts, and an outline, you can print the Notes pages you learned to create in Chapter 12. These can be used as speaker notes for yourself, or as a reference for your audience.

Here's the general procedure for printing Notes pages:

• Choose File, Print.

• From the Print drop-down list, select *Notes Pages*.

• From the Print Range box, select the range option you want.

Figure 13.12   **The printed outline**

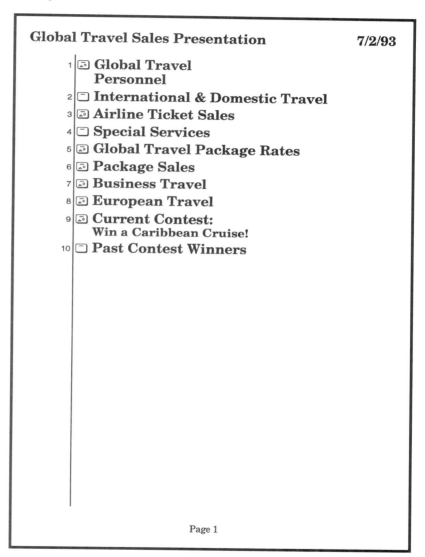

Global Travel Sales Presentation   7/2/93

1. Global Travel Personnel
2. International & Domestic Travel
3. Airline Ticket Sales
4. Special Services
5. Global Travel Package Rates
6. Package Sales
7. Business Travel
8. European Travel
9. Current Contest: Win a Caribbean Cruise!
10. Past Contest Winners

Page 1

- Check the Black & White Only print option.
- Click on OK.

Let's print a Notes page:

1. Move to slide 9.

2. Click on the **Notes button** (located at the bottom of the screen, it displays a miniature slide with notes below it) to move to Notes view.

3. Observe the notes. You created a Notes page for this slide in Chapter 12.

4. Choose **File, Print**.

5. From the Print drop-down list, select **Notes Pages**.

6. In the Print Range box, select **Current Slide** to print the Notes page for only the current slide.

7. Check the **Black & White Only** option and click on **OK**.

8. Observe your Notes page printout. It should resemble that shown in Figure 13.13.

PRACTICE YOUR SKILLS

Throughout the course of this book, you have learned how to create a professional-looking presentation. Now you'll use several of these skills to create the presentation shown in Figure 13.14.

Note: This practice exercise is quite long. It is not necessary to finish the entire practice in one sitting, however. Feel free to work on it over an extended period of time. Make sure you save it whenever you stop, though. Then, next time you sit down, you can begin where you left off.

Let's begin creating the presentation:

1. Create a new presentation (Chapter 7).

2. Type the title **Global Travel** and delete the Body object (Chapter 7).

Figure 13.13　　**The Notes page for slide 9**

Figure 13.14   **The completed SKILLS4.PPT presentation, printed as slides**

Figure 13.14   **The completed SKILLS4.PPT presentation, printed as slides   (Continued)**

Figure 13.14   **The completed SKILLS4.PPT presentation, printed as slides (Continued)**

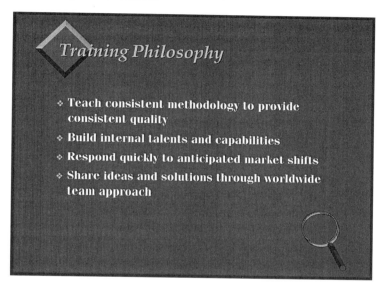

Figure 13.14   **The completed SKILLS4.PPT presentation, printed as slides (Continued)**

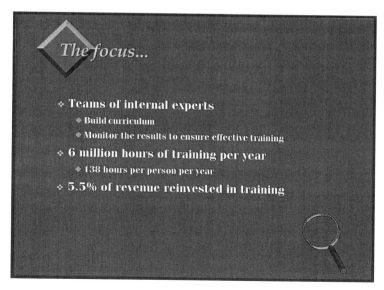

Figure 13.14   **The completed SKILLS4.PPT presentation, printed as slides (Continued)**

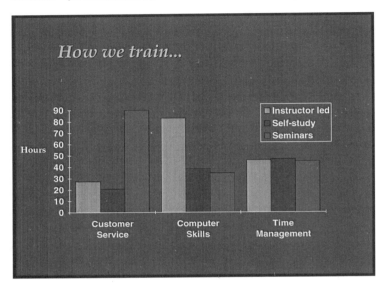

3. Use the **Text tool** to type the following text at the left center of the slide:

   Training

   Perspectives

4. Change the size of the text you typed in step 3 to **54 point** and add a text shadow. (Hint: Use the **Text, Style** command to add a text shadow.)

5. Select the text object **Training Perspectives** and use the **Object** menu to add a gray shadow.

6. Add a new slide and type the title **Training Philosophy** (Chapter 7).

7. Type the following bulleted body text for slide 2 (Chapters 2 and 3):

   Teach consistent methodology to provide consistent quality

   Build internal talents and capabilities

Respond quickly to anticipated market shifts

Share ideas and solutions through worldwide team approach

8. Switch to Outline view (Chapter 2).

9. Create a new slide and increase the view to 50 percent (Chapter 7).

10. Type the title **The focus...** for slide 3 (Chapter 3).

11. Type the following Body text for slide 3 (Chapter 3):

    Teams of internal experts

    Build curriculum

    Monitor results to ensure effective training

    5.5% of revenue reinvested in training

    6 million hours of training per year

    138 hours per person per year

12. Demote the following lines one level:

    Build curriculum

    Monitor results to ensure effective training

    138 hours per person per year

13. In Slide view, move the bulleted item **5.5% of revenue reinvested in training** below the bulleted item **6 million hours of training per year** (Chapter 3).

14. Change the Body object's line spacing to **1.10** for slides 2 and 3 (Chapter 3).

15. Insert a new slide after slide 1 (Chapter 2).

16. Type the title **Global Travel** and delete the Body object.

17. Save the file as **SKILLS4.PPT**.

18. Run the slide show.

19. Apply the **DIAMONDV.PPT** template to the presentation (Chapters 6 and 10).

20. Add a new slide (slide 5) to the end of the presentation, then type the title **How we train...** and delete the Body object.

21. Draw a **Graph object** the approximate size of the Body object you just deleted (Chapters 8 and 9).

22. Clear the data from the datasheet, if necessary (Chapter 9).

23. Input the following information into the datasheet (Chapter 8 and 9):

	Instructor led	Self-study	Seminars
Customer Service	27.4	20.7	90
Computer Skills	83	38.6	34.6
Time Management	45.9	46.9	45

(Hint: You can resize the cells in the datasheet to see all the data in each cell.)

24. Set the data series to **Series In Columns** (Chapter 9).

25. Exit Microsoft Graph and return to the presentation, updating the chart on the slide.

26. Resize and reposition the chart, if necessary.

27. Add the label **Hours** to the y-axis (Chapter 8).

Now let's edit the Slide Master:

1. Move to the Slide Master and change the level-2 bullet to a diamond. (Hint: With the insertion point in the level-2 bullet, choose **Text, Bullet** and use the **Monotype Sorts** font.)

2. View slide 4. The level-2 bullet should now be a diamond.

3. Return to the Slide Master.

4. Open the clip-art file **ACADEMIC.PPT** and view, in Slide view, the magnifying glass (slide 21) (Chapters 5 and 10). (Hint: Double-click on the slide number to move to Slide view.)

5. Select and copy the magnifying glass and close the file **ACADEMIC.PPT**.

6. Paste the magnifying glass into the Slide Master.

7. Scale the magnifying glass to 50 percent (Chapter 10). (Hint: Select the magnifying glass and use the **Object Scale** command.)

8. Move the magnifying glass to the lower-right corner of the Slide Master.

9. Save the file.

10. Run the slide show.

11. Turn off the background items on slide 5 (Chapter 10).

12. Move to slide 2 and insert the picture **FOCUSOBJ.WMF** (Chapter 11).

13. Move slide 2 ahead of slide 1 (Chapter 12). (Hint: Switch to Slide Sorter view to move the slides.)

14. Add transitions to the slides. Have the slides advance automatically after 6 seconds (Chapter 12).

15. Add builds to slides 3 and 4 (Chapter 12).

16. Add the following speaker's note to slide 5 (Chapter 12):

   Global Travel believes that better training makes better employees and happier customers.

17. Save the file.

18. Run the slide show.

19. Print the Notes page for slide 5.

20. Close the presentation and exit PowerPoint.

SUMMARY

In this chapter, you learned various techniques to help you manage the printing of your presentation. You learned how to change the slide setup, how to change print options, how to print all or part of a presentation, how to print an outline, how to print Notes pages, and how to print Handout pages.

With this chapter, you have completed your foundation of PowerPoint skills. Congratulations! You can now venture out into the real world to create and print handsome, sophisticated PowerPoint presentations.

Here's a quick reference guide to the PowerPoint features introduced in this chapter:

Desired Result	How to Do It
Change the slide setup	Choose **File, Slide Setup**; choose the appropriate Slides Sized For option for your presentation output; choose an orientation option; select a number with which to begin numbering the slides; click on **OK**; if you see a message saying that you may need to edit your slides to fit if you make changes to the slide size, click on **Change** if you decide to go ahead with the change; look at your presentation on screen and print a draft copy to make sure the old format and content fit appropriately in the new size; if necessary, edit the slides or change the size again
Print all or just the current slide	Choose **File, Print**; click on the appropriate Print Range option; click on **OK**
Print a range of slides	Choose **File, Print**; click on **Slides**; type the number of the first slide in the range you want to print; press **Tab**; type the number of the last slide in the range you want to print
Print slides	Choose **File, Print**; select the type of slide printout from the Print drop-down list box; select the number of slides to print from the Print Range box; set the number of copies you want to print; click on **OK**
Add text or graphics to the Handout Master	Choose **View, Handout Master**; select the **Text tool** and place the insertion point on the slide workspace; type the text you want to appear on every Handout page; reposition the text, if necessary, so that it is not overlapping the Handout placeholder for the option (2, 3, or 6) that you want to print; add any clip art or drawings that you want on each Handout page

Desired Result	How to Do It
Print Handout pages	Add the text and graphics you want on each Handout page to the Handout Master; choose **File, Print**; from the Print box, select the appropriate Handout option; from the Print Range box, select the range you want to print; if necessary, set the number of copies you want to print; check the **Black & White Only** print option; click on **OK**
Print an outline	Choose **View, Outline Master** and add any elements that you want on every page; in Outline view, format your outline; choose **File, Print** to open the Print dialog box; from the Print drop-down list, select **Outline View**; in the Print Range box, click on **All**; click on **OK**
Print Notes pages	Choose **File, Print**; from the Print drop-down list, select **Notes Pages**; from the Print Range box, select the range option you want; check **Black & White Only**; click on **OK**

Following this chapter are three appendices: Appendix A, "Installation," walks you through PowerPoint 3.0 installation and printer selection; Appendix B, "Tool Palette and Toolbar Reference," lists the buttons for the Tool Palette and the Toolbar in each of Power-Point's views; and Appendix C, "Keystroke Reference," lists the keystroke equivalents of the mouse and menu commands in this book.

IF YOU'RE STOPPING HERE

If you need to break off here, please exit PowerPoint. If you wish to review material from an earlier chapter or proceed to one of the appendices, please do so now.

APPENDIX A: INSTALLATION

Installing
PowerPoint 3.0 on
Your System

Selecting a Printer
for Use with
PowerPoint

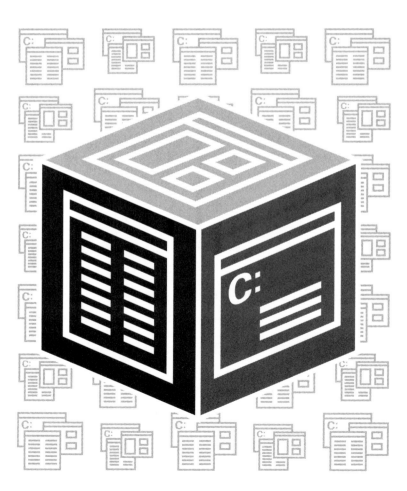

This appendix contains instructions for installing PowerPoint 3.0 on your system and for selecting a printer for use with PowerPoint.

INSTALLING POWERPOINT 3.0 ON YOUR SYSTEM

There are two requirements that must be met before you begin to install PowerPoint 3.0. First, Windows (version 3.1 or higher) must be installed on your computer. If it is not, please install it now. (For help, see your Windows reference manuals.) Second, there must be enough free space on your hard disk to hold the necessary PowerPoint program and data files.

Perform the following steps to meet this last requirement:

1. Make sure you are running in DOS. If Windows is running, please exit to DOS (choose **File, Exit Windows** from the Program Manager window and click on **OK**). The DOS prompt (C:>\ or similar) should be on the screen (change directories, if necessary).

2. Type **c:** (or, if you intend to install PowerPoint on another hard drive, type the letter of this drive followed by a colon) and press **Enter** to log on to your hard drive.

3. Type **dir** and press **Enter**. DOS lists the files contained in the current directory and, at the very end of this list, reports the number of free hard-disk bytes.

4. Observe this number. You need at least 8,000 kilobytes (8,000,000 bytes) of free hard-disk space to install the minimum PowerPoint configuration needed to perform the hands-on activities in this book. You need at least 14,700 kilobytes (14,700,000 bytes) of free hard-disk space to install the complete PowerPoint program. We strongly recommend installing the complete PowerPoint program, as it offers several advanced PowerPoint options that—although not covered in this book—may prove very useful to you at a later date.

5. If necessary, delete sufficient files from your hard disk to free the space required for your desired PowerPoint installation (8,000 or 14,700 kilobytes). Be sure to back up any files that you want to save before deleting them!

6. Type **dir** and press **Enter**. DOS should now report at least 8,000,000 or 14,700,000 free hard-disk bytes. (If not, repeat step 5.)

Note: In addition to these requirements, you must have at least 2 megabytes of memory (with 4 megabytes recommended) and a 3.5-inch high-density (1.44 megabyte) disk drive.

Now that you've met the basic requirements, you can begin the actual PowerPoint 3.0 installation:

1. Start **Windows**.

2. Insert the disk labeled *Setup* (Disk 1) in the appropriately sized disk drive.

3. Activate **Program Manager**. (If Program Manager is running as an icon, double-click on the icon to open it into a window. If Program Manager is running in a window, click on the title bar of the window to activate it.)

4. Choose **File, Run** from the Program Manager menu.

5. Type **a:setup** (if the Setup disk is in drive A) or **b:setup** (if the disk is in drive B). Press **Enter** to start the PowerPoint installation program.

6. When the Welcome window appears on your screen, click on **Continue**.

7. If you are prompted to enter your name and organization, follow the on-screen directions to do so. Click on **Continue** when you are done.

8. Follow the on-screen instructions to enter the hard-disk directory where you will install PowerPoint. Click on **Continue** when you are done. If asked whether you wish to create this directory, click on **Yes**.

9. A dialog box appears, showing two installation options: Complete and Custom. If you want to install the complete PowerPoint program (as discussed in the previous section) and you have freed up the necessary 14,700 kilobytes of hard-disk space, click on the **Complete Installation button**. If you want to control the installation of PowerPoint, click on the **Custom Installation button**. (**Note:** The dialog box says that 13,700K (kilobytes) are needed for complete installation and tells you how many you have free. The extra megabyte that we had you free up is for the PC Learning Lab data files that you'll use in the hands-on activities of this book.)

10. At this point, the installation program begins to copy files from the Setup floppy disk onto your hard disk. A dialog box appears, informing you of the progress of the installation procedure; the procedure is complete when the indicator

reaches 100 percent. (You can click on Cancel at any time to cancel the installation.)

11. When you are asked to insert a new Setup disk, please do so.

12. When the installation procedure is complete, click on **OK**. You are returned to Windows. (With DOS 6.0, this dialog box is a little different; if you're using DOS 6.0, click on **Restart** to return to Windows.) To start PowerPoint, simply open the newly created Microsoft PowerPoint group and double-click on the **Microsoft PowerPoint 3.0 icon**.

SELECTING A PRINTER FOR USE WITH POWERPOINT

PowerPoint presentations normally print to the default printer (which is set in the Windows Control Panel). But you can choose another printer in PowerPoint:

1. Start **PowerPoint**. Do not close the startup presentation.

2. Choose **File, Print Setup**. A dialog box appears, displaying a list of the printers currently installed on your system. They are displayed as possible printers for both the Slides box and the Notes, Handouts, And Outline box. You can select one printer for slides and another for the other components of a presentation, if you want to.

3. In the Slides or the Notes, Handouts, And Outline box, click on **Specific Printer**, select your printer from the Printer list (you might have to scroll), and click on **OK**. You can now use this printer with PowerPoint.

4. If the printer you want does not appear on the list (even after scrolling), install the printer on your system—for instructions, refer to your Windows documentation—and then begin again with step 1 of this printer selection procedure.

APPENDIX B:
TOOL PALETTE AND
TOOLBAR REFERENCE

PowerPoint includes several buttons on the Tool Palette and Toolbar that activate commands or allow you to create objects on the slides. There are so many buttons that it can be daunting to try to figure them all out. However, if you take the time to learn what these buttons do, they can make your life easier and save you time when working with a presentation. Figures B.1, B.2, B.3, and B.4 identify the PowerPoint Tool Palette and Toolbar buttons.

Figure B.1 **The Tool Palette**

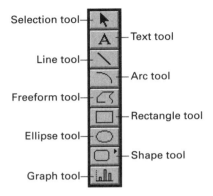

Figure B.2 **The Toolbar in Slide view and Notes view**

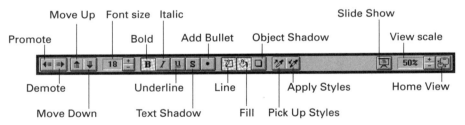

Figure B.3   **The Toolbar in Outline view**

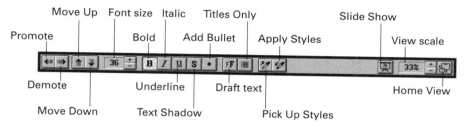

Figure B.4   **The Toolbar in Slide Sorter view**

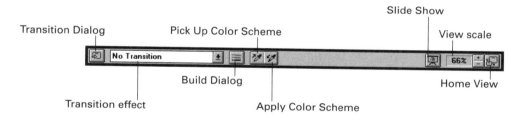

APPENDIX C: KEYSTROKE REFERENCE

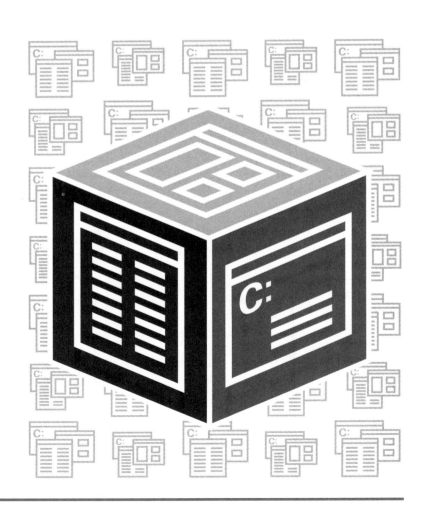

In PowerPoint, many of the actions that can be performed with the mouse can also be performed with the keyboard. Choose the method—or combination of methods—that works best for you. Tables C.1 through C.8 list PowerPoint actions and the corresponding keystrokes required to perform them.

Table C.1　　**Moving Around in a Presentation**

Action	Keystroke
Next slide	PgDn
Previous slide	PgUp
First slide	Ctrl+PgUp
Last slide	Ctrl+PgDn
Next object in stacking order	Tab
Previous object in stacking order	Shift+Tab
Move insertion point one word to left	Ctrl+left arrow
Move insertion point one word to right	Ctrl+right arrow
Move insertion point up one paragraph	Ctrl+up arrow
Move insertion point down one paragraph	Ctrl+down arrow
Move insertion point to beginning of line	Home
Move insertion point to end of line	End

Table C.2　　**Selecting Text and Objects**

Action	Keystroke
Next object	Tab
Previous object	Shift+Tab
Extend text selection	Shift+arrow keys
Add to or subtract from selection	Shift+*click on left mouse button*

Table C.3   **Editing Text and Objects**

Action	Keystroke
Create a new paragraph	Enter
Create a new line in a paragraph	Shift+Enter
Create a new slide	Ctrl+n
Increase font size	Ctrl+Shift+>
Decrease font size	Ctrl+Shift+<
Draw a straight line	*Press* Shift *while drawing*
Duplicate object	Ctrl+d
Ignore grid and guides	*Press* Alt *while drawing*
Resize from center	*Press* Ctrl *and drag resize handles*
Restore shape	*Double-click on handle*
Undo the last action	Ctrl+z
Copy text or object	Ctrl+c
Cut text or object	Ctrl+x
Paste text or object	Ctrl+v
Edit object	Ctrl+e
Show/hide ruler	Ctrl+r
Find/replace	Ctrl+f
Bring forward	Ctrl+=
Send backward	Ctrl+-
Group	Ctrl+g
Ungroup	Ctrl+h
Regroup	Ctrl+j
Show guides	Ctrl+y

Table C.4   **Formatting Text and Objects**

Action or Attribute	Keystroke
Plain text	Ctrl+t
Bold	Ctrl+b
Italic	Ctrl+i
Underline	Ctrl+u
Align left	Ctrl+[
Center	Ctrl+\
Align right	Ctrl+]

Table C.5   **Working with Microsoft Graph**

Action	Keystroke
Clear datasheet	Del
Select entire datasheet	Ctrl+a

Table C.6   **Working in Outline View**

Action	Keystroke
Move to next Body or Title object	Ctrl+Enter
Promote paragraph	Alt+Shift+left arrow
Demote paragraph	Alt+Shift+right arrow
Move paragraph up	Alt+Shift+up arrow
Move paragraph down	Alt+Shift+down arrow
Create a new slide	Ctrl+n

Table C.7   **Working with Presentations**

Action	Keystroke
Create a new slide	Ctrl+n
Open a presentation	Ctrl+o
Close a presentation	Ctrl+F4
Save a presentation	Ctrl+s
Print a presentation	Ctrl+p
Exit PowerPoint	Alt+F4

Table C.8   **Miscellaneous Commands**

Action	Keystroke
Help	F1
Cancel	Esc
Switch between graphics and text selection	F2

INDEX

Imagination.
Innovation. Insight.
The How It Works Series from Ziff-Davis Press

"... a magnificently seamless integration of text and graphics ..."

Larry Blasko, The Associated Press, reviewing *PC/Computing How Computers Work*

No other books bring computer technology to life like the *How It Works* series from Ziff-Davis Press. Lavish, full-color illustrations and lucid text from some of the world's top computer commentators make *How It Works* books an exciting way to explore the inner workings of PC technology.

ISBN: 094-7 Price: $22.95

ISBN: 129-3 Price: $24.95

PC/Computing How Computers Work

A worldwide blockbuster that hit the general trade bestseller lists! *PC/Computing* magazine executive editor Ron White dismantles the PC and reveals what really makes it tick.

How Networks Work

Two of the most respected names in connectivity showcase the PC network, illustrating and explaining how each component does its magic and how they all fit together.

ISBN: 133-1 Price: $24.95
Available: October

ISBN: 166-8 Price: $15.95 Available: October

How Macs Work

A fun and fascinating voyage to the heart of the Macintosh! Two noted *MacUser* contributors cover the spectrum of Macintosh operations from startup to shutdown.

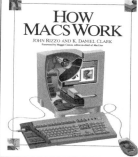

ISBN: 146-3 Price: $24.95

How Software Works

This dazzlingly illustrated volume from Ron White peeks inside the PC to show in full-color how software breathes life into the PC. Covers Windows™ and all major software categories.

How to Use Your Computer

Conquer computerphobia and see how this intricate machine truly makes life easier. Dozens of full-color graphics showcase the components of the PC and explain how to interact with them.

All About Computers

This one-of-a-kind visual guide for kids features numerous full-color illustrations and photos on every page, combined with dozens of interactive projects that reinforce computer basics, making this an exciting way to learn all about the world of computers.

ISBN: 155-2 Price: $22.95

Available at all fine bookstores or by calling 1-800-688-0448, ext. 100. Call for information on the Instructor's Supplement, including transparencies, for each book in the How It Works Series.

The Quick and Easy Way to Learn.

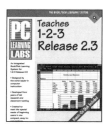

MAXIMIZE YOUR PRODUCTIVITY WITH THE TECHNIQUES & UTILITIES SERIES

ISBN: 054-8
Price: $39.95

Borland C++ Techniques & Utilities

Master programmer Kaare Christian leads this performance-oriented exploration of Borland C++, version 3.1. Focusing on object-oriented programming using the Borland class libraries, he shows you how to increase productivity while writing lean, fast, and appealing programs.

PC Magazine DOS 6 Techniques & Utilities

Based on his national bestseller *PC Magazine DOS 5 Techniques and Utilities*, Jeff Prosise puts essential tools and techniques into your hands with this power-user's guide to DOS 6. The two disks are packed with 60 powerful utilities created specifically for this book.

ISBN: 095-5
Price: $39.95

Techniques & Utilities Series book/disk resources from Ziff-Davis Press are designed for the productivity-conscious programmer or power user. Expert authors reveal insider techniques and have written on-disk utilities and support files so you can apply new skills instantly. If you're a serious programmer or user who wants to get things done quickly and work more effectively, then these are the ideal guides for you.

Look for more performance-oriented titles in the months ahead.

ISBN: 035-1
Price: $39.95

ISBN: 010-6
Price: $39.95

ISBN: 008-4
Price: $29.95

PC Magazine Turbo Pascal for Windows Techniques & Utilities

Neil J. Rubenking guides programmers through the power and intricacy of programming in Turbo Pascal for Windows. Included are two disks that contain all the source code examples from the text.

PC Magazine Turbo Pascal 6.0 Techniques & Utilities

This is the ideal guide for serious users who want to get things done. Neil J. Rubenking reveals tips and techniques that will enable you to unleash the full power of Turbo Pascal 6.0.

PC Magazine BASIC Techniques & Utilities

This guide presents an unprecedented level of coverage of BASIC's internal operation for the QuickBASIC and BASIC 7 programmer. Ethan Winer reveals insider techniques that will allow you to dramatically increase your productivity with BASIC.

ZIFF-DAVIS
ZD
PRESS

Available at all fine bookstores, or by calling 1-800-688-0448, ext. 102.

Insider Networking Secrets Revealed by Renowned Experts Frank J. Derfler, Jr., and Les Freed

Frank J. Derfler, Jr., and Les Freed have pooled their knowledge to create the most extensive guides to networking and communications. Active in the PC industry since its birth, Freed is the founder of DCA's Crosstalk division, and Derfler is senior networking editor of *PC Magazine* and the writer of the magazine's "Connectivity" column. You can be assured you are learning from highly respected experts in the computer industry with the most up-to-date information available.

With the wisdom of Derfler and Freed, you will boost your network system performance and productivity in no time.

PC Magazine Guide to Windows for Workgroups

Both users and administrators will get up and running fast and enjoy an instant boost in workgroup productivity with the help of this concise, easy-to-read guide.

ISBN: 120-X
Price: $22.95

PC Magazine Guide to NetWare

Les Freed and Frank J. Derfler, Jr. present tips, tricks, and techniques that make this best-selling book/disk package the essential survival guide to NetWare.

ISBN: 022-X
Price: $39.95

PC Magazine Guide to LANtastic

Best-selling authors and networking experts Frank J. Derfler, Jr., and Les Freed show you how to master the full power of LANtastic.

ISBN: 058-0
Price: $19.95

PC Magazine Guide to Connectivity, Second Edition

This supercharged second edition of the connectivity bible from Frank J. Derfler, Jr., includes *PC Magazine*'s most up-to-date product information, plus a special section on modem communication. You'll receive two disks that contain a full-featured e-mail program, performance-testing utilities, and many other application and utility programs.

ISBN: 047-5
Price: $39.95

PC Magazine Guide to Modem Communications

Acclaimed experts Les Freed and Frank J. Derfler, Jr., cover the fundamentals of modem communications, and provide scores of tips and insights on purchasing the right equipment and using bulletin board systems and modems for business applications. A valuable companion disk includes scripts for accessing on-line services, a file compression/decompression utility, and many more time-saving programs.

ISBN: 037-8
Price: $29.95

PC Magazine Guide to Linking LANs

Network authority, Frank J. Derfler, Jr., shows you the most effective ways to share network resources with the LAN down the hall or around the globe. This essential guide gives practical advice on quality, cost, and compatibility for dozens of popular products.

ISBN: 031-9
Price: $39.95

Available at all fine bookstores, or by calling 1-800-688-0448, ext. 104.

Ziff-Davis Press Survey of Readers

Please help us in our effort to produce the best books on personal computing.
For your assistance, we would be pleased to send you a FREE catalog
featuring the complete line of Ziff-Davis Press books.

1. How did you first learn about this book?

Recommended by a friend . . . . ☐ -1 (5)
Recommended by store personnel . . . . ☐ -2
Saw in Ziff-Davis Press catalog . . . . ☐ -3
Received advertisement in the mail . . . . ☐ -4
Saw the book on bookshelf at store . . . . ☐ -5
Read book review in: _____ ☐ -6
Saw an advertisement in: _____ ☐ -7
Other (Please specify): _____ ☐ -8

2. Which THREE of the following factors most influenced your decision to purchase this book? (Please check up to THREE.)

Front or back cover information on book . . . ☐ -1 (6)
Logo of magazine affiliated with book . . . . . . ☐ -2
Special approach to the content . . . . ☐ -3
Completeness of content . . . . ☐ -4
Author's reputation. ☐ -5
Publisher's reputation . . . . ☐ -6
Book cover design or layout . . . . ☐ -7
Index or table of contents of book . . . . ☐ -8
Price of book . . . . ☐ -9
Special effects, graphics, illustrations . . . . ☐ -0
Other (Please specify): _____ ☐ -x

3. How many computer books have you purchased in the last six months? _____ (7-10)

4. On a scale of 1 to 5, where 5 is excellent, 4 is above average, 3 is average, 2 is below average, and 1 is poor, please rate each of the following aspects of this book below. (Please circle your answer.)

Depth/completeness of coverage	5	4	3	2	1	(11)
Organization of material	5	4	3	2	1	(12)
Ease of finding topic	5	4	3	2	1	(13)
Special features/time saving tips	5	4	3	2	1	(14)
Appropriate level of writing	5	4	3	2	1	(15)
Usefulness of table of contents	5	4	3	2	1	(16)
Usefulness of index	5	4	3	2	1	(17)
Usefulness of accompanying disk	5	4	3	2	1	(18)
Usefulness of illustrations/graphics	5	4	3	2	1	(19)
Cover design and attractiveness	5	4	3	2	1	(20)
Overall design and layout of book	5	4	3	2	1	(21)
Overall satisfaction with book	5	4	3	2	1	(22)

5. Which of the following computer publications do you read regularly; that is, 3 out of 4 issues?

Byte . . . . ☐ -1 (23)
Computer Shopper . . . . ☐ -2
Corporate Computing . . . . ☐ -3
Dr. Dobb's Journal . . . . ☐ -4
LAN Magazine . . . . ☐ -5
MacWEEK . . . . ☐ -6
MacUser . . . . ☐ -7
PC Computing . . . . ☐ -8
PC Magazine . . . . ☐ -9
PC WEEK . . . . ☐ -0
Windows Sources . . . . ☐ -x
Other (Please specify): _____ ☐ -y

Please turn page.

6. What is your level of experience with personal computers? With the subject of this book?

	With PCs	With subject of book
Beginner...............	☐ -1 (24)	☐ -1 (25)
Intermediate..........	☐ -2	☐ -2
Advanced.............	☐ -3	☐ -3

7. Which of the following best describes your job title?

Officer (CEO/President/VP/owner)........ ☐ -1 (26)
Director/head......................... ☐ -2
Manager/supervisor................... ☐ -3
Administration/staff.................. ☐ -4
Teacher/educator/trainer............. ☐ -5
Lawyer/doctor/medical professional....... ☐ -6
Engineer/technician.................. ☐ -7
Consultant.......................... ☐ -8
Not employed/student/retired........... ☐ -9
Other (Please specify): _____ ☐ -0

8. What is your age?

Under 20............................ ☐ -1 (27)
21-29............................... ☐ -2
30-39............................... ☐ -3
40-49............................... ☐ -4
50-59............................... ☐ -5
60 or over.......................... ☐ -6

9. Are you:

Male................................ ☐ -1 (28)
Female.............................. ☐ -2

Thank you for your assistance with this important information! Please write your address below to receive our free catalog.

Name: _____

Address: _____

City/State/Zip: _____

Fold here to mail.   1544-03-01

BUSINESS REPLY MAIL
FIRST CLASS MAIL   PERMIT NO. 1612   OAKLAND, CA

POSTAGE WILL BE PAID BY ADDRESSEE

Ziff-Davis Press
5903 Christie Avenue
Emeryville, CA 94608-1925
Attn: Marketing

n TO RECEIVE 5¼-INCH DISK(S)

The Ziff-Davis Press software contained on the $3\frac{1}{2}$-inch disk included with this book is also available in $5\frac{1}{4}$-inch format. If you would like to receive the software in the $5\frac{1}{4}$-inch format, please return the $3\frac{1}{2}$-inch disk with your name and address to:

Disk Exchange
Ziff-Davis Press
5903 Christie Avenue
Emeryville, CA 94608